The Aging Networks

Kelly Niles-Yokum, PhD, MPA, is an associate professor of gerontology, University of La Verne, California. Dr. Niles-Yokum also serves as a managing editor for *Gerontology and Geriatrics Education*, the official journal of the Association for Gerontology in Higher Education. She is active in national and regional gerontology organizations. Dr. Niles-Yokum's research interests include social policy and aging, including the lived experience of programs and services, the oldest-old, end-of-life issues, and empowerment in later life. Dr. Niles-Yokum, with Dr. Wagner, authored the previous edition of *The Aging Networks*.

Donna L. Wagner, PhD, is the interim dean of the College of Health and Social Services, New Mexico State University. Prior to this she was the founding director of gerontology, Towson University, Maryland. Her ongoing research on family caregiving and employment includes a history of workplace eldercare programs, a study of "best practices" in workplace eldercare, two national studies on long-distance caregiving, an examination of gender in the workplace, out-of-pocket spending for family caregivers domestically and within the emergency unit (EU), and policy analysis and briefs on the topic of employed caregivers and programs that support them. Dr. Wagner is a fellow of both the Gerontological Society of America and the Association of Gerontology in Higher Education. She is the president of the Association of Gerontology in Higher Education (2014–2016), treasurer of the Board of Directors of the National Alliance for Caregiving, and past president of the Older Women's League (OWL). Dr. Wagner, with Dr. Niles-Yokum, authored the previous edition of *The Aging Network*.

The Aging Networks

A Guide to Programs and Services

Eighth Edition

Kelly Niles-Yokum, PhD, MPA
Donna L. Wagner, PhD

SPRINGER PUBLISHING COMPANY
NEW YORK

Springer Publishing Company, LLC
11 West 42nd Street
New York, NY 10036
www.springerpub.com

Acquisitions Editor: Sheri W. Sussman
Composition: Newgen Knowledge Works

ISBN: 978-0-8261-9659-0
e-book ISBN: 978-0-8261-9661-3
Instructor's Manual ISBN: 978-0-8261-9409-1
PowerPoint Slides ISBN: 978-0-8261-9408-4

Instructor's Materials: Instructors may request supplements by emailing textbook@ springerpub.com

14 15 16 17 / 5 4 3 2 1

The author and the publisher of this Work have made every effort to use sources believed to be reliable to provide information that is accurate and compatible with the standards generally accepted at the time of publication. The author and publisher shall not be liable for any special, consequential, or exemplary damages resulting, in whole or in part, from the readers' use of, or reliance on, the information contained in this book. The publisher has no responsibility for the persistence or accuracy of URLs for external or third-party Internet websites referred to in this publication and does not guarantee that any content on such websites is, or will remain, accurate or appropriate.

Library of Congress Cataloging-in-Publication Data
Niles-Yokum, Kelly.
The aging networks: a guide to programs and services / Kelly Niles-Yokum, Donna L. Wagner.—
Eighth edition.
    pages cm
Includes index.
ISBN 978-0-8261-9659-0 (alk. paper)—ISBN 978-0-8261-9661-3 (e-book)
1. Older people—Services for—United States. I. Wagner, Donna L. II. Title.
HV1461.G44 2015
362.60973—dc23
                                                                          2014035776

Printed in the United States of America by Gasch Printing.

Contents

Preface

The eighth edition of *The Aging Networks: A Guide to Programs and Services* has been substantially changed from previous editions. Rather than including descriptive sections that introduce the array of aging network organizations to the reader, we have focused on nine chapters that are organized to provide information, insight, and the perspective of experts. Links to additional information are infused throughout the text to foster additional independent exploration. This edition is designed to encourage independent examination of the issues addressed in the text by the reader.

In preparing the text, we became more convinced than ever that aging services are at a critical junction. In 2015, the Older Americans Act will turn 50 years old. There were 16.5 million older Americans in the United States in 1960 compared with 41.4 million today (U.S. Census, 2014). While the aging network professionals are working diligently to update and ensure that the growth of the older population is addressed in the design and delivery of services, other factors are influencing the success of these efforts. The Older Americans Act has not been reauthorized since 2006. Funding for some programs that are critical for the most vulnerable of the nation's elders has been flat in the recent past. Finally, we are just coming out of a 20-year period during which the increase in the number of elders was viewed as a threat to our economy. Although some commentators continue to view the increase in older Americans as a "dependency" problem, the aging of the commentators themselves and the increasing number of older Americans in the workforce are evidence to the contrary. In the meantime, however, there are increasing numbers of vulnerable elders who are facing economic difficulties as well as health problems that adversely affect the quality of their "golden years." These are the elders whom the Older Americans Act was designed to support.

In order to keep the Older Americans Act relevant, additional changes to the programming and staffing will be required. There is a shortage of professionals who have been educated and trained to serve older adults effectively in all areas: medical, wellness, social services, and community-planning. And there is a lack of consensus about what needs to be done to ensure that the aging network programs are sustained and enhanced to address the changing needs and growing demand for support from both the older adults and their family caregivers. The solution to this is not only found in funding but in the engagement of students at all levels and in all disciplines. We have attempted to make changes to the aging networks that would better engage students in the study of the aging networks and in the exploration of the alterations needed to enhance those networks.

WHY DO WE CALL IT
THE AGING NETWORKS?

We made the decision to refer to the network as "the networks" for many reasons; most important because it is clear that there are in fact a whole host of "networks" in place that have grown over time to attempt to address issues related to population aging. The evolution of the infrastructure that supports older adults and their families has occurred and now includes such a broad scope of providers and organizations—not for profit, public, private, faith based, and volunteer, for example—that referring to it as one singular network seemed to minimize its enormous impact and reach.

The text includes chapters focusing on the following topics:

- Demography
- Older Americans Act legislation and the networks
- Community-based services
- Aging in place
- Income security
- Elder justice and disaster preparedness
- Workforce issues
- Global aging
- Persistent and emerging issues

An Instructor's Manual and PowerPoint slides are also available to supplement the text. *To obtain an electronic copy of these materials, faculty should contact Springer Publishing Company at textbook@springerpub.com.*

Acknowledgments

We are eternally grateful to our loved ones, who supported us through this process. Thank you, Peter, David, David Jr., and Charles for tolerating us as we were obsessed with this project.

Many thanks to our editor, Sheri W. Sussman, for her guidance, patience, and vision.

Thanks to our contributors for sharing their expertise and for making the book this strong.

Introduction

*A*s the field of gerontology grows and the population of older adults continues to increase, the need for an educated workforce becomes a critical factor in our ability to provide a good old age for everyone in our society. While the aging networks provide a strong foundation for supportive services and programs for older adults, we have also made great strides in our programs, services, and educational opportunities for those interested in the aging of our society. In order to continue to add to our successes, we must also be cognizant of the changing face of aging now and in the future.

In order to fully understand the current status and future development of programs and services created for older Americans, it is necessary to review the historical steps that have brought us to where we are now—the only country in the world that has publicly funded age-entitlement programs and services. Although we have come a long way, there is no doubt that we will have to be proactive in our approach to population aging so that we can address not only persistent but future challenges.

The Administration on Aging (AoA, 2014) provides a time line of historical steps from 1920 to 2014. Here are some of the highlights:

1920   The Civil Service Retirement Act provided a retirement system for many governmental employees.

1935   The Social Security Act was passed; provides for old age assistance and Old-Age and Survivors Insurance.

1950   President Truman initiated the first National Conference on Aging, sponsored by the Federal Security Agency.

1952 First federal funds appropriated for social service programs for older persons under the Social Security Act.

1956 Special Staff on Aging established within the Office of the Secretary of Health, Education, and Welfare (HEW), to coordinate responsibilities for aging. Federal Council on Aging created by President Eisenhower.

1958 Legislation introduced in Congress calling for a White House Conference on Aging.

1960 Social Security Administration eliminated age 50 years as minimum for qualifying for disability benefits, and liberalized the retirement test and the requirement of a fully insured status.

1961 First White House Conference on Aging held in Washington, DC.

1962 Legislation introduced in Congress to establish an independent and permanent Commission on Aging.

1965 Older Americans Act (OAA) signed into law on July 14, 1965. It established the Administration on Aging (AoA) within the Department of Health, Education, and Welfare (HEW), and called for the creation of State Units on Aging.

William Bechill named first Commissioner on Aging.

Medicare, Title XVIII, a health insurance program for the elderly, was established as part of the Social Security Act.

Medicaid, Title XIX, a health insurance program for low-income persons, was added to the Social Security Act.

1967 OAA extended for 2 years, and provisions made for the AoA to study the personnel needs in the aging field.

Age Discrimination Act signed into law.

AoA moved from the Office of the Secretary of Health, Education, and Welfare (HEW) and placed in the newly created Social and Rehabilitative Service Agency within the department.

1969 OAA Amendments provided grants for model demonstration projects, Foster Grandparent, and Retired Senior Volunteer Programs.

1971 Second White House Conference on Aging held in Washington, DC.

1972 A new Title VII was created under the OAA authorizing funds for a national nutrition program for the elderly.

1973 OAA Comprehensive Services Amendments established Area Agencies on Aging. The amendments added a new Title V, which authorized grants to local community agencies for multipurpose senior centers, and created the Community Service Employment grant program for low-income persons aged 55 years and older, administered by the Department of Labor.

1974 Title XX of the Social Security Amendments authorized grants to states for social services. These programs included protective services, homemaker services, transportation services, adult day care services, training for employment, information and referral, nutrition assistance, and health support.

OAA Amendments added transportation under Title III model projects.

The National Institute on Aging created to conduct research and training related to the aging process, and the diseases and problems of an aging population.

Title V of the Farm and Rural Housing Program of 1949 expanded to include the rural elderly as a target group.

1975 OAA Amendments authorized grants under Title III to American Indian tribal organizations. Transportation, home care, legal services, and home renovation/repair were mandated as priority services.

1978 Congregate Housing Services Act authorized contracts with local public housing agencies and nonprofit corporations, to provide congregate independent living service programs.

OAA amendments required each state to establish a long-term care ombudsman program to cover nursing homes.

1981 Third White House Conference on Aging held in Washington, DC.

OAA reauthorized; emphasized supportive services to help older persons remain independent in the community.

1984 Reauthorization of the OAA clarified and reaffirmed the roles of State and Area Agencies on Aging in coordinating community-based services, and in maintaining accountability for the funding of national priority services (legal, access, and in home).

1987 Omnibus Budget Reconciliation Act provided for nursing home reform in the areas of nurse aide training, survey and certification procedures, and preadmission screening, and annual reviews of persons with mental illness.

Reauthorization of the OAA added six additional distinct authorizations of appropriations for services: in-home services for the frail elderly; long-term care ombudsman; assistance for special needs; health education and promotion; prevention of elder abuse, neglect, and exploitation; and outreach activities for persons who may be eligible for benefits under supplemental security income (SSI), Medicaid, and food stamps. Additional emphasis was given to serving those with the greatest economic and social needs, including low-income minorities.

The Nursing Home Reform Act (Omnibus Budget Reconciliation Act) mandated that nursing facility residents have "direct and immediate access to ombudspersons when protection and advocacy services become necessary."

1990   Americans with Disabilities Act extended protection from discrimination in employment and public accommodations to persons with disabilities.

Cranston-Gonzalez National Affordable Housing Act reauthorized the U.S. Department of Housing and Urban Development (HUD) Section, 202 Elderly Housing program, and provided for supportive service demonstration programs.

Age Discrimination in Employment Act made it illegal, in most circumstances, for companies to discriminate against older workers in employee benefits.

1992   Reauthorization of the OAA placed increased focus on caregivers, intergenerational programs, protection of elder rights and called for a 1995 White House Conference on Aging.

The elevation of Commissioner on Aging to Assistant Secretary for Aging.

OAA amendments added a new Title VII "Vulnerable Elder Rights Activities," which included the long-term care ombudsman; prevention of elder abuse, neglect, and exploitation; elder rights and legal assistance development; and benefits outreach, counseling, and assistance programs.

1993   Fernando M. Torres-Gil was sworn in as the first Assistant Secretary for Aging in the Department of Health and Human Services on May 6, 1993.

1995 White House Conference on Aging convened from May 2 to 5, 1995, in Washington, DC.

Marked 30th anniversaries of OAA, Medicare, Medicaid, and the Foster Grandparent Program.

Marked the 60th anniversary of Social Security.

1999 Designated the International Year of Older Persons: A Society for All Ages.

2000 OAA Amendments of 2000 signed into law (P.L. 106–501), establishing the new National Family Caregiver Support Program, and reauthorizing the OAA for 5 years on November 13, 2000.

2001 U.S. Department of Health and Human Services (HHS) Secretary, Tommy G. Thompson, released $113 million for first National Family Caregiver Support Programs grants to states on February 15, 2001.

2005 The fourth White House Conference on Aging was held in Washington, DC.

2006 Medicare Part D Prescription Drug program (part of Medicare Prescription Drug, Improvement and Modernization Act [MMA]) went into effect.

The Lifespan Respite Care Act (administered by AoA) is enacted.

OAA Amendments of 2006 signed into law (P.L. 109–365), embedding the principles of consumer information for long-term care planning, evidence-based prevention programs, and self-directed community-based services to older individuals at risk of institutionalization. OAA was reauthorized for 5 years on October 17, 2006.

2009 Kathy Greenlee appointed by President Obama as fourth Assistant Secretary for Aging.

2010 The Patient Protection and Affordable Care Act is enacted.

2011 First of the nation's baby boomers turn 65.

CLASS (Community Living Assistance and Supports) program, part of the Affordable Care Act, is designated to be administered by the AoA.

Kathy Greenlee appointed as Administrator of the CLASS program in addition to serving as Assistant Secretary for Aging.

2012 The Administration for Community Living (ACL) is established. The new federal agency connects the AoA, the Administration on Intellectual and Developmental Disabilities, and the HHS Office on Disability. The new agency is responsible for increasing access to community supports, while focusing attention and resources on the unique needs of older Americans and people with disabilities across the life span.

And, in 2014, we are still awaiting reauthorization of the OAA. It was last reauthorized in 2006 after which it was to be reauthorized again in 2011. We are still waiting.

Another set of factors contributing to the growth of the aging networks and related programs and services for older persons was and continues to be the increase in numbers of researchers, educators, program directors, providers, practitioners, and entrepreneurs with interests in aging. The earliest gerontologists were primarily researchers from the biological sciences who were later joined by researchers from the psychological and social sciences.

Aging Organizations Timeline

1942 American Geriatrics Society (AGS) established.

1945 The Gerontological Society of America (GSA) established to "promote the scientific study of aging."

1949 GSA holds its first annual scientific meeting in New York, NY.

1950 National Committee on Aging is formed and later renamed the National Council on Aging (NCOA) 1960.

1954 Western Gerontological Society (WGS) is formed.

1974 Association for Gerontology in Higher Education (AGHE) established.

1985 WGS becomes the American Society on Aging (ASA).

1998 Association for Gerontology in Higher Education (AGHE) partners with GSA as the Educational Unit.

Coinciding with increasing interest in aging research among academics was the advent of gerontology and geriatric education programs in institutions of higher education. In the 1970s, the federal government made monies available to colleges and universities for research on aging and related curriculum (Title IV, OAA). The evolution of the discipline of gerontology has brought us from humble beginnings to where we are today, with a myriad of higher education offerings from minors in gerontology to doctoral programs. In order to continue to add to our successes, we must also make room for those who have a background in and competencies related to gerontology, whether it is in the classroom, on the front lines, or developing policies and programs. That is our challenge.

This edition of *The Aging Networks* is not only a guide to programs and services and related issues and challenges, but a call to action. We challenge you, the reader, to read this book with a an eye toward critical reflection, including thoughtful examination of your own ideas about aging and what it means to grow old, what it means to grow old in your local community, and how you can help to ensure that all of us have a good place to grow old.

REFERENCE

Administration on Aging (2014). *Historical evolution of programs for older Americans.* Retrieved from http://www.aoa.gov/AoA_programs/OAA/resources/History.aspx

Older Americans and the Consumers of the Aging Networks

Older Americans are increasingly diverse in a variety of ways, including their racial and ethnic backgrounds, religion, spirituality, income, education, and sexual orientation. Chapter 1 presents relevant statistical data on the older population as an important background to the planning and development of programs. We will also address the current status of older Americans and the social, political, and economic consequences of the demographic shifts we are going through today and must be prepared to face tomorrow.

CHAPTER ONE

The Demographics of Aging Today

Older adults, defined as those older than 65 years, now comprise 13.3% of the U.S. population. More than 1 out of every 8 Americans are "old" by this estimate, with more than 41.4 million Americans 65 years of age and older (U.S. Census Bureau, 2012). The baby boom generation is driving the increase in the percentage and numbers of Americans older than 65 years. By 2020, it is projected that 1 out of every 5 Americans will be 65 years and older. In this chapter, we discuss the current status of older Americans and the social, political, and economic consequences of the demographic shifts we are going through today.

All over the country, communities are discussing the increase in the older population with terms like "tsunami," complaining that we cannot afford this increase of elders, or worse, that the growth in the aging population will require resources that otherwise would have gone to our children. These messages are a function of a lack of information and understanding about what aging means today coupled with ageism. Although this book is primarily about aging services and programs, not all older Americans need help. In fact, the "bonus years" that many Americans are enjoying as a result of expanded life expectancy and, for many, an expanded health span, are allowing today's elders to redefine old age.

Population aging occurs when both the birth rate and death rate are low. Population aging also results in an increase in the median age of a society—the median age today in the United States is 37 years, projected to increase to 39 by 2030. Table 1.1 illustrates the aging of Americans since 1900.

This chapter reviews some of the elements of population aging, including life expectancy and the changing social characteristics of the "new" cohorts entering old age, such as increasing diversity among the older cohorts and increasing educational attainment. Health status, the

TABLE 1.1
Number of Elders in the United States Between
1900 and 2030 (Projected)

1900	3.1 million (actual)	4.1% of the total U.S. population
1920	4.9 million (actual)	
1940	9.0 million (actual)	
1960	16.6 million (actual)	
1980	25.5 million (actual)	
1990	31.2 million (actual)	
2000	35.0 million (actual)	
2010	41.4 million (actual)	
2020	56.0 million (projected)	
2040	79.7 million (projected)	21% of the total U.S. population

Source: U.S. Department of Health and Human Services [HHS], Administration on Aging, Administration for Community Living (2013).

trend toward aging in place, and the relationship between educational attainment and poverty will be discussed. In addition, we will look at the old-old and centenarians and finish the chapter with a discussion of the new "work and retirement equation." The objectives of this chapter are to make you curious about:

(a) *How long you will live*

(b) *How your family will manage the old age of its oldest members and plan for the aging of younger members*

(c) *What the increase of older adults might mean for you personally*

(d) *And, how your own lifestyle and life span might offer you additional opportunities that were unavailable to your grandparents and great-grandparents*

LIFE EXPECTANCY

Life expectancy is increasing. In 2011, a woman who reached the age of 65 years could be expected to live an additional 20.4 years and a man 17.8 years. In 2011, a child born would likely live to the age of 78.7 years—approximately 30 years longer than a child born in 1900 (U.S. Department of Health and Human Services, 2013). Demographers point out that a good part of the life expectancy that we enjoy today derives from a reduction in death rates for youth. However, the U.S. Census Bureau data suggest that between 1990 and 2007, there has been a reduction in death rates of Americans between the ages of 65 and 84 years. The 90+ population has been growing faster than younger older adults and, as a result, the size of this subgroup has increased in numbers proportionately to the older population (He & Muenchrath, 2011).

*Using the Social Security Administration's life expectancy calculation table, how long will you live?**

Although life expectancy is increasing in the United States, this increase is not necessarily associated with concomitant increases in disability and dependence among those older than 65 years. In fact, compression of morbidity has increased the health span as well as the life span of most older adults. As we shall see in this text, increasing life expectancy has afforded many older than 65 years the chance to work longer, start businesses after retirement from a lifelong career, and make important and meaningful contributions to their community and families. Between 1993 and 2010, adults older than 62 years who were in the workforce increased by 33% for men and 62% for women (Johnson, 2011). Many factors have influenced this increase in older workers, including Social Security policy changes, better health status, and the changing nature of the workplace as a result of technological advances. Workforce involvement, community leadership, and the changing lifestyles of older Americans are not the harbinger of dependency that the term "tsunami" conjures up. Rather, there is a much more complicated picture associated with an increasing older population.

What are the implications of an increase in the older population?

Population aging is occurring around the world at varying rates. Population aging started in Sweden and France as a result of a decline in birth rates in the 19th century (Uhlenberg, 2013). However, a decline in birth rates is not the only cause of population aging; a decrease in mortality rates is also necessary for a nation to experience population aging. Demographers point out that a number of factors influence the specific rates and consequences of population aging in different countries. For example, China now is home to 20% of all the people on the planet older than 65 years. The size of this segment of China's population is, of course, related to the number of people living in China. The speed of the growth

---

* See the Social Security Administration's website (www.ssa.gov).

of the aging of China is also a function of enforced one-child policies to address the absolute size of the population. Despite the fact that China is aging rapidly, it is also a nation that is improving economically; an interesting contrast for those who associate population aging with economic challenges. Nonetheless, China does not have a strong pension program for its growing older population and at some point this may lead to a weaker economy for the country. Because of the one-child policy, Chinese elders are also unlikely to have more than one child to support them when they are no longer working. Many European nations have strong pension and health programs that support the elders in the country. In the United States, we are seeing an increase in older Americans remaining in the workforce, particularly during the recent recession. Today's American elders are healthier and better educated than older Americans in the past.

Every nation will experience population aging in its own unique way. As population aging occurs, there will be changes in the social structures of the society to accommodate the changes that population aging creates. Demand for older workers and/or older community volunteers may increase. New businesses and new technology will emerge to address both the problems and opportunities associated with population aging. And, with any luck, ageism will be diminished and not increased. In a recent study of baby boomers and older adults regarding long-term services and supports (LTSS) planning, Robison, Shugrue, Fortinsky, and Gruman (2014) found that the majority of respondents (two thirds) expected that they would need LTSS in the future. Baby boomers were more likely than older adults to report that they planned to move into an apartment or retirement community, or to live with an adult child. As population aging occurs, there will likely be an increase in the awareness of the challenges of late life and more people will not only plan for their own futures, but develop new models of lifestyles for their old age.

What do you think your life will be like in an aging world?

SPOTLIGHT ON THE 90+ POPULATION

The Census Bureau issued a report on the 90+ population in 2011, and not surprisingly, the 90+ population was predominately female—with a ratio of 3:1 (He & Muenchrath, 2011). Women continue to outlive men and among the oldest-old population this gender advantage is particularly dramatic. This gender longevity advantage also affects the ratio of women who are widowed (84.2%) in this age group compared to men (49.3%). A higher proportion of the 90+ group lived in poverty (14.5%) than the 65- to 89-year-old group (9.6%). Poverty rates were the highest among Blacks (25%), with Hispanics (21%)

close behind. Whites (13.3%) and Asians (16.0%) had a lower incidence of poverty than Blacks and Hispanics. In terms of living arrangements, Asians and Hispanics were the least likely to live alone among 90+ elders. Forty percent of women and 30% of men who were 90+ lived alone. This is comparable with the percentage of 90+ elders living in a household with others—32% of women and 53% of men live with others in a household.

Advanced age is a risk factor for institutionalization because of higher disability rates among the old-old. Twenty-five percent of women and 14.5% of men who are 90+ reside in an institutional setting. Almost all (98.2%) older adults living in a nursing home had a disability. Those living in a nursing home were more likely than those living alone or in a household to have a cognitive limitation and limitation in the ability to manage their own personal care. Self-care limitations are highly correlated with a need for nursing home care.

Centenarians

Centenarians, those who live to 100 years of age, are a growing and interesting subset of the older population. Today there are 53,364 Americans older than 100 years (U.S. Census Bureau, 2012). The proportion of centenarians to other age groups in the population is 1.73 per 10,000 people. In proportion to people aged 65 years, the centenarians are 0.19 or 19 per 10,000. This proportion of centenarians in the United States contrasts with those in Japan (3.43 per 10,000), the United Kingdom (1.92 per 10,000); and France (2.70 per 10,000). There was a 28.4% increase in the size of the centenarian population in the United States between 2000 and 2010. Supercentenarians are 110 years of age or older. This elite group numbered 330 in the United States in 2010.

The majority of centenarians (82.5%) were Whites, 12.2% were Blacks, and 2.5% were Asians. Living arrangements for centenarians varied by race/ethnicity. Those with the highest likelihood of living in a household with others were centenarians who referred to themselves as "Some Other Race" (74.2%), Hispanics (66.8%), and American and Alaska Indians (64.7%). Those who were the least likely to live with others in a household were Whites (26.4%) and non-Hispanics (28.9%). These two groups (White and non-Hispanic) were most likely to be living in a nursing home.

What is your opinion about living to 100 years? The probability of living to 100 years at birth is increasing. However, some researchers caution that obesity rates and other health-related factors could result in a decrease in life expectancy over time. Go to the Centenarian Project's life expectancy calculator to see if you are likely to achieve 100 or more years of life (www.livingto100lifeexpectancycalculator).

RACIAL AND ETHNIC DIVERSITY

The older population is becoming more diverse in terms of race and ethnicity. In 1970, 89.5% of the population older than 65 years was White and 15.9% was born in a foreign country (Seltzer & Yahirum, 2013). By 2009, 80% of the older population was White. During this same time frame, the Hispanic elder population increased from 1.9% to 7%. The place of birth of those born outside the United States shifted from 77.6% from Europe in 1970 to 30.4% in 2009. The number of people from Asia increased during that same time period from 3.7% to 27.1%, and those from Latin America increased from 6.3% in 1970 to 35.5% in 2009.

Projections of diversity among elders suggest that this trend will accelerate in the coming years. Parker (2011) reports that by 2030, the Hispanic elder group will increase by 238% and the Asian and Pacific Islanders by 285%. The U.S. Census (2013) projects that the percentage of racial and ethnic minority elders will increase from 16% of the older population in 2000 to 28% of the older population in 2030. Between 2012 and 2030, the percentage of White elders will increase by 54% and that of older racial and ethnic minority elders will increase by 125%. This diversity among older adults will alter the ways in which older Americans live their lives and the ways in which the aging network will configure programs and services to support elders in the United States.

Despite the fact that senior advocacy groups speak out against stereotyping, there is a continued tendency to discuss elders as a homogeneous group whose values and beliefs are defined by their age. In reality, the cultural backgrounds among the present generation of individuals older than 65 years are enormously varied.

Two demographic facts about this population are important in the field of aging: (a) the median age of foreign-born individuals is above 52 years and (b) the foreign-born population is very diverse. Differences in cultural attitudes toward aging and the use of services, as well as a lack of fluency in English among foreign-born elders may create problems for service providers as they attempt to implement aging programs that are inclusive.

HEALTH STATUS OF OLDER ADULTS

Nearly half (44%) of older adults living in the community rated their personal health as excellent or very good. African Americans, American Indians, older Asians, and Hispanics were less likely to rate their personal health as excellent as that of older Whites. Nonetheless, most older adults have at least one chronic condition—the most common ones include arthritis, heart disease, cancer, diabetes, and hypertension (U.S. Department of Health and Human Services, 2013). Older Americans are more likely than younger Americans to have shorter hospital stays (about three times the rate) and once admitted, they tend to stay longer. Finally, older Americans visit their doctors more frequently than younger Americans. In 2012, 96% of older Americans reported that they had a regular health care provider. In spite of the fact that 93% of elders in the United States have health care coverage through Medicare, 12.2% of their total spending is on out-of-pocket health costs. This contrasts with younger Americans who spend only 6.7%. On average, older consumers spent $3,076 for health insurance, $786 for medical services, $714 for drugs, and $193 for medical supplies in 2011.

Managing chronic illness is an important strategy for health aging. Limitations in the activities of daily living (ADL) are highly correlated with a need for assistance in late life. Elders who are 85+ are at maximum risk of limitations. ADL is a measurement of functional independence and consists of the ability of an individual to independently manage personal care—bathing, showering, dressing, eating, using the toilet, and "transferring"—getting in and out of chairs and bed. In 2010, 46% of those 85 years and older had limitations in walking independently compared to 17% of those 65 to 74 years of age and 28% of those between 75 and 84 years. Disability and limitations in ADL or the instrumental activities of daily living (IADL) are associated with the need for assistance and, in some cases, the need to move into a nursing care facility.

Even with limitations in ADLs and IADLs, most elders remain in the community with help from their adult children, friends, or home health providers. Only 3.6% of older adults lived in institutional settings, such as a nursing home, in 2011. The percentage living in an institutional setting increases by age group with as many as 11% of the 85+ age group in this living situation.

Alzheimer's disease (AD) and related dementias are the most talked about and feared diseases associated with aging. It is true that the likelihood of having dementia increases with age. To date scientists continue to explore the cause of dementia and seek a potential cure for this debilitating disease. Up to now there is no cure for this progressive disease that will, over time, result in death. As the disease progresses, families are faced with difficult care decisions and expenses that are not covered by insurance. The Alzheimer's Association (2014) reports that after the age of 65 years, the risk of getting the disease doubles every 5 years and at age 85 years, an individual has a 50% chance of developing the disease. Although there are many questions about the disease, it is assumed that genetics and overall health status of the individual are associated with the illness.

A 2013 study of people older than 65 years in England and Wales found that, in the past two decades, dementia rates among older people have dropped by 25%. This trend was also detected in a study of Danish elders. Researchers suggest that the likely reason for the drop is overall better health and higher educational attainment of the population. The trends in the United States have not been assessed but National Institute on Aging scientist Dallas Anderson described these studies as "rigorous and…strong evidence" (Kolata, 2013). If these trends are found in the United States, it will be a basis for new projections of the future costs of AD in the nation.

Other studies confirm the importance of good health and educational attainment when it comes to longevity and wellness in old age. Jay Olshansky et al. (2012) of the University of Chicago conducted a study that found that life expectancy was declining for those with low educational attainment. White women who have not completed high school have a life expectancy of 73.5 years, whereas White women who completed college have a life expectancy of 83.9 years. Among White men, those without a high-school degree had a life expectancy of 67.5 years, whereas those with a college or better degree had a life expectancy of 80.4 years.

AGING IN PLACE

Most older Americans prefer to reside independently in the community. "Aging in place" is not only a goal for the individual elder, but a policy goal of the Older Americans Act and the programs and services that are funded by this Act. Throughout this text, we will be featuring strategies and programs that support this goal. Community-based services and programs are available in all areas of the country to provide assistance needed by elders who are living in the community. In 2012, 72% of the older men and 46% of older women were living with a spouse. More than a third (36%) of older women lived alone compared to 19% of older men.

In 2011, more than half of those older than 65 years lived in nine states: California, Florida, New York, Texas, Pennsylvania, Ohio, Illinois, Michigan, and North Carolina. Florida has the highest percentage of elders (17.6%), with Maine (16.3%) and West Virginia (16.2%) close behind. Alaska has the lowest percentage of elders (8.1%).

Older adults have a high rate of home ownership; of those households headed by an older person in 2011, 81% are homeowners. Sixty-five percent of older homeowners owned their homes without a mortgage. Only 19% of households headed by an elder were rentals (U.S. Department of Health and Human Services, 2013).

EDUCATIONAL ATTAINMENT AND POVERTY AMONG ELDERS

The educational attainment of older Americans is increasing. In 1970, only 28% of older adults had completed high school. In 2012, 81% of older adults had completed high school. Educational attainment is increasing among all elders regardless of their race or ethnicity, but White elders are more likely to have a high-school diploma than Blacks, Asians, Hispanics, or Native Americans. There is a close association among educational attainment, health status, and income; so this increase is good news for future elders, if in fact, this educational attainment trend continues.

Households with families headed by an individual 65 years and older had a median income in 2011 of $48,538. The median income for older individuals for the same time period was $27,707 for men and $15,362 for women. Primary income sources for elders were Social Security, asset income, earnings, and pensions. For more than a third of elders (36%) Social Security payments made up 90% or more of their total income. This heavy reliance on Social Security was more likely to be for nonmarried elders (46%) than married ones (27%).

In 2011, 8.7% of people older than 65 years lived below the poverty level. When using the new gauge—the Supplemental Poverty Measure—which includes regional variations in cost of living, the percentage of older adults living in poverty was estimated at 15.1%. According to the National Poverty Center of the University of Michigan (n.d.), 22% of all children younger than 18 years lived in poverty in 2010. Breaking this down according to race or ethnicity, we see that 38.2% of Black children, 35% of Hispanic children, and 13.6% of Asian children lived in poverty in 2010. Among White children, 12.4% lived in poverty.

Among Americans older than 65 years, we see a similar pattern of poverty. Although, in 2011 to 2012, 8.7% of older Americans were living in poverty, 17.3% of Black elders and 18.7% of Hispanic elders were living in poverty. Older women were more likely than older men to live in poverty (10.7% for women compared to 6.2% for men) as were people living alone (16.5%). The racial and ethnic differences persist in old age as well. Highest poverty rates were observed for older Hispanic women living alone (38.8%) and older Black women living alone (32.2%; U.S. Department of Health and Human Services, 2013).

Geographic differences in poverty among elders range from a low of 5.7% living below the poverty line in Delaware to a high of 13.5% in Mississippi (U.S. Department of Health and Human Services, 2013).

THE NEW WORK/RETIREMENT EQUATION

The concept of retirement is a relatively new phenomenon. Munnell (2011) reminds us that in the 1880s older men's work participation declined as they became eligible for Civil War pensions. Later there was another large decline of men working when Social Security was enacted and as the workforce began to benefit from employer retirement plans. Men aged 55 to 64 years began to retire earlier. However, this trend of early retirement for men began to reverse in the 1980s as a function of shifts in pension types from defined-benefit plans to 401K plans, which are less generous over time; higher educational levels; and improved health coupled with a growing number of jobs that no longer rely on physical exertion. The average age at retirement for men increased from 62 years to 64 years at this time. Women's workplace participation has also increased significantly, in part because few women were in the labor force before 1950. The average age of retirement for women is now 62 years (Munnell, 2011).

Choosing between retiring and working is more viable for today's 60+ population because of better health and an increase in life expectancies. However, it is expensive to retire and very expensive if you retire at age 62 and look at an additional 30 or more years of life. Certain work sectors are examining new models for retirement transitions. For example, it is common today to see universities rehiring retired professors to teach on a part-time basis. Some businesses are exploring phased-in retirement models, whereas others are hiring older workers as part-time employees—a situation that might be preferred by some older workers who want and need to work but who also prefer having more free time for other activities.

Burtless (2013) examined the relationship between educational attainment, which, as described above, is increasing, and delayed retirement, and found that about half of the increase in older retirement for men was a function of educational attainment. He suggests that additional educational attainment will be slower in the future and, as a result, we might see a slowing of the trend toward longer working lives. However, we are currently in the midst of the aging of the baby boom generation, which has redefined every stage of their lives by their sheer numbers. Many boomers have no intention of retiring, whereas others retire as soon as they can. Obviously, the financial ability to retire is a driver of the retirement decision as is personal health and the health of a spouse. Nonetheless, the median age of the workforce is increasing due to the aging of this generation and its size. Although there is no precise prediction of how Americans will manage their work lives in the future, one thing we are seeing today is that there are more options and more flexibility for different choices than in the past. This is a good thing for many workers in the baby boom generation and for those who follow.

One last note on the workers who follow the baby boomers. There are many misconceptions about the labor force among labor force participants. One of the persistent misconceptions is that older workers are keeping jobs that would otherwise go to younger workers, and their engagement in the workforce is a negative force for the younger workers looking for jobs. According to experts, there is no evidence to support the idea that retaining or hiring older workers keeps younger workers out of the labor force—even during a recession. Overall, the economic benefit of older workers in the workforce accrues to the society and to other age groups (Munnell & Wu, 2012).

The recent recession has led to a near-record unemployment for older workers (55+). In 2010, the unemployment rate for workers who were 55+ was 7.1%, slightly lower than the record rate of 7.2% in 2009. This unemployment rate is lower than that for younger workers but when an older worker becomes unemployed, she or he is unemployed for longer periods than younger workers. In 2010, workers who were 55+ spent an average of 35.5 weeks unemployed compared to 23.3 weeks for 16- to 24-year-olds and 30.3 weeks for the 25- to 54-year-olds. Despite the higher unemployment rates during the recession, labor force participation increased for the 55+ population. About 40% of this age group was employed in 2010. The U.S. Bureau of Labor Statistics suggests that the increase in labor force participation for this group during the recession was due to the replacement of defined benefit retirement plans with contribution plans and the recession's adverse effects on the value of assets (U.S. Bureau of Labor Statistics, U.S. Department of Labor, 2010).

STAKEHOLDERS AND CONSUMERS OF THE AGING NETWORK OF SERVICES

The demographics of the aging population reveals only a part of the importance of a strong network of aging services for older adults today and into the future. The aging network of services for older adults in the United States consists of a patchwork quilt of community-based agencies, communities, housing units, and specialized health providers supported by government funding and the private marketplace. The consumers of these services include older adults as well as younger adults with long-term care needs, family caregivers and friends who help those with chronic care needs, and an array of people who have special needs and interests in the aging network. As the older population becomes more diverse over time, so do other stakeholders and consumers. In order to provide a foundation for understanding why the aging network matters, we will provide a brief review of some of these stakeholders and the forces that are likely to alter the characteristics of these stakeholders in the future.

Caregivers—Family and Fictive Kin

The largest nonelder stakeholder group today is family caregivers. Family caregivers provide an essential service to their older relatives and to our nation's long-term care system. It is estimated that the imputed value of the services they provide at no cost to our nation's long-term care budget was $234 billion in 2011—more than half of the total long-term supports and service expenses for that year (Congressional Budget Office, 2013). A recent survey conducted by Pew Research Center found that approximately 40% of U.S. adults actively care for older adults (Fox, Duggan, & Purcel, 2013). Almost 50% of the sample in the study predicted that they would be caring for an older family member in the future. Not included in this survey is the estimate of the out-of-pocket costs spent by these family members to cover medical and support services needed by their family member or friend *in addition* to the hands-on support they were also providing. A 2007 study found that family caregivers spend an average of $5,531 a year out of pocket for needed goods and services (National Alliance for Caregiving [NAC], 2007). There are demographers who predict that the availability of these family caregivers will diminish into the future for a variety of reasons, including smaller family size, resistance of adult children to assume the role of a caregiver, more older adults entering late life as a single person (never married, divorced, or widowed), and childlessness.

In addition to family caregivers, there are "fictive kin" who provide ongoing support and assistance to an elder. These are individuals who are not related by marriage or blood, but are nonetheless committed to the well-being of the elder they are helping. Barker (2002) estimated that as many as 10% of the community-residing elders were supported by "fictive kin." As the changes described above begin to take place, fictive kin are likely to be a growing group of stakeholders. Both family and fictive kin caregivers are able to manage their own lives and responsibilities when there is a strong and responsive aging network of services and programs to rely on.

Grandparents Raising Grandchildren

The number of grandparents who are raising their grandchildren is increasing. In 2010, 1 out of 14 American children was living in a household headed by a grandparent (Scommengna, 2012). More than half of the children living in a multigenerational household were being raised by grandparents who reported that they have the primary responsibility of the grandchild. Between 2005 and 2010 there was a 16% increase in the number of grandparents raising grandchildren—from 2.5 million in 2005 to 2.9 million in 2010. Financial problems related to unemployment, health care costs, or home foreclosure were drivers of the multigenerational household in which three generations reside together. For the households with a "skipped generation," grandparents have assumed responsibility for the grandchildren due to parents' substance abuse, mental illness, incarceration, death, or child abuse. These grandparents often face difficult circumstances related to emotional problems experienced by the child as well as challenges related to their own aging. The National Family Caregivers Support Program, which you will read about later in this text, has included these households as eligible for services and there are programs that serve both the grandparents and the grandchildren. Other related programs and agencies have been started to assist these grandparents.

Lesbian, Gay, Bisexual, and Transsexual Elders

Older lesbian, gay, bisexual, and transsexual (LGBT) individuals comprise a group of elders who face a complicated set of circumstances in old age. Some of these elders have been disenfranchised from their family members due to attitudes of kin about their sexual identity. Older gays may have spent the majority of their lives keeping their sexual identity private from family and friends due to the stigma that was present when they were becoming adults. They may be reticent to join visible groups in place to support aging elders or, more likely, live in a community that lacks programs for LGBT elders. The aging network of services has been slow in embracing this group of elders and, even in large metropolitan areas, programs specifically designed for this group may be lacking. However, there are now assisted-living facilities, nursing homes, and community agencies designed to serve this population. SAGE, the national advocacy group for gay, lesbian, bisexual, and transgender elders, has been working on behalf of this group of elders since 1978. It is the largest and oldest advocacy group for this population. In February 2010, the U.S. Department of Health and Human

Services awarded a grant to SAGE and 10 other advocacy groups to start the National Resource Center on LGBT Aging. This resource center has raised the awareness of the needs of the LGBT community and the importance of programs and resources for this group of elders to enhance their ability to live independently in the community. This group, an historically silent group of elders, now has a voice and is working to ensure that LGBT aging issues are taken seriously and that programs are developed to address their concerns and needs.

Older Veterans

In 2010, half of the men older than 65 years were veterans (Federal Interagency Forum on Aging, 2012). There were few women (1%) with veteran status beyond the age of 65 years but this is expected to change over time. However, veterans are likely to be men primarily through 2020 due to the makeup of our military historically. Nonetheless, women will be eligible to use long-term services available to veterans through marriage, and the programs that are designed to assist veterans with long-term needs through LTSS will likely see an increase in demand for the services. This is due to the fact that the increase in veterans (and likely their eligible spouses) older than 85 years is dramatic. Between 2000 and 2010, the number of men with veteran status beyond the age of 85 years increased from 400,000 to 1.3 million. The proportion of men older than 85 years went from 33% to 68% in 2010.

The services available to aging veterans are the same as those available to nonveterans with additional enhancements. Veterans are, of course, eligible to use any service that is an age-eligible service funded by the Older Americans Act and other services that are funded by other sources but a component of the aging network. In addition, there are long-term care benefits for veterans that help those with long-term care needs remain in the community with support and also provide financial support for assisted living and other residential treatment options. Additional information about these programs can be found in Chapters 2 and 3 of this book.

Aging Network Professionals

The many aging network professionals who work in community agencies; health care settings; and for federal, state, and local government as well as advocacy organizations are also consumers of the Older Americans Act programs. These professionals are supported by and participate in the evidence-based studies that lead to practice changes and innovations in the way in which programs are delivered and supported for older adults. They often benefit from the older workers who participate in Title V programs. The "Perspectives" section of this chapter addresses the issue of further considering the changes that need to be made in theory and practice, and Mark Brennan-Ing reminds us that LGBT older adults must be a part of this consideration.

CONCLUSIONS

In conclusion, these professionals are not only a part of the aging network, but are beneficiaries of the network as practice evolves and changes and evidence-based changes emerge over time. The aging network professionals of today are critical to the future of the networks of tomorrow. They will need the resources and training to ensure that the practice changes and innovations we have mentioned are implemented and pave the way for a good old age for all of us.

PERSPECTIVES

LGBT OLDER ADULTS, SOCIAL CARE, AND COMMUNITY-BASED SERVICES

Mark Brennan-Ing, PhD
Director for Research and Evaluation
ACRIA, Center on HIV and Aging and
Adjunct Assistant Professor
New York University College of Nursing
New York, NY

Given our limited knowledge of LGBT aging, one area of concern is this population's ability to access adequate social care as they age. As defined by Cantor and Brennan (2000), social care includes the broad-based system of informal social network resources (family and friends) and the network of community-based formal services (senior centers, home health care). The social care network

(continued)

is considered to be a vital component of helping people to age in place independently and maintain a decent quality of life.

Research suggests that the older LGBT population may have different health needs when compared with their heterosexual counterparts, affecting their needs for social care. LGBT individuals report poorer health than the general population and have higher rates of disability. HIV/AIDS is also a dominant health issue within the LGBT community. Data from the Centers for Disease Control and Prevention (2013) show that 55% of all new HIV infections occur among men who have sex with men (MSM), and 17% are diagnosed among adults aged 50 years and older. Care for older lesbian and bisexual women is often compromised because they are reluctant to disclose their sexual identities to health care providers, fearing poor treatment or negative reactions. These high rates of morbidity along with a high prevalence of mental health issues and substance use suggest that many LGBT adults will face health challenges as they age and will require assistance from their social care networks.

LGBT older adults do not have the robust informal social resources that typify heterosexuals. Social networks of older LGBT adults are characterized by reliance on the "family of choice" (close friends and neighbors), in contrast to the biological family or "family of origin" that is the foundation for most heterosexuals. There are limits in the capacity of the family of choice to provide care over the long term, especially if decision making is required. The absence of blood ties between the family of choice and the older LGBT adult can result in conflicts with the biological family. The lack of legal recognition of same-sex partners in many jurisdictions excludes them from making health care and caregiving decisions. Given their limited social networks, older LGBT adults will need to rely on community-based services to meet their needs. LGBT older adults face barriers when accessing care, including the assumption of heterosexuality, lack of same-sex partner recognition, and disparate treatment by providers resulting from negative attitudes toward the LGBT population.

Without concerted efforts to address the unique issues of LGBT aging and to create intentionally a safe and welcoming space, it remains likely that LGBT older adults will be reluctant to access community-based services. It is imperative that mainstream providers improve their LGBT cultural competency through training and capacity building. Many aging providers are open

(continued)

to receiving such training and better serving older LGBT adults. It is important that such programs be evaluated in terms of efficacy and best practices, and LGBT cultural competency should be mandated for providers receiving local, state, or federal funding.

CRITICAL THINKING QUESTIONS

1. *Is 65 years of age a good indicator of "older" today? Should it be increased and, if so, what might be the implications of that increase?*

2. *Because there is a big difference in poverty rates by race/ethnicity for both elders and children, how might the increasing diversity in the older population affect the overall well-being of the older population? Is there something that can be done to address racial and ethnic differences in poverty?*

3. *Do you or other members of your family have a stake in the success of the programs and services designed for older adults? If not, will you in the future?*

4. *How long do you want to work? What do you think about people of "retirement age" working?*

REFERENCES

Alzheimer's Association. (2014). Retrieved from http://www.alz.org.

Barker, J. (2002). Neighbors, friends, and other nonkin caregivers of community-living dependent elders. *Journal of Gerontology: Social Sciences, 57B(3)*, S158–S167.

Bureau of Labor Statistics, U.S. Department of Labor. (2010). *Issues in labor statistics: Record unemployment among older workers does not keep them out of the job market. Summary 10–04.* Retrieved March 2010 from http://www.bls.gov

Burtless, G. (2013). Can educational attainment explain the rise in labor force participation at older ages? *Issue in Brief*, No. 13–13. Center for Retirement Research at Boston College. Retrieved from http://www.ccr@bc.edu

Cantor, M., & Brennan, M. (2000). *Social care of the elderly: The effects of ethnicity, class and culture.* New York, NY: Springer Publishing Company.

Centers for Disease Control and Prevention. (2013). *HIV Surveillance report: Diagnoses of HIV infection and AIDS in the United States and Dependent areas, 2011*; Vol. 23. Retrieved from http://www.cdc.gov/hiv/statistics/basics.

Congressional Budget Office. (2013). *Rising demand for long-term services and supports for elderly people.* Washington, DC: U.S. Government Printing Office. Retrieved from www.cbo.gov.

Federal Interagency Forum on Aging-Related Statistics. (2012). *Older Americans 2012: Key indicators of well-being.* Washington, DC: U.S. Government Printing Office.

Fox, S., Duggan, M., & Purcel, K. (2013). Family caregivers are wired for health. Pew Research Internet Project. Retrieved from http://www.pewinternet .org/2013/06/20/family-caregivers-are-wired-for-health.

He, W., & Muenchrath, M. N. (2011). *American community survey reports, ACS-17, 90+ in the United States: 2006–2008.* Washington, DC: U.S. Government Printing Office.

Johnson, R. (2011). The growing importance of older workers. *Public Policy and Aging Report, 21*(4), 26–30.

Kolata, G. (2013, July 16). Dementia rate is found to drop sharply, as forecast. *The New York Times.* Retrieved from http://www.nytimes.com/2013/07/17/ health/study-finds-dip-in-dementia-rates.html?_r=0

Munnell, A. H. (2011). What is the average retirement age? *Issue in Brief,* No. 11–11. Center for Retirement Research at Boston College. Retrieved from ccr@bc.edu

Munnell, A. H., & Wu, A. Y. (2012). *Are aging baby boomers squeezing young workers out of jobs? Issue in Brief,* No. 12–18. Center for Retirement Research at Boston College. Retrieved from ccr@bc.edu

National Alliance for Caregiving (NAC). (2007). *Evercare study of family caregivers: What they spend, what they sacrifice.* Bethesda, MD: Author.

National Poverty Center. (n.d.). *Poverty in the United States: Frequently asked questions.* University of Michigan, Gerald R. Ford School of Public Policy. Retrieved from http://www.npc.umich.edu/poverty/

Olshansky, J., Antonucci, T., Berkman, L., Binstock, R. H., Boersch-Supan, A., Cacioppo, J. T.,...Rowe, J. (2012). Differences in life expectancy due to race and educational differences are widening, and many may not catch up. *Health Affairs, 31*(8), 1803–1813.

Parker, V. (2011). The importance of cultural competence in caring for and working in a diverse America. *Generations, 34*(4), 97–102.

Robison, J., Shugrue, N., Fortinsky, R. F., & Gruman, C. (2014). Long term supports and services planning for the future: Implications form a statewide survey of baby boomers and older adults. *The Gerontologist, 54*(2), 279–313.

Scommengna, P. (2012). *More U.S. children raised by grandparents.* Population Reference Bureau. Washington, DC. Retrieved March 12, 2014, from http:// www.prb.org/Publications/Articles/2012

Seltzer, J. A., & Yahirum, J. (2013). *Diversity in old age: The elderly in changing economic and family contexts.* Retrieved from http://www.s4.brown.edu/US2010/ Data/.../report/1062013.pdf

Uhlenberg, P. (2013). Demography is not destiny: The challenges and opportunities of global population aging. *Generations, 37*(1), 12–18.

U.S. Census Bureau. (2012). *2010 Census special reports. Centenarians: 2010, C2010SR-03.* Washington, DC: U.S. Government Printing Office.

U.S. Department of Health and Human Services, Administration on Aging, Administration for Community Living. (2013). *A profile of older Americans: 2012.* Retrieved February 2, 2014, from http://www.aoa.gov/Aging_Statistics

Older Americans Act Legislation and the Aging Networks

*T*his section provides an in-depth examination of the Older Americans Act (OAA) and related federal legislation. The complexity of existing and new legislation will be quickly evident, but an understanding of titles and acts discussed is imperative for students and practitioners interested in the field of aging if we are going to be fully cognizant of the importance of being proactive in the face of an aging society. Chapter 2 will help you think about why older adults received such a comprehensive legislative package of protections and services in the 1960s but today are often seen as "not worthy" of the support they are receiving and to consider the changes necessary to update the aging networks and what they provide.

CHAPTER TWO

Older Americans Act Legislation and the Evolution of a Network

In 1965, the Congress passed three important pieces of legislation that, over time, would shape and define the nation's approach to its growing older population. Medicare was enacted to ensure that older adults had the health care they needed and Medicaid was passed to provide access to health care for low-income Americans. And, the Older Americans Act (OAA) became the law of the land. In the more than 40 years since its passage, the OAA has been largely responsible for the development of the aging network of services and the structure that is in place today to provide home- and community-based services to older adults in their communities. This chapter will briefly outline the history and structure of the OAA and review the aging network of services and the network's development. In addition, we will provide an overview of the first major change in the operation of the OAA since its inception in 1965. In 2012, the Administration on Aging (AoA) was merged into a larger agency, the Administration for Community Living (ACL) and is no longer an independent aging agency. This new agency combines the federal work of advocacy and services for both the aging and the disability communities.

This chapter is designed to make you curious about:

(a) *Why older Americans received such a comprehensive legislative package of protections and services in the late 1960s and today are often seen as "not worthy" of the support they are receiving*

(b) *What changes are necessary to update the aging network of services to meet the needs of changing cohorts*

(c) *How the 2015 White House Conference on Aging's agenda can move the discussion forward about what older Americans will need in the future as their numbers grow.*

In 1950, a "National Conference on the Aging" was convened by the Federal Security Agency in the District of Columbia. The Federal Security Agency was the precursor to the Department of Health, Education and Welfare (HEW) in 1953. Between 1939 and 1953, the Federal Security Agency had responsibility for social and economic security, education, and health, including the new Social Security Administration. In the late 1940s, President Truman was advocating for a national health insurance to be funded by a payroll tax. Soon after the National Conference on Aging, the Social Security Administration's Annual Report (1951) recommended health insurance for all beneficiaries of Social Security. Throughout the 1950s, as Congress was considering the expansion of Social Security, disability and the new unemployment system, issues related to the aged, were included in the national conversation.

In 1959, the Senate Committee on Labor and Public Welfare established a special committee to study the "Problems of the Aged and Aging." In 1960, the study "The Aged and Aging in the United States: A National Problem" was unveiled. At the time of the study, 9% of the population in the United States was older than 65 years. There were 16 million older Americans and it was projected that by 1975 there would be 20 million older Americans. The 1960 report identified the following areas as important to address in order to improve the quality of life of older Americans:

- *Financing for health services*

- *Equal opportunity in employment; the report suggested that a "senior citizens service training program" be set up for those older than 45 years(!)*

- *Income adequacy; the report estimated that "at least half" of older Americans were unable to afford basic necessities of life and their income was half of that of younger Americans.*

- *Housing; the study reported that many older Americans lived with their family because they had no other alternative; it recommended that a minimum of 10,000 housing units per year be developed for low-income elders.*

■ *Community services and a professional workforce; recommendations*
included expansion of community services, evaluation of existing
services, and the creation of training programs—both academic and
applied programs.

■ *The creation of a "U.S. Office of the Aging" to ensure advocacy and*
quality improvements.

The 1960 report was an important precursor to the passage of Medicare
and the OAA. In just 5 years, Congress enacted legislation that would
ensure older Americans had affordable health care and legislation that
would create the aging network (OAA). More importantly, the objec-
tives of the act and the titles that authorize each area of activity are con-
sistent with this early report.

THE OLDER AMERICANS ACT

The OAA was enacted, in part, as a result of the first White House
Conference on Aging, which took place in 1961. The White House
Conference on Aging was convened to bring together advocates and
stakeholders to discuss issues facing older Americans and to make recommendations for national policy that might address issues related to aging.
Congress has reauthorized the Act several times since its initial passage.
As this book is being prepared (2014) there are House and Senate bills
before Congress for the reauthorization of the OAA. It has not been reauthorized since 2006. The OAA is an entitlement based on age. Americans
who are 60+ are entitled to use its programs regardless of health status,
income, or other personal characteristics. For some programs, local service providers can request a contribution, but no one can be turned away
because he or she cannot or will not make this contribution. Community-
based services are targeted for those elders with highest need, and OAA
funding is supplemented by state and local funding to ensure that services are available for those with the most need.

The AoA is an agency of the Department of Health and Human
Services (HHS) and was created by the OAA reauthorization of 1965. Until
2012, the AoA was an independent agency with the sole responsibility for
programs and services funded by the OAA. The purpose of the OAA is
defined by its objectives. These objectives and the Act also established a
new role for the federal and state governments in assuring the well-being
of older adults (O'Shaughnessy, 2008).

OBJECTIVES OF THE OAA: TITLE I

1. An adequate income in retirement in accordance with the American standard of living.

2. The best possible physical and mental health that science can make available and without regard to economic status.

3. Obtaining and maintaining suitable housing, independently selected, designed, and located with reference to special needs and available at costs that older citizens can afford.

4. Full restorative services for those who require institutional care; and a comprehensive array of community-based, long-term care services adequate to appropriately sustain older people in their communities and in their homes, including support to family members and other persons providing voluntary care to older individuals in need of long-term care services.

5. Opportunity for employment with no discriminatory personnel practices because of age.

6. Retirement in health, honor, and dignity—after years of contribution to the economy.

7. Participating in and contributing to meaningful activity within the widest range of civic, cultural, educational and training, and recreational opportunities.

8. Efficient community services, including access to low-cost transportation, which provide a choice in supported living arrangements and social assistance in a coordinated manner and which are readily available when needed, with emphasis on maintaining a continuum of care for vulnerable older individuals.

9. Immediate benefit from proven research knowledge, which can sustain and improve health and happiness.

10. Freedom, independence, and the free exercise of individual initiative in planning and managing their own lives; full participation in the planning and operation of community-based services and programs provided for their benefit; and protection against abuse, neglect, and exploitation (42 U.S.C. § 3001).

These objectives articulate a lofty policy goal for the benefit of older Americans. The other titles of the Act address specific policy initiatives

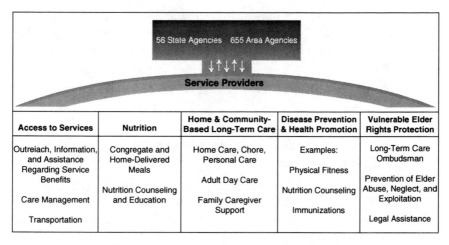

Access to Services	Nutrition	Home & Community-Based Long-Term Care	Disease Prevention & Health Promotion	Vulnerable Elder Rights Protection
Outreiach, Information, and Assistance Regarding Service Benefits Care Management Transportation	Congregate and Home-Delivered Meals Nutrition Counseling and Education	Home Care, Chore, Personal Care Adult Day Care Family Caregiver Support	Examples: Physical Fitness Nutrition Counseling Immunizations	Long-Term Care Ombudsman Prevention of Elder Abuse, Neglect, and Exploitation Legal Assistance

FIGURE 2.1   Major services of the aging network.
Source: O'Shaughnessy (2008).

and programs that address the policy intent of the Act. Title II sets out the language required to establish the AoA, which is under the supervision of the Assistant Secretary of Aging, who is appointed by the president and confirmed by the Senate. Since its inception, AoA has developed and organized the aging network (Figure 2.1), which consists of State Units on Aging (SUA), the local Area Agency on Aging (AAA) network, and thousands of service providers who work directly with older adults. Title II also establishes the National Eldercare Locator Service to provide information about aging services.

Since 1965, there have been several amendments and changes to the OAA that have both expanded the service network and modified eligibility for services. There have been many changes to the OAA since 1965 and we focus on some of the more important changes below.

EXPANSION OF THE SERVICE NETWORK AND MODIFICATION OF ELIGIBILITY

1973—The 1973 amendments provided the authorization to establish the AAA network to plan, monitor, and coordinate services at the local level. There are currently 655 AAAs throughout the nation. The 1973 amendments also reduced the age of entitlement for OAA services from 65 to 60 years.

1978—The home-delivered meals program was begun and the Long-Term Care Ombudsman Program became a requirement for all states. The AoA was charged with being the advocate across federal agencies for older Americans.

1987—Title III priorities set for access services, in-home programs, and legal services.

1992—A separate title (Title VII) was set up for all "elder rights protection activities," including the Long-Term Care Ombudsman Program and a program to prevent elder abuse and exploitation.

2000—The National Family Caregiving Support Program (NFCSP) was started. The initiation of this program expanded the focus of OAA activities and the service population to include younger informal caregivers for an older person.

2006—Congress authorized the AoA to begin disease-prevention and health-promotion programs to serve elders with chronic disease. The amendments also funded the "Choices for Independence" initiative and, among other things, established the Aging and Disability Resource Centers (ADRCs) in partnership with the Center for Medicare and Medicaid Services.

2009—Congress funded the Lifespan Respite Act, which had been passed in 2006 as part of the Title XXIX of Public Health Service Act. AoA selected 12 states for funding in 2009. These states expanded their life span respite services, working to recruit and train respite workers and providing caregiver training. Family Care Alliance and partners were selected to develop the Life Span Respite Resource Center to support all life span respite activities nationwide.

2012—The AoA is combined with disability programs, including the Office on Disability (OD) and the Administration on Developmental Disabilities (ADD) under the new DHHS unit the ACL.

TITLE III: GRANTS FOR STATE
AND COMMUNITY PROGRAMS ON AGING

Title III is the title that is used to fund and design state and community programs on aging. This title outlines the types of services that should be provided at the local level in order to develop "comprehensive and coordinated services" enabling older adults to maintain "maximum independence" (Sec. 301). There are four service areas that are funded through

Title III—supportive services, nutrition, family caregiver services, and the disease-prevention and health-promotion services. The supportive services include an array of services designed to assist older Americans to remain independent in the community and to avoid unnecessary institutionalization.

Supportive services include access services such as information and referral assistance, care management, and transportation. Home- and community-based services such as chore services, personal care services, and adult day services are also included in the supportive service array of assistance. Nutrition services available include congregate meal programs and home-delivered meal programs that serve elders who are limited in their ability to attend congregate meal programs. As the number of frail elders has increased, the demand for home-delivered meals has outpaced that of congregate meals. The family caregivers services included in Title III are specifically authorized through the NFCSP and include special programs for family caregivers, care management, and educational programming to support family caregivers, respite services, and adult day services.

Title III programs include the chronic disease self-management program (CDSMP) designed to foster health of older adults through education and health behavior changes. This program has been a widely disseminated and has provided CDSMP skills for older adults throughout the nation. Community support services, such as legal services, mental health services, and adult day programs, are eligible to receive support through Title III depending on the local AAA plan and the State Unit on Aging plan.

The SUA are required to pass along all Title III funds allocated to the AAAs. The use of Title III funds is determined by plans developed at the AAA level and at the state level. In fiscal year (FY) 2012, funding for Title III programs represented 71% of the total OAA funding. Nutrition services were funded at $816.3 million, supportive services at $366.9 million, family caregiver services received 153.6 million, and health promotion received $20.9 million, for a total of $1,357.7 billion (Napili & Colello, 2013).

Key Consumers of Title III

Title III consumers include the professionals and agencies within the aging network of services who rely on funding from the OAA as the basis of support and leverage of local dollars and older adults who are served by nutrition programs, community centers, transportation services, care management and adult day services, health services, and supportive services. Family caregivers are supported by programs in this title through the National Family Caregiver Support Program, including programs for family caregivers, care management, educational programming, and respite programming and adult day services.

TITLE IV: ACTIVITIES FOR HEALTH, INDEPENDENCE, AND LONGEVITY

Title IV of the OAA has been the primary funding mechanism for grants that have supported research on the development of the aging network and the needs of older Americans—funding intended to create new approaches to service delivery and training. Title IV funds were invested in the development of the gerontological workforce from the first cohort of trained researchers and educators in gerontology in the 1970s to training in special skill sets, such as mental health interventions among direct service workers. The funds invested in research led to the development of centers of excellence in gerontology around the country, many of which are still operating today—at the University of Southern California, Duke, Portland State University, and the University of Massachusetts—Boston to name a few. Before the focus of Title IV was changed to one of independence, health, and longevity, it was focused on education and training (Sec. 410) "to improve the quality of service and to help meet critical shortages of adequately trained personnel for programs in the field of aging" and included funding for "Multipurpose Centers of Gerontology" to develop training, conduct research, and to "incorporate information on aging into the teaching of biological, behavioral, and social sciences at colleges and universities" (Sec. 412).

Title IV funds were used to evaluate the development of new innovations in the aging network of services, such as the development of the AAA network, the future of senior centers, adult day programs, and more recently, the consumer-directed programs that allow older persons to control their own service providers and environment.

Title IV now funds the ADRCs in 43 states, and other initiatives to assist those at risk of institutionalization to remain in the community, and centers that support special issues of importance to elders, including the National Alzheimer's Call Center, National Education and Resource Center on Women and Retirement, National Resource Centers on Native Americans, National Minority Aging Organizations, National Technical Assistance Resource Center for LGBT Elders, Multigenerational Civic Engagement, and Elder Rights Support Activities. Between 2011 and 2012, Title IV program funding of $27.1 million was reduced by 72% to $7.7 million. This was because the Innovations Program was eliminated from Title IV. That program had been engaged in funding the development of the Chronic Disease

Management Programs now funded and ongoing through Title III funding, and other demonstration models that were moved from the evidence-seeking stage to the developed stage are now funded elsewhere.

Key Consumers of Title IV

The consumers of these programs include both older Americans and family caregivers as they benefit from improved access to services and educational resources as well as improved and innovative programs. In addition, providers of services in the aging network are consumers of the work funded by Title IV as they participate in the demonstration of new and innovative programming themselves and incorporate findings of the evaluative work into their own practice.

TITLE V: SENIOR COMMUNITY SERVICE EMPLOYMENT PROGRAM

Title V funds senior employment programs for low-income older adults. This title is administered by the Department of Labor and is managed by national organizations and states. Unemployed persons 55 years of age and older who are in the low-income group (125% of the federal poverty level) are eligible to receive training and subsidized employment opportunities through the program. The Senior Community Service Employment Program (SCSEP) is, for many adults, an ongoing essential income source and, for others, a stepping stone to unsubsidized employment. Funding for Title V programs was $443.25 million in 2012. The AoA has requested that Title V programs be moved from Department of Labor management to AoA management in order to effect integration between the employment programs and the supportive services of OAA. Napili and Colello (2013) report that in order for this shift to occur Congress would have to enact legislation authorizing the move. Since the 2012 administrative request, no further action has been taken on this proposal.

Key Consumers of Title V

Low-income older adults are a key consumer group of this title through the provision of subsidized employment in the community, training opportunities, and an option for transitioning into new jobs as they complete their time in a Title V position. The community organizations that host these older workers are also consumers of this title. The individual assigned to them is paid by Title V and not the organization. When there is a good match between the older worker and the organization there is an opportunity for other workers at the organization to experience firsthand the value of older workers and for the older workers to gain new skills and experiences that will help them in the future.

TITLE VI: GRANTS FOR NATIVE AMERICANS

This title authorizes funds for Native American tribes to develop social and nutritional services for the aged. In addition to Indian tribal organizations, Native Hawaiian organizations are also covered under this program. This set-aside for tribes and indigenous organizations recognizes the autonomy of these groups as well as the special needs of the elders that are best addressed within their cultural environment. Total funding for Title VI was $33.965 million in 2012. This funding was distributed to 256 tribal organizations. Funds may be used for transportation, home-delivered and congregate meals, home care services, caregiver services, as well as information and outreach programs. In addition, respite services may be funded as can counseling and support groups.

Key Consumers of Title VI

Members of Native American and Hawaiian tribes are key consumers of funding in this title. In addition to the elders, family members are supported by information and outreach programs, respite programs, and counseling and support groups.

TITLE VII: VULNERABLE ELDER RIGHTS PROTECTION ACTIVITIES

Title VII has two major components: The State Long-Term Care Ombudsman Program and the Elder Abuse Prevention Program. The set-aside of a separate title for all elder rights protection programs demonstrates a commitment to addressing the very serious issues associated with elder abuse, neglect, and exploitation as well as the protection of the rights of older Americans. The Patient Protection and Affordable Care Act (ACA) contained the Elder Justice Act, an Act that is designed to strengthen the protection available to vulnerable elders through adult protective services, better coordination between federal and state offices, and training and research centers. Although not part of Title VII, this new program will likely influence the way this title operates and is funded over time. More about this new initiative will be covered later on in this book. The State Long-Term Care Ombudsman Program is responsible for the well-being of adults who are living in long-term care facilities. Staffing in most states is a combination of professionals and volunteer ombudsmen. The ombudsman's role in protecting the rights of older Americans is to work as an advocate to resolve situations that may occur between the preferences and rights of older residents living in long-term care facilities and the facility administration and staff.

Key Consumers of Title VII

The key consumers of Title VII programs are those older adults who are vulnerable and have adverse experiences with administrators or staff of residential facilities or family members or friends in the community who are exploiting or abusing the elders. Other consumers of the program supported by this title include facility administrators/owners, members of the legal community who are advocates for older adults, and the law enforcement community involved in investigating and prosecuting perpetrators of elder abuse. In addition, health professionals are consumers of information developed and disseminated by the advocacy network supported by these programs that allow them to better evaluate and treat their older patients.

THE NEW 2012 AOA

Since 1965, the AoA has been an independent agency within the DHHS. The function of AoA has been to administer the programs funded by the OAA and act as the central clearinghouse for aging-related information and advocacy. In 2012, the AoA became a part of the ACL, also housed in the DHHS. As we were thinking about this new edition of the aging networks, we wondered how this change might affect the operation of OAA programs and whether the voice of advocacy for older Americans might be lessened as a result of it no longer being an independent administrative agency. We asked Greg Link, Aging Program specialist in the AoA and the manager of the National Family Caregivers Act programs, to prepare an essay for the text that provided the reader with information about the change, why it occurred, and what we might expect as a result of this change.

PERSPECTIVES

OPERATIONAL CHANGES AFFECTING THE AOA

Perspective on ACL
Greg Link, MA
Aging Program Specialist
Administration on Aging
Office of Supportive and Caregiver Services
Washington, DC

The Administration for Community Living

In April 2012, the creation of the ACL, a new operating division within the DHHS, was announced. The establishment of the ACL is a notable achievement in the federal landscape because it created a single organization devoted to strengthening and enhancing DHHS's efforts to support seniors and people with disabilities. The creation of the ACL occurred in response to the growing need to better understand, advocate for, and support the needs of seniors and people with disabilities. This section highlights key events leading up to the creation of the ACL, describes the structure and function of the new agency, and describes how the AoA and the programs it supports continue to be a mainstay in the lives of frail older adults and their family caregivers.

(continued)

Olmstead and the Community Living Initiative

The groundwork for the creation of the ACL lies in the Supreme Court's 1999 *Olmstead* decision, which reaffirmed the belief that all Americans, including people with disabilities and seniors, should be able to live at home with the support they need and participate to the fullest extent in communities that value their contributions. Since then, the federal sector, in partnership with states and communities, has worked to operationalize the directives contained in *Olmstead* to create meaningful and lasting change in the long-term services and supports (LTSS) landscape nationwide.

In June 2009, the 10th anniversary of the *Olmstead* decision, DHHS launched the Community Living Initiative (CLI) to promote cross-federal partnerships to advance the mandates of that decision. The CLI develops and implements strategies for increasing the availability of meaningful community-living opportunities for older adults and persons with disabilities. The passage of the ACA in March 2010 broadened the scope of the CLI by creating new opportunities for states to promote and support community living for people with disabilities and enhancing the focus on the relationship between LTSS and accessible and affordable health care.

Led by a Coordinating Council made up of representatives from across DHHS, the primary goals and objectives of the CLI are to ensure that LTSS are person centered, culturally competent, inclusive, sustainable, efficient, coordinated, and transparent. Working groups lead department-wide efforts to implement CLI goals and objectives by focusing broadly on the barriers that prevent persons with disabilities and older adults from realizing meaningful lives as part of their community.

One such barrier to full community participation is the fragmentation often present in the development, implementation, and administration of LTSS programs. When this happens, it can be difficult for programs to comprehensively understand, advocate for, and support the needs of persons with disabilities and older adults. Similarly, such silos can often make it difficult for consumers to access needed services and supports. To address this issue, public-sector entities sometimes turn to

(continued)

interdepartmental realignment as a means to more efficiently and inclusively address the issues it is charged with overseeing. In this respect, the creation of ACL is intended to enhance and strengthen DHHS's efforts to address matters pertaining to aging and disability policy.

The Administration for Community Living

That all people, regardless of age and disability, live with dignity, make their own choices and participate fully in society.

—*ACL Vision Statement*

Formally announced by DHHS Secretary Kathleen Sebelius on April 2, 2012, the creation of the ACL involved three components within DHHS—the AoA, the Office of Disabilities (OD), and the Administration for Developmental Disabilities (ADD), including the office supporting the President's Committee for People with Intellectual Disabilities (PCPID). As part of the reorganization, ADD was renamed the Administration for Intellectual and Developmental Disabilities (AIDD) to more fully reflect the scope of the populations served by its programs.

At the federal level, the ACL is intended to sharpen the focus on finding common solutions to community living for all individuals, regardless of age or disability. ACL seeks to realize more fully the Obama administration's vision of ensuring "the fullest inclusion of all people in the life of our nation" by focusing on the following objectives:

- Reduce the fragmentation that currently exists in federal programs by addressing the community-living service and support needs of both the aging and disability populations

- Enhance access to quality health care and LTSS for all individuals

- Promote consistency in community-living policy across other areas of the federal government

(*continued*)

■ Complement the community infrastructures, as supported by Medicaid and other federal programs, to better respond to the full spectrum of the needs of seniors and persons with disabilities

The organizational structure for ACL includes the following major operational components:

■ Office of the Administrator (OA)

   ● ACL Regional Support Centers

■ AoA

■ AIDD

■ Center for Disability and Aging Policy (CDAP)

■ Center for Management and Budget (CMB)

Although the creation of ACL involved three distinct operational divisions within DHHS, the organizational expertise, focus, and resources of the respective components involved have remained unchanged. AoA and AIDD exist as distinct organizations within the overall structure of ACL, with daily management of the respective AoA and AIDD programs and operations continuing relatively unchanged. The range of programs serving seniors and caregivers authorized in the OAA continue operation under ACL's AoA. Programs for people with intellectual and developmental disabilities and their families continue to be led by ACL's AIDD.

Within ACL, coordination of federal activities on behalf of older Americans and persons with disabilities occurs within the newly created CDAP. The CDAP supports, plans, coordinates, and oversees the implementation of programs and initiatives designed to overcome barriers that prevent older Americans and persons with disabilities from fully participating and contributing inclusively in community life. In this role, CDAP and its four offices work across all components of ACL to develop and implement federal policies and programs to address the needs of older individuals and persons with disabilities.

(continued)

AoA and the Aging Services Network Today

The OAA of 1965 continues to be the foundation of the Aging Services Network by focusing on ensuring the well-being of older adults and their family caregivers. The Network is comprised of 56 SUA and territorial units on aging, 618 AAAs, 256 Indian Tribal and Native Hawaiian organizations, nearly 20,000 direct service providers, and hundreds of thousands of volunteers. AoA's core programs, authorized under the seven titles that make up the OAA, help seniors remain at home for as long as possible. These services fall into broad categories, including:

■ Access assistance in the form of outreach, information, care management, and transportation services

■ Nutrition programs, such as home-delivered and congregate meals, and nutrition counseling and education

■ Home- and community-based LTSS, such as home and personal care services, chores, adult day care programs, and family caregiver support services

■ Disease-prevention and health-promotion programs focusing on improvement of physical fitness, prevention of falls, and better management of chronic diseases and disabilities

■ Ensuring that the rights of our most frail elders are protected through long-term care ombudsman; elder abuse, neglect, and exploitation prevention service; and legal assistance programs

Analysis of AoA's FY 2011 performance data (the most recent year for which data are available as of this publication) and trends demonstrates that the Aging Services Network is highly effective in meeting established targets and outcomes. Although units of service delivery have declined in recent years, largely due to flat funding and inflationary factors, program evaluation data

(continued)

continue to demonstrate that the services provided by the Aging Services Network are highly effective. For example:

■ *OAA programs help frail older Americans remain independent in their homes and communities.* Older adults with three or more impairments in activities of daily living (ADL) are at a high risk of nursing home placement. In FY 2003, the Aging Services Network served home-delivered meals to 280,454 clients with three or more ADL impairments. By FY 2011, that number grew to 358,376—a 30% increase and an example of the Network's ability to effectively target and serve vulnerable seniors.

■ *OAA programs are efficient.* In addition to helping frail older Americans remain in their homes and communities, OAA programs are doing so in an efficient and cost-effective way. Over the years, Aging Services Network providers have increased the numbers of clients served per million dollars of OAA, Title III funds. For example, in FY 2011, the Network served 8,881 people per million dollars of OAA funds.

■ *OAA programs build system capacity.* By staying true to their original intent as outlined in Section 301 of the OAA, Aging Services Network programs "encourage and assist State agencies and Area Agencies on Aging to concentrate resources in order to develop greater capacity and foster the development and implementation of comprehensive and coordinated systems." This is demonstrated most clearly by the fact that for every dollar of OAA funds expended, nearly $3 of state/local and other sources are leveraged to increase the state's capacity to meet service needs.

■ *OAA programs are valued by consumers and are of high quality.* The 2012 National Survey of Older Americans Act Participants (Administriation on Aging, 2013) demonstrates that the services provided by the Aging Services Network are essential to helping seniors remain independent, support family caregivers in meaningful ways, and are highly regarded by consumers. For example:

● 77% of congregate meal participants indicated that they ate healthier foods as a result of the program

(continued)

- 59% of consumers receiving congregate meals said that the program helped them remain at home

- 86% of homemaker recipients indicated that as a result of the services they receive, they are able to live independently

- 85% of caregivers served indicated that as a result of the supportive services they received, it was easier to continue providing care to their loved one

- 74% of caregivers felt less stress as a result of the services they received

The effectiveness of Aging Network programs is due in large measure to the creativity and responsiveness of SUAs, AAAs, and local providers. With leadership from AoA, the Network continues to design programs and services that promote consumer choice and independence, translate research into practice, and address the needs of family caregivers. For example:

- Through demonstration programs funded under Title IV of the OAA and in partnership with the Centers for Medicare and Medicaid Services (CMS), AoA has supported states and communities in developing ADRCs to provide person-centered, no-wrong-door approaches for accessing a range of long-term services and support options for persons of all ages with a disability and their families.

- In 2008, ACL and the Veterans Health Administration (VHA) began a partnership to serve veterans of all ages at risk of nursing home placement through the Veterans Directed Home and Community Based Services (VD-HCBS) program. The VD-HCBS program provides veterans the opportunity to self-direct their long-term supports and services and continue to live independently at home.

- With grants from the 2012 ACA Prevention and Public Health Fund (PPHF), states are delivering evidence-based health-promotion and disease-prevention programs employing the latest research to empower older adults to take care of their health.

(continued)

■ Through Public Health Service Act–funded programs like the Alzheimer's disease, Supportive Services Program, and Lifespan Respite Care Program, states are implementing evidence-based interventions to support family caregivers of individuals with Alzheimer's disease and related dementias and developing statewide coordinated systems of accessible and high-quality respite services.

For nearly 50 years, the OAA and the AoA have guided the work of the Aging Services Network to provide services to nearly 11 million older adults and their family caregivers every year. As the principal advocate for older Americans at the federal level, the AoA will continue to advance the concerns and interests of older people and provide leadership to the Aging Services Network, promote the design and delivery of cutting-edge programs and services, and advocate for the needs of our most frail older citizens and their family caregivers.

The creation of the ACL grew out of the belief that all Americans, including people with disabilities and older adults, should be able to live at home with the supports they need and to participate fully in their communities that value their contributions. To that end, ACL, via its multiple program areas, will work with states, tribes, community providers, families, and a host of public and private entities to design public policies and programs, protect the rights of elders, prevent abuse and neglect, promote self-determination and independence, and facilitate access to needed LTSS.

ACL Strategic Goals: 2013 to 2018

Goal 1: Advocacy—Advocate to ensure the interests of people with disabilities, older adults, and their families are reflected in the design and implementation of public policies and programs.

Goal 2: Protect rights and prevent abuse—protect and enhance the rights of older Americans and prevent the abuse, neglect, and exploitation of older adults and people with disabilities.

Goal 3: Individual self-determination and control—work with older adults and people with disabilities as they fully engage and

(*continued*)

participate in their communities, make informed decisions, and exercise self-determination and control of their independence, well-being, and health.

Goal 4: LTSS—enable people with disabilities and older adults to live in the community through the availability of and access to high-quality LTSS, including supports for families and caregivers.

Goal 5: Effective and responsive management—implement management and workforce practices that support the integrity and efficient operations of programs serving people with disabilities and older adults and ensure stewardship of taxpayers' dollars (ACL, 2013).

SERVICE PHILOSOPHY OF THE AGING NETWORK

The objectives of the OAA in Title I set the stage for a service philosophy that continues today, nearly 50 years after its enactment. The Aging Network is dedicated to providing assistance and support to older adults and their informal caregivers that allows them to remain in the community and avoid unnecessary institutionalization. If an older adult requires skilled nursing care in a nursing home, he or she has the right to full restorative care services and to return to the community when able to live independently again. Although not all areas of the country have the full range of services needed to achieve that goal, each area's aging network professionals strive to develop and maintain a continuum of services to allow individuals the freedom of choice about where they live, how they live, and what they do. The OAA and the rules of law support autonomy and independence for persons of advanced age. Older Americans are assumed to be capable of both managing their lives and their decision making independently. Services are provided with OAA funding on the basis of age. Although many services provided by the aging network today request a donation from consumers, this donation is not required for participation in a meal program or activity.

Since the 1990s the aging network has also been focused on "person-centered" services in the community that allow for flexibility and autonomy of the older adult. The person-centered program initiative has been supported by Assistant Secretary for Planning and Evaluation (ASPE), the

Robert Wood Johnson Foundation, and through the development of the ADRC network. The ADRC network is designed to be a one-stop shop for accessing services and supports that are needed to remain in the community in a setting that is chosen by the individual. The ADRCs have developed the No Wrong Door system (NWD) to provide information and help to individuals to develop a person-centered plan through the provision of information and one-on-one counseling. Resources are provided not only to the individual, but also to family caregivers and professionals who assist clients in planning for LTSS and future needs. The NWD program is collaboration among ACL, CMS, and the Veterans Health Administration (VHA). The goal is to streamline the LTSS options available to older adults and persons with disabilities. These programs link individuals to resources in the aging network that are funded by the OAA, LTSS that are funded by Medicaid and VHA, as well as resources that are supported by state funds. There are, according to ACL, 530 NWD centers nationwide that have responded to 25 million requests to provide information about LTSS and other health questions and issues.

REAUTHORIZATION OF THE OAA

The OAA has been both amended and reauthorized many times since its original passage in 1965. The Act is scheduled to be reauthorized every 5 years but has not been reauthorized since 2006. That reauthorization covered the appropriations for the programs of the OAA through 2011. Funding since that time has been on a continuing resolution and none of the bills introduced to reauthorize the OAA has been acted on in Congress. The National Association of Area Agencies on Aging (N4A) has four recommendations that they are advocating for the next reauthorization:

- To preserve the person-centered nature of the Older American Acts programs that recognize the importance of the local community aging services

- To strengthen the role of the aging network of services and integrate these services more effectively with health—physical and mental—services

- To increase the level of funding to support the services needed by a growing number of old-old Americans in greatest need of supportive services and their caregivers. N4A points out that Older American Act programs have resulted in a "three-to-one" return on investment in community service support.

▓ To strengthen the capacity of the aging network through initiatives that will increase competencies; provide evidence on outcomes; evaluations; and address staff and volunteer training, development, and retention (N4A Policy Priorities, 2013).

It is unclear when the reauthorization of the OAA will occur. When the Congress debates the reauthorization there will be many issues coming up for discussion. O'Shaughnessy (2011) points out several challenges to the OAA programs now and in the future. One of these challenges is a growing population eligible for and in need of programs offered by the OAA and a limited budget to support the costs of these programs. In order to keep up with the needs of elders in the community, many AAAs have become social entrepreneurs, developing supplemental funding from several sources to expand the existing federal allocations. The structure of the aging service's decentralized planning and service model has also led to variability in the services available to older adults and, in some cases, variability in the quality as well. In addition, as mentioned in the first chapter of this book, the older population is becoming more heterogeneous and diverse as well as expanding in size. This adds additional pressure on the aging network as it tries to accommodate changing "consumer" preferences and needs while also trying to manage the expanding market for services that are limited due to limited funding.

The aging networks are, in addition to unpaid family caregivers, the primary provider of long-term care services or long-term services and support. As the old-old group increases in size, the demand for LTSS will also increase and it is unlikely that the increase in funding for these services will keep pace with the need. A thoughtful reauthorization is needed in order to manage our aging future and to ensure that services are adequate, of high quality, and provided by trained and a well-managed workforce.

Changes in the Allocation of Funding: Improved Equity?

Since its inception, the OAA has been an entitlement program based on age and, more recently, special status such as being a family caregiver. Although some programs funded by OAA ask consumers to make a contribution to the costs of the program, that is, meal programs requesting a donation of a certain amount, these contributions are voluntary and no one can be turned away if he or she is unable to pay. Funding levels of OAA have been limited and most aging network services and programs are required to use additional resources to support the programs of importance to older adults. At the local level, federal funds are supplemented by funds collected from community foundations, United Way and other sources. The N4A estimates that each federal dollar leverages $3. Nonetheless, funding for OAA programs is not able to meet the demand for services. For example, the home-delivered meals are not adequately funded to provide meals to all of the elders who qualify for the program. There are waiting lists in many American communities. In 2012, the Government Accountability Office (GAO) conducted a study of OAA programs to identify better ways to allocate funding that targets needs (GAO, 2012). Their report was designed to examine strategies to ensure that the funds are being used in a targeted and efficient way. Their study found that the allocation of OAA funds based on the number of state residents 60 years and older was not consistent with equitable targeting of funds to those with the most need. States are required to target elders with the greatest economic and social needs due to low income or being at risk of institutional placement or isolation due to social, geographic, language, race, or ethnic culture.

The GAO used the state of Louisiana and the state of Colorado as examples of the inequitable allocation formula. Louisiana has 83,000 more people with at least one ADL limitation than Colorado but Louisiana receives a higher allotment of OAA funding because Colorado has more people aged 60+. They recommend that using ADL estimates to allocate need would result in a more equitable distribution to states of OAA funds. Another way to modify the allocation, adjusting for the relative difference in the costs of wages, food, and other "inputs" needed to manage the programs, would also provide better equity. Finally, an allocation partially based on a state's taxable resources would also lead to better equity.

The White House Conference on Aging

The first White House Conference on Aging was convened in 1961, just 1 year after the landmark study on aging in America was unveiled. This conference has been an aging network event of importance since that time. The 1961 White House Conference on Aging participants, who were selected from around the country, worked on the development of issues of importance to American elders and developed recommendations about programs needed to meet the needs of these elders. Four years later, the OAA was passed and the aging network was funded and built with an organized system of agencies that were designed to foster not only the involvement of older Americans but also the communities they served in order to address the needs of older Americans. The AAA network was developed and the SUA were also created in order to construct the framework of the aging network. And, of course, the AoA was created to oversee the project and entrusted with ensuring the welfare of older adults over time.

There have been White House Conferences on Aging approximately every 10 years since then. However, it has not always been an easy thing to convene the conferences. In 1981, the White House Conference on Aging process for delegate selection and "control" of the agenda, which emerged from the event, was "politicized" and became a political party issue. For a great read and interesting peek into political workings around aging, see *The Politicalization of the 1981 White House Conference on Aging, A Report Presented by the Chairman of the Select Committee on Aging, House of Representatives, Ninety-Eighth Congress* (Select Committee on Aging, 1984). The conflict began in the spring of 1981 when President Reagan proposed a cut in Social Security benefits by $82 billion in the subsequent 5 years. There were protests and public demonstrations, and Congressmen were lobbied to work against this proposal. Even though the administration withdrew the proposal after the uproar, this continued to be a hot-button issue and was slated as the number one topic for the upcoming 1981 White House Conference on Aging. Eight weeks before the conference was to begin, the executive director and assistant director of the conference were fired and replaced. Delegates to the conference began to complain that they had been called with a "suspicious" survey regarding their opinions about the administration, the organizations they belonged to, and so on. The conference was convened "amid suspicion, tension, and frank partisanship" (Select Committee on Aging, 1984, p. viii). The report reads like a mystery novel and is a fascinating snapshot of the history of the aging network.

At the time of the writing of this text, President Obama had included funds for a White House Conference on Aging to be convened in that fiscal year.

CONCLUSION

The OAA programs form the center of the aging networks and services for elders in the United States. Although there have been organizational changes affecting OAA programs and the AoA, many issues need to be addressed. For example, should the federal program continue to be a program that is an entitlement based on age or should an individual's level of need be the primary factor in allocation of OAA resources? With the number of older Americans increasing, the life expectancy being high, and with more older Americans remaining in the workforce longer, should 60 years continue to be the age of entitlement for services? Obviously, little can be done without reauthorization of the OAA and we continue to wait for that to occur. It is important that we not only continue to advocate for reauthorization but discuss changes that are needed, if any, in the Act based on the changing nature of the older American population.

In the meantime, innovations within the aging network are occurring as a result of collaborative work among ACL, the Veterans Administration (VA) programs, CMS, and the many local agencies and organizations that have as their goal the advocacy and support of older Americans.

CRITICAL THINKING QUESTIONS

1. *What are some potential challenges and opportunities associated with intradepartmental reorganizations such as the one that created the ACL?*

2. *As a result of bringing together three separate entities from across DHHS, what potential benefits could be realized with respect to ACL's ability to advocate on behalf of its target populations?*

3. *How can the structure of the ACL support AoA's advocacy on behalf of older Americans and their family caregivers?*

4. *What are the benefits to older adults and their families of maintaining the programs of the OAA as entitlement programs according to age? Are there any disadvantages?*

5. *Identify some of the issues that might be controversial in the upcoming White House Conference on Aging.*

6. *What do you think are the most important topics to discuss during the White House Conference on Aging?*

REFERENCES

Administration on Aging (2013). *2012 national survey of older Americans act participants*. Retrieved from http://www.agid.acl.gov/DataFiles/NPS/

Administration for Community Living (2013). *ACL strategic plan 2013-2018*. Retrieved from http://www.acl.gov/About_ACL/StrategicPlan/docs/ACL_ Strategic_Plan.pdf

Government Accounting Office. (2012). *Older Americans Act: Options to better target need and improve equity*. US Government Accountability Office Report to the Ranking Member, Special Committee on Aging, U.S. Senate. Retrieved from http://www.gao.gov.

Napili, A., & Colello, K. (2013). *Funding for the Older Americans Act and other aging services programs*. Congressional Research Service. Retrieved December 5, 2014, from http://www.crs.gov

N4a Policy Priorities. (2013). *Promote the health, security and well-being of older adults*. Retrieved October 5, 2014, from http://www.n4a.org

O'Shaughnessy, C. (2008). *The aging services network: Accomplishments and challenges in serving a growing elderly population*. National Health Policy Forum, Background Paper, April 11. Washington, DC: George Washington University. Retrieved November 7, 2014, from http://www.nhpf.org

O'Shaughnessy, C. (2011). *The aging services network: Serving a vulnerable and growing elderly population in tough economic times*. National Health Policy Forum, Background Paper No. 83, Dec. 13. Washington, DC: George Washington University. Retrieved January 5, 2014, http://www.nhpf.org

Select Committee on Aging. (1984). *The politicization of the 1981 White House Conference on Aging: A report presented by the chairman of the Select Committee on Aging, House of Representatives, Ninety-Eighth Congress*. Washington, DC: U.S. Government Printing Office.

Community-Based Services, Aging in Place, Income Security, and Well-Being in Later Life

*M*any of the programs and services included in this section have common elements. Adult day centers and multipurpose senior centers use transportation and have major social components, for example. Although we often discuss providing "services" or "serving" older adults, the attempt is to differentiate between programs and services, terms often used synonymously. As defined, "programs" contain individual elements; "services" include many of the same elements combined under a larger umbrella. The focus is on programs vital to the well-being of older adults: information, referral, and outreach; mental health programs; transportation; elder justice; and nutrition programs are just a few we will be addressing in Section Three.

Chapter 3 introduces community-based services provided by the aging networks and segues into Chapter 4, where we address the community supports provided by the aging networks to help older adults age in place. Income security is a critical issue for older adults and is addressed in Chapter 5 along with an historical overview of legislation. Chapter 6 covers elder justice and disaster preparedness, an increasingly important issue for our aging society.

CHAPTER THREE

Community-Based Services

The broad array of community-based services for older adults has developed over time as a result of the Older Americans Act (OAA) and the Administration on Aging (AoA) and the funding allocated to this Act by Congress. Senior centers were built, staffed, and funded. Home-delivered and congregate meals were developed and implemented nationwide. And the range of services was developed and sustained as a result of the Area Agency on Aging (AAA) network. This network was established to provide every community a local focus for its investment in programming for older adults. The AAAs, of which there are now 629 in the country, were envisioned to be this focal point. In addition, the aging network includes 256 tribal and Native Hawaiian organizations (Napili & Colello, 2013). These organizations plan and coordinate the service networks in their geographic locations. Service networks vary across the country but most include the following services provided by a combination of OAA funding, state funding, and local funding:

- *Meals programs*
- *Senior centers*
- *Adult day programs for elders with care needs*
- *Family caregiver programs*
- *Information and referral services*
- *Senior transportation*
- *Health-promotion centers*

In addition, other federal and state funds support elder justice services, such as Adult Protective Services and the Ombudsman Program. Finally, home health and other health-related programs are supported by Medicare for beneficiaries, public health funding, and Medicaid funding. It is a complex weave of funding and service models that are supported by nonprofit and charitable organizational providers as well as state, county, and city providers. OAA funding supports the Eldercare Locator service, which is a service designed to assist callers identify services throughout the country.

In this chapter, we will explore the elements of the aging network and how they work together in the community to provide assistance to consumers. In addition, we discuss family caregiving and the importance to not only the care recipients, but the long-term care system and society as well. A brief review of effectiveness data collected by the AoA follows along with a discussion of persistent issues currently being addressed through innovations and research to develop evidence-based models of care. After reading the chapter, you will be curious about:

(a) *How services are integrated to provide older adults with the highest quality possible for maximum support and well-being*

(b) *What social benefits are derived from the programs and the interaction between program participants*

(c) *How long-term services and supports (LTSS) can be better managed and paid for to support those who need long-term support and services*

(d) *How this network can and will evolve over time to serve the changing cohorts of older adults*

THE DEFAULT LONG-TERM CARE SERVICE NETWORK—FAMILY AND FRIENDS

Most older adults who need help would prefer to receive this help from their family or friends. Although many elders are independent, there are situations during which even the most independent elder will need a helping hand. Adult children, other relatives, and, at times, neighbors and friends provide this extra help. In a Select Committee report issued in 1987, unpaid care provided by family and friends was estimated to make up 80% of all of the long-term services used by older Americans (Select

Committee on Aging, 1987). Current research on family caregiving suggests that this continues to be the primary source of help when help is needed. Family caregivers take on tasks that range from helping an older adult with shopping and lawn maintenance to complicated health tasks after a hospitalization. In a recent study conducted by the Pew Research Center, approximately 40% of all American adults were engaged in some caregiving for an elder or adult with long-term care needs (Pew Research Center, 2013). The Congressional Budget Office estimates that family and friends provided services on an unpaid basis worth $234 billion in 2011; or the equivalent of 55% of the total LTSS expenses in the United States. In 2011, nursing home care made up 31% of the LTSS budget and home- and community-based services were 14%; the remainder of the value of LTSS was provided on an unpaid basis by family and friends.

Although most family caregivers report that they received personal satisfaction from the caregiving tasks they performed, there are also many costs associated with providing this care. Caregivers are often required to make workplace accommodations and some actually leave the workplace as a result of their caregiving responsibilities. The National Alliance for Caregiving (NAC)/AARP survey of family caregivers (2009) revealed that as many as 10% of the employed caregivers left the workplace. Family caregivers also do more than hands-on care; they often purchase goods and services that the care recipient cannot afford. This out-of-pocket spending can pose a difficult burden on families with limited incomes. Caregivers spend an average of 19 hours a week on caregiving-related activities (NAC/AARP, 2009).

The National Family Caregivers Support Program (NFCSP) began in 2000 and is funded through Title III of the OAA. In 2012, the allocation to this program and its activities was $153.6 million. The NFCSP requires that the aging network of services, including the Area Agency on Aging network and the Aging and Disability Resource Center (ADRC) network include family caregivers as consumers of their services. Surveys of family caregivers have found that some of the most pressing needs of caregivers include:

- Information about the underlying illness or condition of the care recipient

- Assistance in identifying the needs of the care recipient and help managing the services that are needed

- Respite services

- Supportive services for caregivers

▨   Assistance with transportation and escort services

▨   Help selecting a home health agency or assisted-living facility (NAC/ AARP, 2009)

Those caregivers who are employed, which includes the majority of family caregivers, also report that they need more flexibility at work, and some support and assistance at work when they need to see to the care of the care recipient.

SERVICES THAT SUPPORT BOTH THE ELDER AND THE FAMILY CAREGIVER

Home-Delivered Meals

Research suggests that 90% of the recipients of home-delivered meals are 60 years or older. In most communities around the nation, there are not enough home-delivered meals to meet the demand. AoA has addressed this problem by allowing local AAAs to shift some funds from congregate meals to home-delivered meals. The home-delivered meals also offer a social connection for the recipients. The person delivering the meal may be the only person the elder sees during the day. The meal delivery becomes a brief social connection for the homebound elder and enables someone to check on his or her well-being. This is particularly important for those elders who live at a distance from their adult children or other family members.

Geriatric Care Management Services

In many AAAs around the country and in affiliated organizations, a family caregiver can receive help in planning for the array of services his or her care recipient needs. Geriatric care management services are provided by nonprofit organizations as well as independent private trained individuals. Some large employers also offer this program to their employees with geriatric care responsibilities. A trained and skilled geriatric care manager can be of assistance to an older wife who needs to design a care system for an older husband; an adult child caring for a parent, a friend, or a neighbor who needs some ideas on ways he or she can support the elder in his or her home; or an elder who needs some advice himself or herself as he or she tries to maintain his or her independence during a health episode. And, of course, this service can be essential for long-distance caregivers who cannot check up on their loved ones themselves.

Transportation Services and Escort Services

Transportation services are essential for older adults living in the community who no longer drive. These services allow them to go to doctor's appointments, visit the senior center, and attend church services. Most publicly funded transportation services, however, are restricted to medical appointments due to a lack of funding. Some communities have started volunteer transportation programs that rely on volunteer drivers using their own automobiles to counter the shortage of funds for transportation.

THE OLDER CAREGIVER

The NAC/AARP survey of family caregivers has demonstrated that an increasing number of caregivers are older themselves. Examination of the 1997, 2004, and 2009 samples of family caregivers suggests that the percentage of caregivers older than 75 years is increasing and that these caregivers have some unique characteristics. Although many of these caregivers are helping an aging spouse, 20% were caring for a friend, 20% were caring for a parent, and 18% were caring for a sibling. The older caregivers reported a higher level of burden than the younger caregivers and were most likely of any age group to report that no one was helping them in their caregiving activities (Wagner & Tagaki, 2010). These older caregivers used respite services and transportation services more frequently than younger caregivers. As the oldest-old population increases, it is likely that we will see an increase in caregiving on the part of this age group, and it is important to remember that their needs for support are likely to be different and more intense than the needs of younger caregivers.

CONSUMER VIEWS: VOICES OF CAREGIVERS

- Joe has been helping his father manage the care he needs as a result of a recent cancer diagnosis. His 85-year-old father does not want to go to the clinic to get his treatment by himself and will only go for treatment if his son takes him and stays at the clinic with him. Recently, Joe reported that, even though he was taking intermittent Family and Medical Leave Act (FMLA) time off (his right protected by federal law) his supervisor at work told him that he would lose his job if he continued to take time off to help his father. Joe, who supports a family of three children, cannot afford to lose his job and is presented with a very difficult dilemma.

Emily is a 35-year-old single woman who is providing care for her father. He is 75 years of age with multiple health problems and is homebound. Emily has recently made the decision to leave her job in order to provide full-time care to her dad. She is convinced that he will not live much longer and needs more help every day than she can provide while working. Emily will give up her job and her income, move into her father's house, and deal with her own future after her father dies.

Joanna is a 25-year-old woman who recently finished a graduate degree and started her career at a company in the Midwest. Her grandmother, who lives on the East Coast, recently was hospitalized and is back home receiving home health care services. Joanna has started flying back to the East Coast every weekend to see to the care of her grandmother. As a result of these weekend trips, Joanna has been unable to socialize with coworkers and neighbors in her new community and is unavailable for weekend work. Although weekend work is not mandatory, Joanna realizes that she is likely to be passed over for promotions as a result of the caregiving choices she has made.

Mary is providing care to her aging husband who is moving into a nursing home because she can no longer care for his personal care needs. He is bed bound now and, at age 89 years herself, it is impossible for her to transfer him, bathe him, or assist with toileting. She is very concerned about her own ability to visit him when he moves into the facility because she no longer drives. Mary and her husband had no children but they do have a niece who lives nearby and Mary is hoping that she will be able to take her to the facility to visit. Mary is afraid of using the public bus system because she is not able to get safely to her seat while the bus is moving and has fallen once before. She has been caring for her husband alone for 10 years.

Note: Names have been changed but these are actual caregiver situations.

THE LONG-TERM SERVICES
AND SUPPORT NETWORK

The aging network of services is designed to support adults with functional limitations to remain as independent and autonomous as possible. Long-term care, once associated with nursing homes, is now taking place in the community, and "aging in place" is not only the preferred choice for most older adults, but also a possibility, in large part because of the aging network of services. These services are the heart of the LTSS system, which serves those with functional limitations. LTSS is defined as the range of support services that are needed by adults of all ages with care needs as a result of a physical or mental limitation that limits their ability to see to all their own care needs (O'Shaughnessy, 2014). Although health care services are important for all adults, regardless of age or functional limitations, it is LTSS that can make the difference between an individual's ability to remain in the community or relocate to a nursing home or care setting in an assisted-living facility. There are an estimated 11 million adults older than 18 years who receive LTSS; 57% are older than 65 years and 43% are between the ages of 18 and 64 years (O'Shaughnessy, 2014).

In addition to LTSS, many adults with care needs depend on their family members or friends to provide support and assistance. In fact, help from family or friends is often referred to as the "default" long-term care system. As described earlier, these unpaid caregivers do a variety of tasks to support the person needing LTSS, including helping him or her with the instrumental activities of daily living (IADLs), which include shopping, transportation, yard care, home care, meal preparation, and money management. Some caregivers also provide help with more intense care needs, such as activities of daily living (ADLs), including toileting, personal care, and feeding assistance. The NAC, an advocacy organization that conducts research and education on family caregiving, conducts a survey of family caregivers every 5 years. This survey suggests that the "average" family caregiver spends about 19 hours a week providing help to a family member; 34% of these caregivers had been helping between 1 and 4 years and 31% had been helping for 5 years or longer. Family caregivers also coordinate the care received by the older adult. For example, an adult daughter or son may arrange for home care services, transportation to and from a senior center or other adult program, and/or manage the health care services needed.

KNOWLEDGE AND MYTHS ABOUT LTSS

Many Americans are poorly informed about LTSS and their importance during old age. As Chapter 1 discussed, the fastest growing subgroup of elders is the old-old. This group is the most likely to need some LTSS. In fact, the U.S. Department of Health and Human Services projects that 70% of Americans older than 65 years will need some form of assistance for an average of 3 years. In 2009, the Mature Market Institute of MetLife conducted a survey to assess the awareness of the American public about long-term care. A little over a third of the respondents (36%) correctly estimated their risk of needing long-term care after the age of 65 years at between 60% and 70%. Most believed that the majority of long-term care was provided in nursing homes and a third believed that Medicare pays for LTSS. In 2013, the NORC [naturally occurring retirement community] Center for Public Affairs Research surveyed 1,019 Americans about LTSS and found that misconceptions about LTSS were persistent. Like the MetLife survey, respondents had little accurate information or understanding about LTSS and nearly half believed that Medicare covered the costs of long-term care. More than half underestimated the cost of nursing homes and 31% underestimated the cost of assisted-living facilities. We list some common myths about LTSS below.

Why is knowledge about LTSS important for the American public? Ideally, each of us would be planning for our old age and likely need for LTSS at some time in our lives. Americans are not even saving for their own retirement and, if there are savings, it is likely to be needed in case of a long-term illness or disability. Understanding the risk of requiring LTSS and the care options is an important step in planning for the future.

What You Should Know About LTSS

▓ There is no safety net or public payer for the cost of LTSS in the United States. The only public payer of LTSS is Medicaid, which requires users to be indigent in order to receive services.

▓ Medicare is an essential health care resource for older people, but LTSS are not paid for by Medicare on a regular basis. Medicare support is limited to home health or rehabilitation services after a hospitalization and only for 100 days.

▓ Although some Americans have long-term care insurance, many insurance providers have left the marketplace and fewer choices are available for those Americans who want to purchase long-term care insurance. The cost of this product is also often prohibitive for the "average" American family.

■ The direct care workforce, the primary paid workforce for LTSS, continues to be poorly trained and poorly paid. There is also a shortage of workers in this workforce that is expected to persist into the future.

The Patient Protection and Affordable Care Act (PPACA) included a public long-term care program, the CLASS Act, which could have created a public fund for supporting LTSS needs of participants. Unfortunately, this program was "voluntary" and viewed as unlikely to attract the large numbers needed to make it financially sound. The CLASS Act was cancelled as a result. Many policy experts suggest that any successful public program would need to be a program that required participation by all Americans.

A recent analysis examines the LTSS planning of baby boomers in a single state, Connecticut, and is based on a needs assessment conducted in the state in 2007. Robison, Shugrue, Fortinsky, and Gruman (2014), report that a majority of baby boomers is expected to need LTSS in the future but few were saving for the costs of these services. Gender was a predictor of planning for LTSS needs, with women more likely than men to report that they were planning ahead. One of the most interesting findings of this analysis was that baby boomers in the sample were likely to report an interest in moving in with their adult children if they needed assistance. This was in contrast to older respondents who were not receptive to this "solution." The authors of the study suggest that multigenerational living arrangements may become more commonplace in the future.

CASE STUDY: BALANCING FAMILY CAREGIVING RESOURCES WITH COMMUNITY LTSS

Ethel Williams is an 85-year-old widow who lives alone in an older neighborhood in suburban America. When she moved into the neighborhood, everyone was moving in to raise their children and there was a cohesive social structure that offered many important resources such as neighbors who were able and willing to watch children when a mom needed to run errands, good schools, and several parks were nearby. The residents of the neighborhood often shared meals and the children were able to play outside safely both during the day and in the early evening. Today, few residents are of Ethel's age and the neighborhood is now home to a diverse group of residents that includes young adults without children, large families with children, and a few intergenerational households. Ethel knows her immediate neighbors only by sight but does have the phone number of her next-door neighbor in case there is an emergency.

Ethel recently stopped driving after getting lost coming home from the grocery store. She now relies on "Meals on Wheels" for food and someone to chat with when the meal comes. Twice a month her adult daughter comes to take her to the grocery store and pharmacy to get refills or products she needs. She tried to attend a senior center during the week to have some social interaction, lunch, and activities, but had to walk to the bus stop, which was several blocks from her house and it became too much for her so she had to stop. On weekends, her adult son and daughter come by to do lawn work and help with housekeeping. She wears a "Life Alert" pendant that she can use to call for help if she were to fall or hear an intruder and now feels safe in her house alone. Recently, Ethel has had difficulty getting in and out of the bathtub/ shower and bathing has become more problematic for her. Her daughter wants her to move into her house but Ethel is hesitant about doing so because she values her independence and does not like the idea of living with her grandchildren and their activities and noise, plus she would have to take one of their bedrooms, which is not something she wants to do to them.

Ethel does not have the financial means to move to an assisted-living facility. In her town, assisted-living centers charge $5,000 a month for the basics, which is well beyond her means. She is not poor enough to qualify for senior housing for low-income elders. Ethel is concerned about the amount of time that her adult children have to spend taking care of her. She still is able to visit her doctor independently because the "dial a ride" program sends a van for her when she has an appointment. In order to remain independent, Ethel will need to plan for help with personal care like bathing. She also is concerned about a few things she has noticed about herself—forgetting to turn off the gas stove when she is finished cooking, having difficulty keeping track of the days and her appointments, and her inability to balance her checkbook. Ethel thinks that she would be better if she was regularly engaged in a senior center or some other group setting where she could spend time socializing and in activities she liked. But she cannot get to a senior center without taking a cab or asking her daughter to drive her there. Because her daughter works all day that is not an option. There are many things that the aging network of services is helping Ethel with, and her children are providing many of the other things for her.

She does not want to ask her daughter to help her with personal care and she is already worried about how much her kids do for her and what the cost is for them in terms of time and resources. Ethel sees only concerns and problems when she looks into her future.

What options might Ethel have for continuing to remain independent when her needs are increasing? How might you advise Ethel?

As Ethel's case demonstrates, the aging network of services provides an essential and important support network for people who experience increasing frailty and need some help with daily activities. As is the case for millions of older Americans, adult children and/or friends or neighbors provide additional assistance to supplement services that an elder uses. In case the children are not in the same town as the elder, many older Americans rely on neighbors, friends, or church or community volunteers. The Supportive Services program funds a range of services designed to help older people like Ethel remain independent in their own homes. For example, Ethel could benefit from a personal care worker, a homemaker, or a chore program, all of which are funded by the Supportive Services program. However, funding is very limited for this program, so much so that services are not available for everyone who needs them. In 2010, access to services (transportation, outreach, and care management) was funded by 17% of the $1.041 billion, and the home- and community-based long-term care (LTSS) services like Ethel needs had only 6% for personal care, homemaker, chore, and adult day care. According to O'Shaughnessy (2011, p. 86), "almost 300,000 older adults received Title III funded personal care, homemaker, or chores services in FY 2010." The funds are targeted to individuals most at risk of losing their independence due to functional limitations.

In a recent article by Kwak and Polivka (2014), the authors investigate the future of long-term care and the aging network. They point out the rapid increase in demand for LTSS and the declining numbers of family caregivers projected to be available in the future. Evidence on the effectiveness and efficiency of the current LTSS system, which relies on the aging network is mixed, but a recent analysis suggests that the Medicaid-funded LTSS have improved health and reduced the likelihood of requiring an institutional care option over time. They caution that the move to address LTSS needs by using for-profit managed care organizations to increase efficiency is not supported by empirical evidence. As demand for LTSS increases over time there is a need for more evidence-based research regarding models that promote the aging network's goal of community independence for as long as possible and "person-centered" approaches to the care.

EFFECTIVENESS AND IMPORTANCE
OF OLDER AMERICAN ACT PROGRAMS

Programs funded by Title II of the OAA include support for the ADRCs that provide one-stop shopping for information about and access to services. The National Eldercare Locator is an online and telephonic service designed to provide callers with information about available services and local Area Agencies on Aging, ADRCs, and other sources of information and assistance nationwide. In addition, the Senior Medicare Patrol educates Americans about Medicare and Medicaid fraud and how to report it. Finally, Title II funds the Pension Counseling and Information Program, which includes six regional projects to help people learn about and gain access to benefits. All these Title II programs work to increase the access of Americans to OAA programs and services.

Title III is the primary funding source for the community services that support older adults in the community. The funds are distributed by the AoA through the State Units on Aging to the community. The total 2012 budget for Title III was $1,358 billion. This budget supported home-delivered meals (145.5 million in fiscal year [FY] 2010); congregate meals (96.4 million); and transportation to medical appointments, grocery stores, and other activities (26 million); 35 million hours of personal care, home-maker, and chore services. In addition, 10 million hours of services in adult day/health programs and preventive health programs (medication management and falls prevention) served 5.9 million individuals (Napili & Colello, 2013).

The access services and the community services supported by the OAA are essential to older Americans who need some support in order to remain in the community. Although services are available for everyone older than 60 years, the targeted elders are those with the most economic or social needs. In FY 2010, nearly 3 million Americans used home-delivered meal, home care, and personal care or case management on a regular basis (O'Shaughnessy, 2011). Almost 8 million people used transportation, information services, and/or congregate meals on a sporadic basis. In FY 2010, 30% of those receiving regular services were living below the federal poverty level and 25% were members of a minority group. Congregate meal programs and transportation service users were the oldest age category assessed—75 to 84 years—(36%) according to an independent study (Shaughnessy, 2011). According to estimates of the National Association of Area Agencies on Aging (N4A), the investment in community services of the OAA leverages significant funds from states, communities, and other organizations at the local level on a three-to-one basis (N4A, 2013).

According to a study conducted by Thomas and Mor (2013), support for older adults to continue living independently in the community can result in savings to states on the cost of LTSS. Their analysis found that increasing the number of people aged 65 years or older who received home-delivered meals would result in annual savings to the Medicaid programs of more than $109 million. Home-delivered meals are, according to the researchers, a strategy for preventing institutionalization. Theresearchers point out that 89% of older adults who experience food insecurity and nearly 90% of older adults who were limited in two or more ADLs were not receiving home-delivered meals. In most communities, the home-delivered meals program has a waiting list due to limited funding and capacity.

THE ADMINISTRATION FOR COMMUNITY LIVING'S INITIATIVE TO PROVIDE LEADERSHIP IN ADDRESSING PERSISTENT PROBLEMS

As mentioned above, OAA funding is not the only funding available to support services for older Americans. Local and state sources supplement OAA funding and federal funding to the Administration for Community Living (ACL) also provide important add-ons to the cafeteria of services available to older Americans. The Lifespan Respite Care Program, Chronic Disease Self-Management Program, National Clearinghouse for Long-Term Care Information, Medicare Enrollment Assistance Program, Elder Abuse Prevention Intervention Program and Alzheimer's Disease Program are supported (Napili & Colello, 2013). These federally funded programs work in conjunction with other aging network programs to provide improved access to needed services and integrated service networks at the community level to benefit older residents. Lifespan Respite Care benefits Americans of all ages who have caregiver burdens that make life complicated. The Chronic Disease Self-Management Program has been embraced nationally through the efforts of Area Health Education Centers and other community-based networks. The curriculum, developed at Stanford University, is designed to empower the individual with chronic disease to take control over his or her own health and wellness. It is a popular program among those who participate and an evidence-based program that supports wellness among people with chronic disease. Medicare enrollment assistance provides needed information to access Medicare for those who are not familiar with participation in a federal program. Furthermore, the National Clearinghouse for Long-Term

Care Information, the Elder Abuse Prevention Program, and Alzheimer's Disease Program are access programs that are designed to work cooperatively with other community-based agencies to better serve individuals in need of support and assistance.

With the ADRC network at the center, a focus on critical pathways of older adults began in 2003 with the engagement of the Centers for Medicare and Medicaid Services (CMS) to design a response to transitions that create challenges for older adults. One of these transitions is that from a hospital stay to the community—either the home of the elder or a short-term (or long-term) residential setting. Without careful assessment and the integration of services and the professionals involved, this transition can have negative consequences for the older person. Unnecessary institutionalization or a return to a home setting that lacks the necessary physical, social, and/or medical supports can result in worsening of the health and well-being and other adverse effects.

In 2010, ACL started the ADRC Evidence-Based Care Transitions Program. This program supports ADRC's role in implementing evidence-based care transition models through training, integration with medical services and facilities, and increasing the awareness of the importance of the transitions. These programs and others as well as research have emphasized the importance of integrating health and community services to address common problems among elders, particularly the oldest-old. ACL is not the only agency working on care transitions. In fact, in addition to CMS, private hospitals and physicians are engaged in this concern as are the Affordable Care Act and the Institute of Medicine (IOM).

In 2001, the IOM issued a report, *Crossing the Quality Chasm*, which outlined the underlying issues of poor care transitions: lack of integration of care, poor organization, and processes that do not lead to a higher quality of care but, in fact, add to the problem of poor care transitions (*Health Policy Brief: Care Transitions*, 2012; IOM, 2001). The IOM report states that almost 20% of Medicare beneficiaries who were discharged from a hospital were readmitted within 30 days, at a cost of $12 billion a year.

CMS began implementation of the Affordable Care Act's Hospital Readmissions Reduction Program (HRRP) in October 2012. This program reduces payments to hospitals that have "excessive" readmissions. This regulatory action provides a necessary incentive for hospitals to take seriously the problems associated with poor care transitions. In a study conducted by McHugh, Berez, and Small (2013), the hospitals that have higher levels of registered nurse staffing have lower readmission rates. In fact, the study found that hospitals with higher nurse staffing had a 25%

reduced likelihood of being penalized compared to hospitals that did not have this higher nurse staffing.

The problems associated with the health of older adults and care transitions is not resolved yet, but the involvement of ACL, CMS, and the provisions of the Affordable Care Act have begun to change the behavior of providers and to create important incentives for professionals to come together to work toward better care transitions. The evidence collected on care transitions suggests that educating patients about their own role in care transitions as well as better information provided to family caregivers and providers, coupled with interprofessional education are all pieces of a change model that will not only save money but provide a higher quality of life for the older adult who is able to experience a smooth transition when care is needed.

Integrating Health and Community-Based Services

In the early days of the OAA programs, specific services were designed to support older adults in either social service models or health models. For example, adult day programs were categorized as either "medical models" or "social models." Senior centers were primarily viewed as social models of services and separate and distinct from health or medical services. Today there is a more consumer-friendly approach to community-based services that provides some integration of programming. For example, virtually all adult day programs have some level of health services—even a visiting nurse who comes in to check on the well-being of the members. Health screening services are ubiquitous in senior centers and wellness programming is an important component of most senior centers. And, the distinction between adult day programs and senior centers is not always based on the status of the older participants. In Maryland, for example, some senior centers offer special programming for residents with dementia. In other states, community-based models are developing that integrate services with health, education, and wellness programming. Breaking down barriers has many advantages for the consumer. For example, an elder may be reticent to go to a therapist to discuss his or her sadness or depression, but within a familiar center, may be happy to talk to a staff about it and receive screening and referral services.

In the community network of services for older adults it is common to find not only the standard community-based providers at monthly meetings but residential staff, nurses, social workers, and home health providers as well. This is a positive trend for the well-being of a community as well as the elders who live in a community. One group of key stakeholders and consumers that is not present at the monthly meeting of community providers is that of family caregivers. However, family caregivers have their own needs and are served by support groups convened by ARDCs or specific services or programs set up under the National Family Caregivers Program, which funds Area Agencies on Aging and ARDCs to provide resource and referral information to family caregivers and to provide special programming as well.

Advocacy groups for family caregivers, such as the National Center on Caregiving–Family Caregiver Alliance and AARP's Public Policy Institute, have been advocating the need for assessment of the family caregiver when the individual care recipient is being assessed. Home and community-based services (HCBS), which are funded through Medicaid, require an assessment of individuals who would receive the services in order to determine the "level of care" they need. Some states have begun to include caregiver assessment in the assessment of the user, and the Commission on Long-Term Care asked CMS to require this assessment of family caregivers if any part of the care plan is dependent on family members. In a recent study conducted by AARP, only 30% of the states were including any family caregiver assessment in their Medicaid HCBS waiver assessments (Kelly, Wolfe, Gibson, & Feinberg, 2013).

Mental Health

Understanding mental health issues, their treatment, and support for older adults with mental health problems continue to be persistent problems. Historically, older adults have been underrepresented in the mental health services. One explanation for the small percentage of older adults being served was the belief that they were reticent to seek help for mental health problems. Cohorts are changing, however, and as more elders enter late life with high educational attainment, the "stigma" associated with the use of mental health services is likely to become less of a barrier to service use. The American Psychological Association (2013) has a list of myths about older adults that attempts to separate fact from fiction. These include:

■ *Dementia is an inevitable part of aging.* The fact is that most older people do not have dementia.

▓ *Older adults have higher rates of mental illness than younger ones, particularly depression.* The fact is that older adults have lower rates of depression than younger adults.

According to the American Psychological Association, the prevalence among older adults of a mental illness is between 20% and 22%. Some elders bring a history of mental illness with them into old age, whereas others may develop a mental disorder in late life. Symptoms of mental illness in late life also may look different for older adults. For example, depression in late life might not include visible signs of sadness. However, research shows that older adults also respond well to treatment.

According to the Substance Abuse and Mental Health Services Administration (SAMHSA), more than 8,000 older adults died as a result of suicide in 2010 (SAMHSA and AoA, 2012). Rates are highest among men. The highest rate of suicide of any aging group is for White males who are 85+. This group has a suicide rate four times that of the overall rate of suicide for all Americans. Death by firearms is the most common means for older adults. Older adults are twice as likely to use firearms as younger adults to commit suicide. Risk factors include depression, prior suicide attempts, hopeless feelings or social isolation, changes in family configurations due to death or other reasons, access to firearms, alcohol or medication misuse, and/or difficulty adjusting to change. Among elders who have committed suicide, more than half (58%) saw a primary care provider within the last month of their lives. Professionals suggest behavioral health interventions, such as screening services and training programs for aging network providers, to better identify those at risk.

In 2006, AoA implemented a State-Based Evidence-Based Disease and Disability Program for older adults. This continues to be a collaboration among the Centers for Disease Control and Prevention (CDC), Agency for Healthcare Research and Quality (AHRQ), CMS, and private foundations. One important model program is the Healthy Ideas (Identifying Depression, Empowering Activities for Seniors; IDEAS). This is an evidence-based depression program to detect and reduce the severity of depressive symptoms in older adults with chronic health conditions and functional limitations through existing community-based case management services. Other evidence-based programs that address mental health issues include Improving Mood-Promoting Access to Collaborative Treatment (IMPACT) and Program to Encourage Active Rewarding Lives for Seniors (PEARLS).

The IMPACT program is designed for primary care settings but is also a tool that could be used within home health care services and chronic disease management. The program encourages elders to become involved in some form of behavioral activity that could include physical activities or participating in a pleasurable activity. Those individuals who wish to engage in some problem-solving treatment receive six to eight sessions of brief therapy with a "depression care manager." The evidence suggests that those receiving IMPACT care were twice as likely to experience a 50% or greater reduction in depressive symptoms as those patients who followed standard care procedures (Centers for Disease Control and Prevention and National Association of Chronic Disease Directors, 2009).

The Pearls Program—Seattle, Washington (www.pearlsprogram.org)

The Pearls Program (www.pearlsprogram.org) is an evidence-based program for depression in late life and for those adults with epilepsy. The program is geared toward older adults (60+) who have symptoms related to minor depression and dysthymic disorder. The program focuses on teaching clients the skills necessary to move to action and make lasting life changes. The program is delivered in the home and designed to be part of a community-based model, primarily through existing service-provision programs. It is a team-based approach that is well suited for individuals with chronic illness.

Alzheimer's Disease

Alzheimer's disease is a condition that primarily strikes older adults. The longer you live, the more likely you are to have Alzheimer's disease. It is poorly understood and includes a number of different types of dementias. More than 5 million Americans have some form of Alzheimer's disease and there are 35 million people in the world with the disease. There is no cure and the disease will cause death. However, some good news about Alzheimer's disease was discussed at the Alzheimer's Association International Conference (2014). According to a CBS/AP News (2014) report about this conference, data from the Framingham Study, which is a longitudinal study funded by the federal government, new cases of dementia dropped 44% in 2009 compared to data from 1978, 1989, and 1996. Also, the age at which new cases developed increased from 80 to 85 years. Similar findings were reported from other European nations. Researchers believe that higher educational attainment and better control of cholesterol and blood pressure were responsible for the decline.

Nonetheless, Alzheimer's disease is a serious public health problem in our aging world. While scientists reported the good news for high-income nations, researchers in Columbia reported that they may have underestimated the rate of dementia in their country and now believe that it is 50% higher than originally reported.

Alzheimer's disease and related disorders are a particularly difficult problem for family caregivers who are providing support for a loved one. There are no publicly funded residential services for persons with Alzheimer's disease or related disorders unless the individual is financially indigent. This would, of course, require a spouse to share the spend-down experience to poverty with only a limited amount of funds to continue living. Most American families cannot afford the very high costs of nursing homes to provide the care for their loved one, costs that can exceed $75,000 a year. There are evidence-based programs in place to support family caregivers and many services at the community level for these caregivers. The Alzheimer's Association has a network of support groups nationwide to help and support family caregivers. Family caregiver advocacy groups provide information and access to community services for family caregivers.

Dr. Mary Mittleman has developed an evidence-based program to support family caregivers of persons with Alzheimer's disease. The New York University (NYU) Caregiver Counseling and Support Intervention has four components: two individual counseling sessions for each caregiver that are tailored to the individual's unique situation, family counseling sessions with both the primary caregiver and family members, a weekly support group, and counseling on an "as needed" basis by phone. Her model of intervention has been demonstrated to not only improve the well-being of caregivers but also delay nursing home placement of the care recipients. The Alzheimer's Disease Supportive Services Program (ADSSP) was created by Section 398 of the Public Health Services Act. Grants were awarded to states to develop interventions for caregivers of persons with Alzheimer's and many states selected the NYU Caregiver Counseling and Support Intervention model to implement.

CONCLUSION

The aging network of services is changing and evolving and is now a composite of governmental and nonprofit services that receive OAA funding, local foundation and state funding, as well as user fees. This nonprofit and governmental network is supplemented by for-profit providers who have their own stake in making sure that older Americans receive high-quality services. In Chapter 4, you will see how this loose network of organizations and professionals works together to make sure that older Americans can remain in the community as long as they wish. Although the development and expansion of this network have been a positive step for many communities, its breadth within a community can make it confusing to the consumer. ADRCs are tasked with reducing this confusion and making needed services accessible to both the older adult and his or her caregiver(s).

CRITICAL THINKING QUESTIONS

1. *Is it always less costly to keep an elder in the community rather than a nursing home or assisted-living facility? Why or why not?*

2. *Can an LTSS network be developed that does not require a family member or friend to provide essential services? How would you manage that development?*

3. *What types of stakeholders are most dependent on the existing LTSS and why?*

4. *What role will technology play in the LTSS of the future and how will it be accessible to the old-old who are caregiving for siblings, spouses, and friends?*

REFERENCES

American Psychological Association. (2013). *What mental health providers should know about working with older adults.* Retrieved July 2, 2014, from http://www.apa.org

CBS News/AP. (2014, July 15). Why Alzheimer's rates may be declining in some countries. Retrieved from http://www.cbsnews.com/news/alzheimers-rates-may-be-declining-in-some-countries

Centers for Disease Control and Prevention and National Association of Chronic Disease Directors. (2009). *The state of mental health and aging in America issue brief 2: Addressing depression in older adults: Selected evidence-based programs.* Atlanta, GA: National Association of Chronic Disease Directors. Retrieved from http://www.cdc.gov/aging

Health Policy Brief: Care Transitions. (2012). *Health affairs.* September 13, 2012. Retrieved from http://www.healthaffairs.org/healthpolicybriefs/brief.php?brief_id=76

Institute of Medicine (IOM). (2001). *Crossing the quality chasm: A new health system for the 21st century.* Retrieved from http://www.iom.edu

Kelly, K., Wolfe, N., Gibson, M. J., & Feinberg, L. (2013). *Listening to family care-givers: The need to include family caregiver assessment in Medicaid Home-and Community-Based Service Waiver Programs.* Washington, DC: AARP Public Policy Institute. Retrieved from http://www.aarp.org/ppi

Kwak, J., & Polivka, L. (2014, summer). *The future of long-term care and the aging network. Generations.* Retrieved from http://asaging.org/blog/future-long-term-care-and-aging network

McHugh, M.D., Berez, J., & Small, D.S. (2013). Hosptials with higher nurse staffing had lower odds of readmission penalties than hospitals with lower staffing. *Health Affairs, 32*(10), 1740–1747.

Napili, A., & Colello, K. (2013). *Funding for the Older American Act and other aging services programs.* Washington, DC: Congressional Research Service. Retrieved May 12, 2014, from www.crs.gov

National Alliance for Caregiving (NAC)/AARP. (2009). *Caregiving in the U.S.* Bethesda, MD: Author. Retrieved from http://www.caregiving.org

National Association of Area Agencies on Aging (N4A). (2013). *N4A policy priorities: Reauthorization of the Older Americans Act.* Retrieved May 5, 2014, from http://www.n4a.org.

O'Shaughnessy, C. (2011). *The aging services network: Serving a vulnerable and growing elderly population in tough economic times.* Background Paper No. 83. National Health Policy Forum, The George Washington University. Retrieved from http://www.nhpf.org

O'Shaughnessy, C. (2014). *The basics: National spending for long-term services and supports (LTSS), 2012.* National Health Policy Forum, The George Washington University. Retrieved May 1, 2014, from http://www.nhpf.org.

Pew Research Center. (2013). *Pew Research Centers internet and American life project.* Retrieved July 15, 2014, from http://www.pewinternet.org/2013/06/20/family-caregivers-are-wired -for health/

Robison, J., Shugrue, N., Fortinsky, R. H., & Gruman, C. (2014). Long-term supports and services planning for the future: Implications from a statewide survey of Baby Boomers and older adults. *The Gerontologist, 54*(2), 297–313.

SAMHSA and AoA. (2012). *Older Americans behavioral health, issue brief 4: Preventing suicide in older adults.* Retrieved from http://www.aoa.gov/AoARoot/AoA_Programs/HPW/Behavioral/docs/Older%20Americans%20Issue%20Brief%204_Preventing%20Suicide_508.pdf

Select Committee on Aging. (1987). *Exploding the myths: Caregiving in America (Committee Publication No. 99–611).* Washington, DC: U.S. Government Printing Office.

Thomas, K. S., & Mor, V. (2013). Providing more home-delivered meals is one way to keep older adults with low care needs out of nursing homes. *Health Affairs, 32*(10), 1796–1802.

Wagner, D. L., & Takagi, E. (2010). *Informal caregiving by and for older adults* [Web log message]. Retrieved February 2, 2010, from http://healthaffairs.org/blog

CHAPTER FOUR

Community Supports
for Aging in Place

Is your community a good place to grow old? As you ponder that question, consider what the World Health Organization (WHO) has put forth as part of their Age-Friendly Cities Programme as a reminder about the critical role of older adults in the communities in which they live: "Making cities and communities age-friendly is one of the most effective local policy approaches for responding to demographic ageing. The physical and social environments are key determinants of whether people can remain healthy, independent, and autonomous long into their old age" (www.who .int/ageing/projects/age_friendly_cities_programme/en/).

The domains addressed by the WHO provide a framework for moving toward creating aging-friendly communities and provide a framework for creating supportive and empowering environments for everyone. Domains include (WHO, 2007):

- *Outdoor spaces and buildings*

- *Housing*

- *Transportation*

- *Social participation*

- *Respect and social inclusion*

- *Civic participation and employment*

- *Communication and information*

- *Community support and health services*

After reading this chapter you may be curious about:

(a) *The age-friendliness of your own community*

(b) *The role that social determinants play in later life and how the aging networks can help to mediate the issues*

(c) *The importance of aging in place and what this might look like for future cohorts of elders*

(d) *The ways to address food insecurity for older adults*

(e) *Why housing is so important and how the aging networks can bridge some of the existing gaps*

(f) *The role of senior centers in the community and how this may continue to evolve*

In recent years, considerable attention has been paid to finding ways to allow and support older persons to remain in the familiar settings of their own homes and communities as they age toward and into the frailty that accompanies aging for many.

This chapter explores issues related to community-based services in the context of aging in place for older adults. This includes a broad range of programs and services available from the aging networks we have in place in this country. We will explore the history of aging in place and the role of the social determinants of health (SDH). It is clear that the new old, the baby boomers, will demand a change in focus in programming and services. The aging networks are making some headway in this area but would do well to promote programs that are "active-aging" focused and grounded in the SDH as the WHO's Age-Friendly Cities Programme is, and ensure that consumer engagement in the design and implementation of programs is included.

For example, the Community Innovation for Aging in Place Initiative was created to "assist frail older adults to remain independent and age in place" (AoA, 2014a). The Lesbian, Gay, Bisexual, and Transgender (LGBT) Aging in Place Initiative, a project funded by AoA and directed by the Los Angeles Gay and Lesbian Community Services Center, aims to address issues of social isolation, providing case management, and training professionals. Specifically, the goals are to: "increase socialization among and between LGBT older adults and provide LGBT seniors with greater access to LGBT-targeted services; establish a central data bank for LGBT-friendly resources and become a resource clearing house; LGBT seniors will have greater access to resources that are LGBT *friendly; and increase the knowledge and awareness of LGBT senior issues and needs among mainstream social service providers. This innovative project directly impacts LGBT older adults in the Los Angeles area, promotes active aging, and addresses issues that cause an impact where this population lives and works, which is a major component of the SDH"* (AoA, 2014a).

A HISTORY OF AGING IN PLACE

The concept of federally supported housing began in the 1930s with the National Housing Act of 1934 (www.youtube.com/watch?v=TzMT8Bk8u4c) and the United States Housing Act of 1937. The 1934 Act inaugurated the first home mortgage program—structuring the private home financing system—under the Federal Housing Administration (FHA). Under the 1937 Act, the government offered subsidized housing to low-income families. Although the primary purpose of this latter legislation was to clear slums and increase employment, new housing resulted. Under the Housing Act of 1949, the national goal of "a decent home and suitable living environment for every American family" was first stated (American Presidency Project, 2014). The Act also included programs for urban renewal, increased funds for subsidized housing, and new programs for rural housing. During the 1950s, housing programs were more directed toward rehabilitation, relocation, and renewal. Section 202 began under the Housing Act of 1959. The program provided low-cost loans to developers of private housing and was the forerunner of later mortgage subsidy programs. In the Housing Act of 1961, below-market interest rate mortgages were initiated to assist rental housing for moderate-income families through section 221(d)(3).

In 1965, two rent-subsidy programs were begun. In one program, residents would pay 25% of their income in privately owned housing units built with FHA financing. Under the Section 23 leasing program, the government would lease regular units for low-income families. In 1968, Congress found that "the supply of the nation's housing was not increasing rapidly enough to meet the national goal of 1949" (U.S. Department of Housing and Urban Development [HUD], 1974, p. 19). Congress then established a production schedule of 26 million housing units—6 million of these to be for low- and moderate-income families over the next 10 years. One of the programs of this act was Section 236, which provided a subsidy formula for rental housing. In 1969, the Brooke Amendment was passed, which limited the amount of rent that could be charged by local housing authorities to 25% of adjusted tenant income.

In September 1973, President Nixon halted all housing programs except for the low-rent public-leasing program, in order that a thorough review could be accomplished of what was then viewed as a spendthrift and inadequate program. Following a study, during which no new federally subsidized housing starts were approved, the Housing and Community Development Act was signed into law in August 1974. The Act removed the suspension that had been placed on construction and required contracts annually of at least $150 million to help finance development or acquisition costs of low-income housing projects. Because most of the money was to be channeled through the new Section 8 program, which was authorized under this Act, funding was slow to begin. Administratively, at least 2 years elapsed before the Section 8 program was fully operational (U.S. Senate, Special Committee on Aging, 1975).

Considering the Role of the
Social Determinants of Health

According to the WHO (2008, p. 3), "the social determinants of health (SDH) are the circumstances in which people are born, grow up, live, work and age, and the systems put in place to deal with illness. These circumstances are in turn shaped by a wider set of forces: economics, social policies, and politics." The WHO's Commission on the SDH (CSDH, 2008) has intentionally adopted a broad definition of the SDH, which is meant to be inclusive of the entirety of the social conditions in which we live and work. In the Commission's final report (2008) they quote Tarlov as a way to provide further context of SDH: "the social characteristics within which living takes place" (Tarlov, 1996, p. 71).

Further, a life-course perspective explicitly recognizes the importance of time and timing in understanding causal links between exposures and outcomes within an individual life course, across generations, and in population-level disease trends. Adopting a life-course perspective directs attention to how SDH operate at every level of development—early childhood, childhood, adolescence, and adulthood—both to immediately influence health and to provide the basis for health or illness later in life (WHO, 2008). Marmot (2005, p. 1099) writes, "The gross inequalities in health that we see within and between countries present a challenge to the world. That there should be a spread of life expectancy of 48 years among countries and 20 years or more within countries is not inevitable."

Key Consumer Views

As part of a class research project, York College of Pennsylvania (PA) students conducted interviews with older adults in York, PA, about their experiences with the "aging network" (Niles-Yokum, 2012–2013). The purpose of the research was to incorporate the perspective of the older consumer and family caregivers who use Older Americans Act (OAA) programs and services. It was our goal to give them a voice and also provide a depth of perspective that will add to our understanding of the experience of using services and programs within the aging network. We were particularly interested in how these programs really work and what they mean to those who live them.

The respondents were interviewed at various senior centers around the York County region and all reported that they were aware of the aging network and related services. Although this is a self-selected group that is perhaps more aware of the aging network in general, they all seemed to be familiar with the term "aging network" and considered their attendance at the senior center, and participation in the programs and services as related to the network. Respondents report using the following services: senior center, paratransit (local senior transportation), Fresh Express (food program), and Meals on Wheels.

When asked how the programs and related services helped them, respondents were clear that they benefited in many ways. A theme throughout the interviews was the importance of the opportunity to socialize and to have a place to go.

> [Senior center] gives us a place to go. I like the dances, the singing, and the extracurricular activities. It's like a family.
>
> It [senior center] helps me with the socialization, being involved in physical activities helping me with my health. Educates me on things to help my health. I'm not sitting at home alone becoming depressed. I'm happy to be here.
>
> Saves us from driving, we go to the store and doctors appointments its free!
>
> I like everything about the senior center, we talk with friends, trips to go on, just getting out of the house.

When asked if they could change anything about the services and programs many reported that they wouldn't change anything. Some reported that they would like to see more "kids" at the senior center and in programs to help. Another suggested that the senior center and other programs extend their hours because they close so early (many close at 3 or 4pm) that the rest of the day is left open.

Although this research was a small component of a service-learning project in an introductory gerontology class, it highlights the fact that the voice of the consumer is critical to the evolution of the aging networks, particularly as we begin to feel the impact of the baby boom generation on usage. The very fact that the majority of senior centers are still called seniors centers is a blatant reminder that change is now the name of the game and change comes most successfully when the stakeholders are at the table.

SUPPORTING AGING IN PLACE—HOUSING

Public Housing

Although the term is often assumed to relate to all forms of subsidized housing, "public housing" was in fact the earliest means of providing adequate homes for low-income elderly. Public housing was established under the Housing Act of 1937. HUD appropriates funds for these complexes. More than 1 million households live in rental units administered by local housing authorities. The authorities maintain the buildings and ensure that low-cost rentals are available to poor families. Rentals are usually set at 30% of the family's income. In addition, HUD provides funds for maintenance of the buildings, and other agencies may provide staff for special programs for older persons.

It is often difficult for older persons to live in public housing units because many local housing authorities require that older residents who need supportive services arrange to have these needs met if they are to remain in the complex. A small percentage of housing authorities (10%) do not allow older persons who are not independent to live in the public housing complex. In 1999, 13% of public housing tenants were seniors. Many of these tenants had aged in place. In recognition of the needs of this population, the National Affordable Housing Act of 1990 allows local housing authorities to charge HUD for the inception of service coordinator positions and for 15% of the cost of services to older tenants. These services may include meals, chore services, transportation, personal care, and health-related services. Approximately half of all public housing units are more than 20 years old. In recent years, the federal emphasis in the field of housing has shifted to other programs, such as Sections 8 and 202.

The Section 8 Existing Housing Program

Authorized under the Housing and Community Development Act of 1974, this program filled the void left by the 1973 moratorium. It provides no direct funding to the developer, but instead pays monthly rent, so that housing can be developed on the private market. Section 8, or subsidized rent, is the rent for a unit in a development receiving federally subsidized Section 8 housing-assistance payments. The Section 8 rent differs from the market rent in that it depends strictly on the amount of income of the tenant. Tenants pay 30% of their adjusted income for rent, with the Section 8 housing assistance payment to the landlord making up the difference between tenant-paid rent and the full-market rent. Tenants are now allowed to pay more than 30% of their income for rent if the public housing authority agrees that the rent is reasonable for both the unit and the family (U.S. Senate, Special Committee on Aging, 1990). The tenant could pay as little as $40 or $50 per month or nearly as high as the market rents, depending on the monthly adjusted income.

Rents under Section 8 cannot exceed the fair market rent for the area as established by HUD. Rents are reviewed annually, and the tenants must move if 30% of their adjusted income meets the fair market rent for that particular housing project. Fair market rents take into account construction costs and maintenance fees for individual locations. Tenants in housing built through Section 202 grants usually receive Section 8 subsidies.

Fair market rates vary widely. In Oakland, California, the fair market monthly rent for a one-bedroom apartment is $1,132; in San Diego, $939; in Atlanta, $815; and in Chicago, $797. In order to qualify for Section 8 subsidies originally, the income of a family of four could not be above 80% of median income in their area of residence. Congressional action between 1981 and 1984 reduced eligibility to 50% of median income, thus making many families ineligible for Section 8 subsidies. Nationally, families with less than 30% of the local median income comprise 75% of the families receiving subsidized rent. Projects with Section 8 rental units are owned by private parties, for-profit and nonprofit organizations, and public housing agencies. Under Section 8, HUD has made 15- or 20-year contracts with private parties for the rental units, unless the project is owned by or financed with a loan or loan guarantee from a state or local housing agency. In this case, HUD will guarantee the rental units for 40 years. Efforts have been made to increase the private guarantee time of 20 years because in some situations it is a disincentive for private parties to become involved in the program.

Any type of financing may be used for the purchase or rehabilitation of a project that houses Section 8 rental units, including HUD–FHA mortgage insurance programs, conventional financing, and tax-exempt bonds. The property owner handles the whole program and is responsible for leasing at least 30% of the subsidized units to eligible families. Under the Section 8 legislation, priority is given to projects with only 20% of their units in Section 8, to guarantee an income mix in the housing project. However, if the rental units are to be used for the elderly, there is no restriction on the number of Section 8 rental units per project. Older persons occupy approximately half of all Section 8 housing.

Purpose of the Section 8 Program

The purpose of the Section 8 program is to develop rental housing for very low-income families within the structure of the private housing market. Section 8 units can exist in houses, small apartment buildings, or any other location that has units to rent. Suburban, rural, and urban areas are equally eligible. However, HUD determines how many Section 8 rental units can be awarded to a given area in each state. Usually, applications far exceed the units available for the specific areas in question.

The Section 8 housing program had a slow beginning after it was authorized in 1974. In 1975, there were 200,000 applications, but only 30 new units actually materialized (U.S. House of Representatives, Select Committee on Aging, 1976). The cumbersome application and administrative procedures were blamed for the delay. Section 8 was an entirely new program involving low-income families. The private financial community— the group that had to generate the construction monies—did not appear ready to fund the building of units that would house Section 8 families until the program had grown to become one of the key housing programs for the elderly. Section 8 covers only the actual rental units but is most successful when combined with other housing construction and service programs.

The Section 202 Program

Authorized under the Housing Act of 1959, Section 202 provides a capital advance at no interest to nonprofit organizations. The advances do not have to be repaid if the housing units remain available to low-income elderly for at least 40 years (HUD, 2014). The rents paid by tenants in Section 202 housing do not usually cover the costs of operating the property. To cover these costs, the program also provides rental assistance to the nonprofit organizations. Rental housing can be provided for the elderly through new construction or rehabilitation of existing structures. The property should include needed support services and can have rooms such as dining halls, community rooms, infirmaries, and other essential services.

These supportive services are largely funded by non-HUD organizations. Many of the nonprofit homes for the aged, such as Cathedral

Residences in Jacksonville, Florida—a large housing complex that serves more than 700 elderly—were partially constructed with money under Section 202. Reaffirming the importance of Section 202, the Section 202 program was very successful throughout the 1960s but was phased out after that time and replaced by Section 236, another federal loan program. However, Section 236 was frozen in 1973, when all federal housing programs were halted to allow for review. Section 202 was reinstated as part of the Housing and Community Development Act of 1974, but it did not return to full activity until the summer of 1975. Under the 1974 act, a $215 million borrowing level was approved for fiscal year (FY) 1975, but it was not used until the following year. Regulations in 1976 reaffirmed the importance of the program in providing both construction and long-term financing for housing projects (U.S. Senate, Special Committee on Aging, 1991). By 2003, 350,000 units had been funded through the Section 202 program.

Typically, 6,000 units of new housing are funded through the program each year. In FY 2002, $783 million was available for Section 202 programs (U.S. General Accounting Office, 2003). In 2004, older persons constituted 85% of the households using the Section 202 program (Government Accountability Office, 2005). Despite this impressive figure, only 8% of very low-income elderly renters were being helped by Section 202 housing.

Private nonprofit corporations and consumer cooperatives are eligible for Section 202 financing. Housing developments under Section 202 cannot exceed 300 units. Section 8 participation is required, and approval of Section 202 loans is based on the feasibility of getting Section 8 financing. In other words, Section 202 construction financing cannot be granted if the number of section writs for a section of the state has already been obligated. Section 202/8 allocations are made in accordance with Section 213, a fair share needs formula. The formula, which determines the number of eligible units for a given geographic area, is based on the following criteria:

1. The number of households with the head or spouse aged 62 years or older

2. The number of such households that lack one or more plumbing facilities

3. The number of such households with incomes less than the regionally adjusted poverty level

4. The prototype production costs for public housing units as adjusted by average cost factors within the loan region.

Target Population of Section 202

The target population for Section 202 programs is an elderly household—one headed by an individual older than 62 years—with income less than 50% of the median income in an area. In 2003, approximately 3.3 rental households in the United States qualified under these income criteria (GAO, 2003). The 1974 Housing Act also specified that 20% to 25% of funds for Section 202 housing must be awarded in rural areas. The residents of the housing must also reflect the racial population of the community. This provision was meant to ensure that minority elderly obtained housing. The projects are required to have either an adequate range of necessary social services or facilitate the access of residents to such services. Although Section 202 projects continue to be built, the size of these projects has dropped substantially. Some of this reduction in size is related to the growth of 202 projects outside of central cities: 22% of the projects occupied after 1984 were built in areas with fewer than 10,000 residents, a figure that is in stark contrast to the 2.2% of the projects occupied before 1975. The 202 program provides 86,000 units for needy older persons around the country (GAO, 2003).

SUPPORTING AGING IN PLACE—SUPPORTIVE SERVICES AND SENIOR CENTER PROGRAMS

According to the Administration on Aging (AoA), Home and Community-Based Supportive Services, established in 1973, provides grants to states and territories using a formula based primarily on their share of the national population aged 60 years and older. The grants fund a broad array of services that enable seniors to remain in their homes for as long as possible. These services include but are not limited to:

■ Access services such as transportation, case management, and information and assistance

■ In-home services such as personal care, chore, and homemaker assistance

■ Community services such as legal services, mental health services, and adult day care. (AoA, 2014b)

Senior centers and adult day services provide services tailored for older adults who live in the community. Senior centers are focused primarily on well elders, whereas adult day services provide a supportive environment for elders who need some assistance and supervision during the day. Providing social opportunities and engagement with peers are at the center of both. Senior centers and adult day services are important to the elders who use them and are often intertwined. Take the case of an older woman who is caring for her husband with Alzheimer's disease (AD). By enrolling her husband in an adult day program a few days a week, she can spend time with her friends taking classes and playing cards at the senior center. Both adult day programs and senior centers provide information about services in the community, health education, and connect the participants and their families with the larger community's calendar of cultural and civic events. And, both types of programs provide consumer information about health and supportive services that benefit the participants and their families.

The first senior center in the United States was started in the 1940s in New York City. The center was started by a group of New York City Welfare Department workers who believed that the older people with whom they were working would benefit from a place to meet, socialize, and organize activities. Senior centers were initially developed as indigenous, locally supported programs set up by nonprofit organizations or local government departments of social service or recreation. The OAA 1973 amendments included a new Multipurpose Senior Centers section that recognized the importance of this program model and facilitated public investment in senior centers. The amendments to OAA in 1978 provided the legislative authority for the development of senior center buildings and the operation of senior centers. Senior centers were constructed as free-standing facilities and, with funding from HUD, were also developed within some housing projects for seniors.

In many communities, the senior center was built as a new, modern building with amenities that allowed a range of activities. In other communities, funds were used to retrofit historic buildings that previously had served as schools or hospitals for their new use as senior centers. There continues to be an active small group of architects and designers who work on the design and retrofitting of senior centers and related-use buildings. Senior centers became more popular and grew from 1,200 centers in 1970 to nearly 15,000 in 1995 (Wagner, 1995).

In 1985, Louis Lowy described the essence of senior centers:

> The uniqueness of the senior center stems from its total concern for older people and its concern for the total older person. It works with older persons not for them, enabling and facilitating their decisions and their actions, and in so doing it creates and supports a sense of community that further enables

older persons to continue their involvement with and contribution to the larger community. (Wagner, 1995, p. 4)

The National Institute of Senior Centers (Wagner, 1995), a membership unit of the NCOA, defines senior centers as follows:

A senior center is a community focal point on aging where older adults come together for services and activities that reflect their experience and skills, respond to their diverse needs and interests, enhance their dignity, support their independence, and encourage their involvement in and with the center and the community (pp. 3–10).

Senior centers are not only the most widely recognized program for elders but also the service most used by older people. In the 1978 OAA amendments, senior centers were identified as "focal points" with the following characteristics: service delivery focal points are organizations that have high visibility and information and services for everyone, provide an array of services and opportunities for elders, take responsibility for identifying new resources and creating linkages with other organizations, and ensure that all information disseminated is accurate and timely.

The 2008 AoA data indicate that there are 6,951 senior centers serving as focal points in the United States. Some senior centers received OAA funding through Title III; in 2008, there were 6,022 centers that received OAA funding. Because senior centers continue to be rooted in the local community, their activities and services vary by community based on available resources and community characteristics. In 1976, Taietz identified two models of senior centers—the voluntary model and the social service agency model (Taietz, 1976). The voluntary model is a center that focuses primarily on social and recreational activities. The social service agency model is a more professionally managed center that provides social services to center participants.

Today's senior centers have evolved beyond these two models and reflect the diversity of the communities they serve as well as the standards established by NISC in their accreditation system. Senior centers can serve as intergenerational programming centers, recreation centers for after-school programs, and a place for the community to meet in the evening to discuss community-specific issues and planning. Senior centers are now also a community resource for residents of all ages to learn how to use a computer.

Pardasani and Thompson (2012) notes six models that were identified by a taskforce involved in a project sponsored by the NISC, the New Models Task Force (NMTF).

- Multigenerational community centers
- Wellness

- Lifelong learning
- Continuum of care/transitions
- Entrepreneurial center
- The Café Program

Their analysis put forth their definition of what makes a center innovative:

- Breadth of the innovation
- Stakeholder involvement extent and type of resources
- Impact on participation
- Potential for replication
- Long-term feasibility

Multipurpose senior centers are not only focal points within communities but also offer a wide array of programs and services. In 2001, it was estimated that 75% of the existing senior centers in the United States were "multipurpose" senior centers. These centers provide volunteer opportunities, classes and educational programming, health services and health education programming, recreational activities, meal programs (see the section "Supporting Aging in Place: Nutrition" for more information), access to transportation and community services, as well as access to national and state benefits and services. Senior centers also provide opportunities for candidates running for public office to reach out to the senior community, for students to learn about older persons through internships and volunteer service, and for researchers. Turner (2004) described the wide array of models as including those that are "single purpose," providing a meal, public and privately managed centers, centers that are free to consumers and others that charge for services, and some centers that serve ethnic groups and others that provide programming and support for frail and special-needs elders.

Turner's study of more than 800 participants from 27 senior centers found that 80% of the participants were older than 70 years and more than half reported that lunch at the senior center was their most important source of nutrition. More than half had been attending the center for more than 5 years. Pardasani (2004) explored the underutilization by minority group elders through a survey of 220 senior center directors in New York State. Because the aging population is increasing in ethnic and racial diversity and is projected to do so into the future, Pardasani was interested in looking at how centers could better recruit and serve this diverse group. Previous research conducted by Krout and others suggests that the "modal" senior center attendee was a White woman. In a study conducted by Krout and reported in 1988, he found that nearly 80% of the senior center participants in New York State were Caucasian (Krout, 1988). Pardasani's findings suggest that multipurpose senior centers and those located in urban areas were most likely to serve the highest percentage of minority elders. Other factors that were related to higher minority participation included targeting ethnic, religious, or racial groups of elders, offering services in more than one language, and having a racially and ethnically diverse professional staff. In other words, programming and diverse staff make a difference.

The successful senior center has an adaptable, flexible program with a menu of activities and programs that appeal to the center user and the community in which the center is located. A center provides access to transportation and cultural events, lunch along with snacks, a few card tables, and a pool table. The card tables and the pool tables area particularly draw for the older men who participate in center activities.

Using a computer, learning a foreign language or sign language, and taking field trips are all typical senior center activities. Increasingly, senior centers have also become a "health club" for community elders. In Baltimore, Maryland, for example, there are fitness centers in the senior centers that are staffed with kinesiologists who help the participants achieve their fitness goals. Some senior centers even have their own swimming pools, banks, and craft shops. The "good old days" of ceramics and bingo have been eclipsed by a diverse set of activities and a diverse set of participants. In many of the urban areas, senior centers are specialized for Asian elders, Hispanic elders, or Russian immigrants, serving ethnic meals and employing bilingual staff.

Accreditation of Senior Centers

In 1999, NISC began a national accreditation program for senior centers. The accreditation process includes a self-study that is done by the senior center. This self-study is guided by standards set by NISC. Baltimore County Department of Aging was the first Area Agency on Aging to have all of its centers accredited. There are currently more than 200 senior centers that hold accreditation in the United States. The accreditation must be renewed periodically and centers are expected to maintain a level of quality in their programming that reflects the changing nature of both the older population and the local community.

In 1995, a conference was convened by NISC and its parent organization, NCOA, to examine the future challenges of senior centers (Wagner, 1995). There was a consensus among participants that change was necessary if senior centers were going to survive into the future and effectively manage the dramatic changes in the older population, including higher education levels and more diversity and the changing nature of financial support for senior centers. A series of recommendations was developed about ways to maintain senior centers as vibrant community organizations that serve not only the older residents but also the larger community.

PERSPECTIVES

SENIOR CENTER CHALLENGES

John A. Krout, PhD
Professor Emeritus
Ithaca College Gerontology Institute
Ithaca College
Ithaca, NY

"This is not your mother's senior center" is a quote that likely describes to a 55- or 60-year-old what the senior center of the 21st century is striving to become. Over the past 30 years or so, senior centers have experienced their own life-cycle change as participants (who often also served as volunteers) have "aged in place." Although tremendously varied in terms of programs and user characteristics, centers have historically operated from a "nutrition, recreation, and socialization" model. In many communities, especially in rural and central city areas where seniors have fewer resources, this model still has relevance. However, even 30 years ago, some senior centers offered wellness and educational programs to attract the growing number of more active elders. Today, the large majority of senior centers recognize that the new wave of 60+ baby boomers are demanding new program options and that centers need to shape a new image to compete with the increasing number of activity options available to the 60+ from

(continued)

the private sector. As they shape this new image, I would suggest that centers neither repudiate nor forget their history, but rather build on the strengths they now have. Above all, have an answer to the question, "How will we know when we are successful (by what criteria will this be measured)?" What major challenges/opportunities will senior centers face as they transition to the future? They are the same ones that centers have faced since Little House opened its doors 50 years ago:

- Attracting participants

- Garnering funding

- Having attractive space and programs

- Recruiting and retaining effective staff and volunteers

- Establishing a community identity and positive image

- Finding ways to serve elders of varying interests and abilities

What fundamental actions do I think that senior centers need to take in the 21st century?
Below are some suggestions:

- Identify goals and develop strategic plans to address the interests of baby boomers and current center participants

- Identify the "image" the center wants to project and market it accordingly

- Have space that expresses that image and programming

- Define and stake out their "place" in their community's "activity menu"

- Define the organizational and personal linkages needed to be successful

- Know the demographics of their potential users and service area—for the next 25 years

- Be entrepreneurial in funding and identify private-sector tie-ins—assume the "old" sources will dry up

- Do not be afraid to dream!

SUPPORTING AGING IN PLACE—
ADULT DAY SERVICES

Adult day services are professional programs designed to meet the needs of adults in a community-based setting. As part of the home- and community-based long-term care array of services, adult day services provide a supervised support environment for elders and other adults with cognitive, developmental, and physical health problems. Adult day services models emerged in 1947 with the development of a geriatric day hospital opened by the Menninger Clinic. In the early days of adult day service programs, this service was referred to as "adult day care." This term was controversial among advocates for older adults because of its association with child care. Although some older programs may continue to use the term "adult day care" in their title and marketing material, professionals prefer the term "adult day services."

The National Adult Day Services Association (NADSA) represents the adult day service organizations and has a long history of working toward improving the quality of these services, as well as expanding the research and awareness of the importance of this service for both older adults and their family caregivers. NADSA was started in 1979 and was originally a unit of the NCOA. Dabelko, Koenig, and Danso (2008) point out that the development and the growth of adult day services have largely been a function of adapting to the external environment—in this case, the increasing number of older adults with dementia, physical frailty, and other functional limitations, along with a policy focus on aging in place and reducing the excessive costs of institutionalization. A 2008 study conducted by the MetLife Mature Market Institute of adult day services and home care costs articulated the efficiency of adult day services in the continuum of home- and community-based services. In 2008, the average daily rate for adult day services was $64.00 a day (MetLife Mature Market Institute, 2008). This compares with an average hourly rate of $20.00 for a home health aide and $18.00 for a homemaker/companion.

Adult day services are available under a range of auspices from nonprofit organizations to profit-making organizations. NADSA reports that approximately 78% of the adult day centers are operated on a nonprofit or public basis; 22% are for-profit organizations. Based on the national census conducted by Partners in Caregiving in 2004, NADSA reports that the majority of the centers (70%) are affiliated with other organizations such as skilled nursing facilities, medical facilities, or multipurpose senior organizations. This census also revealed that adult day centers provide services for 150,000 participants every day. According to NADSA there are 4,601 day programs operating in the nation today—this is a 35% increase from the estimated 3,407 programs identified in the 2004 census.

Medicaid waivers and Title III of the OAA funding for home- and community-based services, which prevent premature institutionalization, are important sources of revenue for adult day services. Income-eligible elders are able to attend adult day services under the waiver programs. Other adult day service participants pay for the service out of pocket.

These programs provide a range of services, including transportation between the program and the participant's home, social activities, meals and snacks, personal care such as help with toileting and grooming, and therapeutic activities such as physical exercise and cognitive activities. In the 1970s, there were two models of adult day services—the medical model and the social model. Today there are three models: a social model that also includes some health services, a medical model that provides therapeutic and health-related services with some social services, and a specialized service model that serves participants with specific conditions such as AD and related disorders or developmental disabilities. The federal government does not regulate adult day service programs, but most states have guidelines in place and/or an agency (health departments or department of aging) that monitors adult day services. In addition, there is a voluntary system of accreditation for adult day services that was developed by NADSA in 1998 and is managed by the Commission on the Accreditation of Rehabilitation Facilities (CARF). NADSA leadership specifically selected CARF to manage this accreditation because of its focus on rehabilitation, the centerpiece of the philosophy of adult day service development in the late 1990s. Accreditation has been slow to catch on within the industry, and the 2004 census found that only 6% of the centers were accredited and that two thirds of those surveyed reported that they had no plans to pursue accreditation.

Future funding sources that are based on performance and quality indicators rather than payment for services may make this accreditation more important to adult day services. Participants in adult day service programs come with a range of health conditions. More than half (52%) of the participants have some cognitive deficit. The average age of a center participant is 72 years, and two thirds of the participants are women (NADSA, 2010). Therapeutic and rehabilitative services are important components of an adult day service program and will likely become more important in the future. In a study conducted in Massachusetts, Silverstein, Wong, and Brueck (2010) set out to explore the extent to which the adult day service programs were addressing the needs of persons with AD. They were particularly interested in how the centers served persons with early onset of the disease, a situation in which caregivers commonly report that there are few appropriate program options. Their survey found that, within the 70% of programs that had services specifically designed for persons with AD, 71% provided early-stage services, 63% provided late-stage services, and 43% provided end-stage services. Nearly half (44%) of the sites reported that they provided services for persons younger than 65 years. The researchers indicated that most centers were engaged in stage-specific therapeutic services and, when necessary, individualized planning was undertaken to ensure that the program was meaningful and appropriate for the early-onset participant. This study highlights some of the compelling issues that the home- and community-based service network will be facing in the future as the demand for specialized programming increases with the aging of the baby boomers.

Adult day services are also an important source of respite services for family caregivers (Arch National Respite Network and Resource Center, 2010). In addition to the professional therapeutic attention to the day-service participant, staff also needs to view the family caregiver as a beneficiary of the services. Family caregivers need help in fostering the transition to adult day service programs. Bull and McShane (2008) analyzed the transition to and from the adult day program to better understand the role of the family caregiver in this transition. In their sample, half of the families received help from a care manager assigned to them by the Department on Aging who helped them identify programs. Geographic proximity was one criterion of importance to this care manager. Family caregivers were interested in safety, staffing ratio, types of activities offered, cleanliness, and a "good fit" with the interests of the elder.

Family caregivers encouraged the older care recipients by giving them "pep talks" and helping them dress and get ready for the van to pick them up. Good relationships between the family caregiver and the staff helped in the adjustment of the caregiver, as did positive reports provided by the care recipient. Their study found that adjustment to adult day services was facilitated by regular attendance at least 3 days a week. Most adult day services operate only 5 days a week, providing services during the day. This schedule can help an employed caregiver who works "regular" hours during the week but not the off-schedule worker. Some centers are open on Saturdays, which can free a family caregiver to do errands that day. And a few programs offer evening hours. Both the service array and the schedule may differ if the dominant focus of the adult day service is respite care rather than therapeutic services for the participant. In the future, we may see an expansion of the models of adult day service programs as some begin to focus on the needs of the family caregiver and offer more flexible scheduling and drop-in programming. Balancing the needs of the family with the needs of the participant will, however, continue to be a critical factor in a successful adult day service program. Historically, programs have provided assistance in identifying needed community services, education about caregiving, and information about diseases, such as diabetes and AD, to the families of program participants. We will likely see an expansion of these education and support services on the part of programs that are responding to the life-span respite agenda.

SUPPORTING AGING IN PLACE: NUTRITION

The Congregate Meal Program

Good nutrition is the foundation of good health. The OAA Nutrition Program has been providing nutritional meals to older Americans since 1973, when the amendments to the OAA authorized the Elderly Nutrition Program. Since that time, nutrition programs have been a cornerstone of community-based programs for older Americans. Meal programs have become the most popular and well-received programs of the OAA. This section will address information related to the congregate meal program. The purpose of the nutrition program is to reduce hunger and food insecurity, foster social participation, and encourage health promotion. The OAA authorizes the nutrition programs under three Title III programs, including

▪ Congregate Nutrition Services (Title III C1)

▪ Home-Delivered Nutrition Services (Title III C2)

▪ Nutrition Services Incentive Program (NSIP)

The congregate nutrition services are group meals provided in senior centers, senior housing complexes, and other settings to any person older than 60 years. Congregate meal programs provide participants with a nutritious meal as well as an opportunity to socialize with peers. The group meals also offer a venue for nutrition education, community activities, and educational programming. The home-delivered meals are provided to individuals who are homebound. The meals are delivered to the elder's home and, in many cases, the meal is a gateway service to other needed home- and community-based services. These meals are available to persons 60 years and older who are homebound and the spouse of the meal recipient regardless of age (AoA, 1996).

The Nutrition Services Incentive Program

The Nutrition Services Incentive Program (NSIP) is a program that provides additional resources in the form of cash or commodities or a combination of both to supplement the resources available for nutrition programs. In 2008, the congregate meal program served 1,656,330 people. The Title III fund spent on the congregate program was $265.5 million. The total cost of the congregate program was $636.2 million, with Title III providing 42% of the funds needed for the program. There were 909,787 people served by the home-delivered meals at a Title II cost of $228.1 million. The total cost of the program was $755.1 million; Title III covered 30% of this cost. In addition to the meals provided to older Americans, Title III also provides nutrition counseling and education. In 2008, $1.04 million of Title III funds was spent on nutrition counseling and $3.5 million on nutrition education. Title III funds supported 38% of the total costs of nutrition counseling and 57% of nutrition education costs (AoA, 2014c).

History of the Congregate Program

The malnourished elderly have been a part of our society for a long time, but formal, sustained programs to provide for those who do not have personal or financial resources are relatively new. The most significant research prior to the planning and development of a national nutritional program was the 1965 National Study on Food Consumption and Dietary Level sponsored by the Department of Agriculture. This study showed that 95 million Americans did not consume an adequate diet; 35 million of these had incomes at or below the poverty level. Subsequent analysis indicated that 6 to 8 million of those aged 60 years and older had deficient diets. These data laid the foundation for a federal nutrition program for the aged (Cain, 1977). A task force set up to develop recommendations based on the results of the national study recommended demonstration projects for a 3-year period to determine the best mechanisms for delivering nutritional services. Demonstration projects were needed because of the lack of information on how such programs should be designed and, more important, the extent of their effectiveness (Bechill & Wolgamot, 1972). The purpose of the demonstration projects was to "design appropriate ways for the delivery of food services which enable older persons to enjoy adequate palatable meals that supply essential nutrients needed to maintain good health . . . in settings conducive to eating and social interaction with peers" (Cain, 1977, p. 142). Although this overall goal seems straightforward, the demonstrations were expected to examine multiple issues. In addition, to improve the diet of older adults, the meals were to be served in social settings that would allow for the testing of the effects of different types of sites. These sites would be evaluated in terms of their ability to promote increased interaction among the older clients. The effects of a nutrition education program on the eating habits of the elderly would be evaluated, as would the general ability of the congregate meals approach to reduce the isolation of older persons. Of course, the AoA was also concerned about the comparative costs of different methods of preparing and delivering meals and the problems that were entailed in any effort to increase the nutritional quality of the older person's diet (Cain, 1977).

AoA funded 32 demonstration and research projects under Title IV. An intensive evaluation of the demonstrations produced the support for the National Nutrition Program first authorized in the 1973 OAA amendments. The 32 demonstration projects were designed to control for variations in income, living conditions, ethnic background, environmental setting, staffing, and record keeping. This intricate design allowed national guidelines to be developed that would incorporate the successful components of each project. More important, the Title IV projects indicated to the AoA and the U.S. Congress that the proper provision of congregate meals for groups of elderly people fostered social interaction, facilitated the delivery of supportive services, and met emotional needs while improving nutrition.

All persons aged 60 years and above and their spouses are eligible for services under the nutrition program. Special emphasis is placed on serving the low-income and disadvantaged elderly. The centers or sites for congregate meal programs are located in any space appropriate for the serving of congregate meals. The centers can serve as few as 5 or as many as 250 participants on a given day; however, the average center serves between 20 and 60 participants each day.

Congregate Meal Sites

Church basements, schools, high-rise apartments, senior centers, and multipurpose centers are the most common locations for nutrition sites. Because transportation is so important to the success of the program, centers are usually located in high-density areas where walking is possible, or on bus or subway lines. In suburban and rural areas, the centers are located in areas where some form of transportation to and from the center can be provided by the site. Unless the nutrition program is incorporated into senior centers that offer all-day programming, nutrition sites or centers are open up to 4 hours a day. The location of the center, available transportation, and additional resources affect the length of time the program operates daily. Location also affects the type of programming developed by the site. Sites that are not used for other purposes allow greater freedom for alterations, decoration, and storage space than do locations that have other activities scheduled in the same space. Shared space has posed a hardship for many nutrition programs in meeting the national guidelines for program development.

Because the purpose of the nutrition program is to provide both meals and socializing, programming is an important part of the services offered. When the nutrition site is incorporated into a high rise for the elderly, a senior center, or a recreation center, programming is usually part of the additional available resources. When the nutrition site is its own center, programming responsibility rests with the nutrition site managers under the direction of the nutrition project director for the region. Programming is diverse and related to the interests and backgrounds of the participants. The programming available is similar to that found in senior centers, but with special emphasis on nutrition education, meal preparation, buying practices, health maintenance, and physical fitness. Not all participants become involved in the programming. Nutrition screening, assessment, education, and counseling are, however, basic components of the program.

Encouraging Participation

Participants are encouraged to contribute something for the meal. Nutrition centers suggest that individuals, from their own consciences, should determine how much they should and can afford to pay. Nutrition centers furnish envelopes or have similar systems in which participants pay what they feel is appropriate. The 1984 OAA amendments forbid programs from charging for their meals. Voluntary contributions, however, account for about 20% of the costs of congregate and home-delivered meals. Some congregate nutrition programs have adopted the use of posters to encourage older people to contribute for their meals. Others, such as the Columbus County Office for the Aging in New York State, have a suggested contribution scale. State offices on aging also receive surplus commodities or cash to supplement the cost of the meals they provide. The funding provided by the Department of Agriculture is based on the number of meals served with Title III funds. With the limited funding in some local areas relative to the participant demand, participants have decided among themselves to contribute higher amounts so that more people can be served. Local donations and volunteers also help to defray about 14% of the costs of this program (Lieberman, n.d.).

Home-Delivered Meals

Home-delivered meals ("Meals on Wheels") are provided to homebound persons and enable those who cannot buy food or prepare their own meals to have good nutritious meals on a regular basis. Approximately 90% of all those receiving homebound meals are aged 60 years and above. The purpose of the program is to provide either one or two meals per day, 5 days a week. These delivered meals may enable many of these meal recipients to remain living in the community.

Home-Delivered Meals: A Brief History

Programs of home-delivered meals began in England immediately after World War II. The first program in the United States began in Philadelphia in 1955. The longest continuously operating program is Meals on Wheels of Central Maryland, Inc., which began in 1960 in Baltimore and was modeled after the English programs.

Early Models

The early models of home-delivered meal programs were operated locally and largely by volunteer organizations. Originating in a church kitchen, these programs served from 15 to 100 clients, generating payment from clients either through a fixed fee or on a sliding scale. From 30 to 300 volunteers are involved in any given local program. Referrals would come from friends, families, professionals in the field, or the elderly themselves. The number of daily meals and the costs of these meals both depended on the facilities available for meal preparation. Menus, number of meals served, amount, and cost were determined by the local organization sponsoring the program. Volunteers were primarily retirees and nonworking women, each of whom volunteered approximately 2 hours a week. The hot meal was delivered at noontime and, if a second meal was provided, it was a cold evening meal delivered at the same time as the hot meal. The early programs were sponsored by local churches, community groups, or nonprofit organizations and were largely self-sufficient, based on the fees charged to the participating clients.

The Active 1970s

In the early 1970s, government funds resulted in either new programs under government sponsorship or links between nonprofit local programs and government agencies. With the introduction of these new support mechanisms, uniform standards, quality control, and uniformity began. The 1978 amendments to the OAA for the first time designated a separate authorization for home-delivered meals. This program was to be administered through the nutrition program. In some situations, there were no preexisting home-delivered meal programs. AoA-funded home-delivered meal programs primarily served clients who were congregate-site participants, whereas locally funded programs served other eligible clients. Congregate nutrition participants often paid only when they felt they could, whereas those being served by a locally self-supporting home-delivered meal program paid a fixed fee; as a result, the Meals on Wheels cost to a client was often as much as five times higher. This caused confusion when a client moved from one program to the other.

The 1978 legislation allowing separate authorization for home-delivered meals brought this issue of privately operated, largely volunteer groups vis-à-vis federally sponsored programs to a head. The authorizing legislation stated that home-delivered meal programs under the separate authorization were to be administered through the federal nutrition program, with preference for funding given to local preexisting voluntary home-delivered meal programs. Since 1978, OAA funding for home-delivered meals has grown dramatically. In a home-delivered meal program, two volunteers—one acting as a driver, one as a visitor—visit 8 to 10 different clients each day. The volunteers spend 5 minutes with each client while delivering the meal. The home-delivered meal program's primary function is to prepare and deliver the meals, but it also provides a few minutes of friendly visiting. If additional services are needed, the client is referred to other support systems.

Realizing the Importance of the Connections

When the home-delivered meal program is attached directly to the nutrition congregate site, the nutrition participants themselves often package and deliver the meals. In this way, those who are attending can keep in touch with participants who are unable to attend. As was pointed out in Congressional testimony (Cain, 1977), the longer the congregate nutrition program is available, the greater the potential for home-delivered meals remaining part of the program.

One project found that after 3 years, up to 30% of the participants were receiving home-delivered meals because of changes in their physical condition. The interrelation of the two programs is important so that those who are eligible for the nutrition program can continue, even when physical limitations temporarily make visiting the center impossible. The home-delivery program can speed up recovery and perhaps, in many situations, make a return to the congregate site possible.

Federal Appropriations for Congregate and Home-Delivered Nutrition Services

Congregate Nutrition Services Appropriations (Title III C1), 2008 to 2012, are as follows:

Federal Fiscal Year Congregate Nutrition Services Appropriation

FY 2008 $410,716,000

FY 2009 $434,269,000

FY 2010 $440,783,000

FY 2011 $439,901,000

FY 2012 $439,070,000

Home-Delivered Nutrition Services Appropriations (Title III C2), 2008 to 2012, are as follows:

Federal Fiscal Year Home-Delivered Nutrition Services Appropriation

FY 2008 $193,858,000

FY 2009 $214,459,000

FY 2010 $217,676,000

FY 2011 $217,241,000

FY 2012 $216,831,000

NSIP Appropriations, 2008 to 2012, are as follows:

Federal Fiscal Year NSIP Appropriation

FY 2008 $153,429,000

FY 2009 $161,015,000

FY 2010 $161,015,000

FY 2011 $160,693,000

FY 2012 $160,389,000 (AoA, 2014)

INNOVATIONS IN "AGING IN PLACE"—MODEL PROGRAMS

We will continue to see innovations in aging in place. There are a variety of exciting models being developed both in the United States and Europe that give hope that there may be more options in the future that actually fit the consumer rather than the consumer having to fit the environment. There are several models to keep an eye on, including the Affordable Living for the Aging and the National Shared Housing Initiative, The Village Model, and Elder Cohousing. A recent report by the Older Women's League (Wagner, 2014) notes that, "Around the nation there are informal and formal initiatives being tried to improve the quality of LTSS and *living long with care needs*" (p. 36) Below are a few examples:

The Village Movement—www.vtvnetwork.org

The Green House Project—thegreenhouseproject.org

The Eden Alternative—www.edenalt.org

Elder Co-Housing—www.cohousing.org

Beatitudes Campus—www.beatitudescampus.org

CONCLUSION

Would you want to grow old in your community? Would you be able to live independently as you aged? These are critical questions to consider if we want to allow older adults to have choices about where they age. And, as we know, most older adults want to age in place in their own homes and communities. This chapter explored a variety of issues related to community-based services in the context of aging in place for older adults. There are a broad range of programs and services available through the aging networks that help older adults maintain their independence and, as a result, also help informal caregiving networks and families.

As was mentioned earlier The Community Innovation for Aging in Place Initiative has the potential to address many of the issues related to aging in place, including housing choices for LGBT older adults. In an article in the *San Diego Gay & Lesbian News* (Bajko, 2014) the author reminds us that LGBT older adults still "face stark housing choices"—particularly if housing requires a move to city that may be seen as less gay friendly than a city like San Francisco. However, regardless of what community one lives in it is clear that the challenges faced by LGBT older adults are only going to increase if the aging network and the field of aging do not step up to the plate with focused programs and services that target the LGBT community in general.

It is important to view the supports for older adults from the perspective of empowerment and autonomy rather than where we have been in the past with programs that foster dependence and operate from a paternalistic attitude about aging, including the view that professionals know what is best and at the very least, someone other than the older adults themselves knows what is right and what is needed. The aging networks can achieve this by promoting programs that are "active aging" focused and grounded in the SDH as their organizing principles.

CRITICAL THINKING QUESTIONS

1. *Develop a list of criteria you think would be important to consider in selecting an adult day service program. Visit a few program sites on the Internet to investigate whether the information offered addresses your criteria. What recommendations would you make to the program director to improve the site?*

2. *Discuss the differences between a program that is set up as a respite program and a program that is focused on the therapeutic needs of the participant. How might these differences affect the program from the perspective of the participant and from the perspective of the family caregiver?*

3. *Review the WHO Age-Friendly Cities and Communities Program and take a walk through your neighborhood to identify improvements that could be made in your community to create a community for all ages. What existing programs support active aging and foster empowerment?*

4. *Prepare a list of housing-related questions and call the housing authority in your area to set up an appointment to discuss policies and programs related to the elderly.*

   a. *Are there currently waiting lists for senior housing?*

   b. *What are the main challenges in housing policies and programs for the elderly?*

5. *Consider yourself at age 75 years. Will you want to continue to maintain a household and property? Will you want to live with others your own age? Will you want to live in a congregate setting? Make a list of the pros and cons of a variety of living options.*

REFERENCES

Access to Respite Care and Help (ARCH) National Respite Network and Resource Center. (2010). *Adult day care: One form of respite for older adults.* Fact Sheet Number 54. Retrieved June 16, 2010, from http://www.archrespite.org

Administration on Aging (AoA). (1996). *Serving elderly at risk: The Older Americans Act nutrition programs: National evaluation of the Elderly Nutrition Program, 1993–95.* Washington, DC: Author.

Administration on Aging (AoA). (2014a). *Community innovations for aging in place.* Retrieved from http://www.aoa.acl.gov/AoA_Programs/HCLTC/CIAIP/index.aspx

Administration on Aging (AoA). (2014b). *Supportive services and senior centers program.* Retrieved from http://www.aoa.gov/AoARoot/AoA_Programs/HCLTC/supportive_services/index.aspx#purpose

Administration on Aging (AoA). (2014c). *Nutrition services (OAA Title IIIC).* Retrieved from http://www.aoa.gov/AoA_programs/HCLTC/Nutrition_Services/index.aspx#nutrition services

American Presidency Project. (2014). *Harry S. Truman: Statement by the president upon signing the Housing Act of 1949 (July 15, 1949).* Retrieved from http://www.presidency.ucsb.edu/ws/?pid=13246

Bajko, M.S. (2014, April 30). As health falters, LGBT seniors face stark housing choices. *San Diego Gay and Lesbian News.* Retrieved from http://sdgln.com/health/2014/04/30/health-falters-lgbt-seniors-face-stark-housing-choices#sthash.MZ1cVWRw.dpuf

Bechill, W. B., & Wolgamot, I. (1972). *Nutrition for the elderly: The program highlights of research and development nutrition projects funded under Title IV of the Older Americans Act of 1965, June 1968, and June 1971.* Washington, DC: U.S. Government Printing Office.

Bull, M., & McShane, R. (2008). Seeking what's best during the transition to adult day health services. *Qualitative Health Research, 18*(5), 597–605.

Cain, L. (1977). Evaluative research and nutrition programs for the elderly. In J. E. O'Brien (Ed.), *Evaluative research on social programs for the elderly* (pp. 32–48). Washington, DC: U.S. Government Printing Office.

Commission on the Social Determinants of Health (CSDH). (2008). *Closing the gap in a generation: Health equity through action on the social determinants of health. Final Report of the Commission on Social Determinants of Health.* Geneva, Switzerland: World Health Organization.

Dabelko, H., Koenig, T., & Danso, K. (2008). An examination of the adult services industry using the resource dependence model within a value context. *Journal of Aging and Social Policy, 20*(2), 201–217.

Krout, J. (1988). *The frequency, duration, stability and discontinuation of senior center participation: Causes and consequences.* Fredonia, NY: Final Report to the AARP Andrus Foundation.

Lieberman, T. (n.d.). *Hungerwatch: America's elders are waiting for food.* Retrieved January 8, 2005, from http://www.asaging.org/at/at-201/hunger.html

Marmot, M. (2005). Social determinants of health inequities. *Lancet, 365,* 1099–1110.

MetLife Mature Market Institute. (2008). *The MetLife market survey of adult day services & home care costs.* Westport, CT: Author.

National Adult Day Services Association (NADSA). (2010). Retrieved from http://www.nadsa.org

National Council on Aging (NCOA). (n.d.). *Older Americans Act appropriations—Nutrition services.* Retrieved January 8, 2005, from http://www.ncoa.org/content.cfm?sectionID=165&detail=71

National Institute of Senior Centers (NISC). (2010). *Accredited/re-accredited centers. The National Council on the Aging document.* Retrieved October 4, 2010, from http:// www.ncoa.org/strengthening-community-organizations/senior-centers/nisc/

Pardasani, M. (2004). Senior centers: Increasing minority participation through diversification. *Journal of Gerontological Social Work, 43*(2–3), 41–56.

Pardasani, M., & Thompson, P. (2012). Senior centers: Innovative and emerging models. *Journal of Applied Gerontology, 31*(11), 52–77.

Silverstein, N., Wong, C., & Brueck, K. (2010). Adult day health care for participants with Alzheimer's disease. *American Journal of Alzheimer's Disease & Other Dementias, 25*(3), 276–283.

Taietz, P. (1976). Two conceptual models of the senior center. *Journal of Gerontology, 31*, 219–222.

Tarlov, A. (1996) Social determinants of health: The sociobiological translation. In D. Blane, E. Brunner, & R. Wilkinson (Eds.), *Health and social organization* (pp. 71–93). London, UK: Routledge.

Turner, K. (2004). Senior citizens centers: What they offer, who participates and what they gain. *Journal of Gerontological Social Work, 43*(1), 37–47.

U.S. Department of Housing and Urban Development (HUD). (1974). *Housing in the seventies: A report of the National Policy Review.* Washington, DC: Author. Retrieved from http://www.huduser.org/portal//Publications/pdf/HUD-968.pdf

U.S. Department of Housing and Urban Development (HUD). (2014). *Section 202 Supportive Housing for the Elderly Program.* Retrieved from http://portal.hud. gov/hudportal/HUD?src=/program_offices/housing/mfh/progdesc/eld202

U.S. General Accounting Office. (2003). *Elderly housing: Project funding and other factors delay assistance to needy households.* Report to the Special Committee on Aging, U.S. Senate. Retrieved from http://www.gao.gov/assets/240/238383.pdf

U.S. House of Representatives, Select Committee on Aging (1976). *Elderly housing overview: HUD's inaction report.* Washington, D.C.: U.S. Government Printing Office. Retrieved from http://archive.org/stream/elderov00unit/elderov00unit_djvu.txt

U.S. Senate, Special Committee on Aging. (1990). *Developments in aging.* Washington, D.C.: U.S. Government Printing Office.

Wagner, D. (1995). Senior center research in America: An overview of what we know. In D. Shollenberger (Ed.), *Senior centers in America: A blueprint for the future.* Washington, DC: The National Council on the Aging.

Wagner, D. (2014). *Keep calm and manage your future. 2014 Mother's Day Report, long term care.* Washington, DC: The Older Women's League.

World Health Organization (WHO). (2007). *Global age-friendly cities: A guide.* Geneva, Switzerland: Author. Retrieved from http://whqlibdoc.who.int/publications/2007/9789241547307_eng.pdf?ua=1

World Health Organization. (2008). *Closing the gap in a generation: Health equity through action on the social determinants of health.* (Report from the Commission on Social Determinants of Health.) Geneva, Switzerland: Author. Retrieved from http:// www.who.int/social_determinants/thecommission/finalreport/en/index.html

CHAPTER FIVE

Income Security in Old Age

Since the passage of the Social Security Act in 1935, the percentage of elders who live in poverty has decreased dramatically. In fact, there is a lower percentage of people older than 65 years living in poverty today than there are younger people. One estimate suggests that 21.8% of children younger than 18 years were living in poverty compared to 9.1% of those older than 65 years (Desilver, 2014). In 2012 there were 3.9 million Americans older than 65 years living below the poverty level and an additional 2.4 million (5.5%) with incomes of just 125% of the poverty level (Assistant Secretary for Planning and Evaluation [ASPE], 2014). The poverty guidelines set by the federal government to determine eligibility for programs and support in 2014 were $11,670/year for a single person and $15,730 for two-person households (for the 48 contiguous states). Many federal and state programs, such as Supplemental Nutrition Assistance Program (SNAP) and the Low-Income Home Energy Assistance Programs, use 125% or 185% of poverty as the eligibility level.

Prior to the passage of the Social Security Act, older adults who were no longer able to work or who had no independent resources, were entirely dependent on others such as family or friends. The Great Depression was particularly difficult for the older people in our nation who were not likely to find alternative employment if their jobs had been abolished. The United States was a nation of soup kitchens and breadlines; banks were closed and millions of Americans were out of work. The elders were particularly vulnerable during this time if they did not have family who could support them (Figures 5.1 and 5.2). The Social Security Administration website has an interesting and informative history section that includes photos and posters about the rollout of Social Security and a detailed chronology of events related to the development of the social insurance program of Social Security and Medicare (Social Security Administration [2014a]).

FIGURE 5.1   Soup Kitchens in the 1930s.
Source: Social Security Administration (2014a).

This chapter reviews the social insurance programs that support older Americans, poverty rates, and modern retirement compared to "old fashioned retirement," gender differences, income equality, and the broad reach of Social Security. We also cover the mechanics of Medicare and Medicaid. There are three "Perspectives" in this chapter; one addresses the "comfortable retirement" and its differential meaning and possibility, another focuses on women older than 50 years, and the final Perspective piece covers the broad reach of Social Security and its importance to families of all ages.

After reading this chapter, you will be curious about:

(a) *The difference between the historical development of "safety net" programs in the United States compared to European countries*

(b) *Why we require that people receive supported long-term services and supports (LTSS) only by becoming impoverished*

(c) *The changing nature of poverty and what might be done to equalize lifestyles and income*

(d) *Gender differences and ways in which we can equalize the differential*

(e) *Why only older Americans can participate in a single-payer, comprehensive health care system*

SOCIAL INSURANCE

The United States has two important social insurance programs that are of essential importance to older adults—Social Security and Medicare. According to Marmor and Mashaw (2002, p. 169) "Universal social

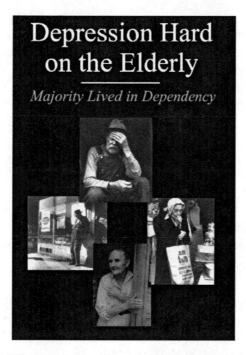

FIGURE 5.2 Poster from the Great Depression.
Source: Social Security Administration (2014a).

insurance programs are preconditions for a workable system of…capitalism and political democracy." Social insurance protects all members of a society from common hazards we all face, including aging, illness, unemployment, and economic downturns. Social Security is a program that the vast majority of Americans participate in during their working years either directly or indirectly through a family status (e.g., nonworking husband or dependent children). Similarly, Medicare is a universal health care program for older persons and persons with special conditions that enable them to be eligible for coverage (e.g., end-stage renal failure) regardless of age. Others who are eligible for Medicare coverage are Americans who have received disability benefits from Social Security for 24 months and those who are disabled as a result of amyotrophic lateral sclerosis (ALS; also known as Lou Gehrig's disease). Individuals with Lou Gehrig's disease do not have to wait 24 months to receive the benefits of Medicare.

The basis of a social insurance program is that everyone participates and everyone is eligible to receive benefits based on the specified "hazards" covered by the program. Regardless of income, for example, Social Security and Medicare benefits are available to all beneficiaries. The design of Social

Security is progressive in that those who have been low-income workers receive a higher "replacement rate" for their lost incomes after they retire. This model has proven to be an important one for low-income people who are less likely than others to have additional resources to assist them in old age. The first social insurance program was developed in 1889 in Germany. See Table 5.1 for historical highlights related to Social Security.

TABLE 5.1
Historical Highlights of Social Security

1881	Germany's Emperor, William I, proposed old-age social insurance to the German Parliament.
1888	Austria enacts compulsory health insurance legislation.
1889	Germany is the first nation to adopt an old-age social insurance program.
1909	First public commission on aging set up in Massachusetts.
1909	Geriatrics as a scientific study began.
1909	First old-age pension bill introduced in Congress.
1910	First survey of economics of elderly conducted in Massachusetts.
1912	The Progressive Party calls for protection hazards of old age, illness, and unemployment by system of social insurance designed for the United States.
1914	First textbook on geriatrics published.
1920	American Medical Association developed first declaration of opposition to any mandatory health insurance by a state or the federal government.
1929	State laws providing workmen's compensation in effect in all but four states.
1934	Francis Townsend and Robert Clements establish Old-Age Revolving Pensions, Ltd.
1935	Roosevelt asks Congress for legislation to help unemployed, aged, poor children and those with physical handicaps.
1935	American Medical Association met in emergency session to oppose mandatory health insurance.
1935	On August 14th President Roosevelt signed the Social Security Bill into law.
1936	Federal unemployment tax of 1% applied to employers of eight or more.
1936	First unemployment check paid under state law in Madison, WI ($15.00).
1937	U.S. Supreme Court declares unemployment insurance provisions of the Social Security Act and old-age pensions constitutional.
1938	National Health Conference convened in Washington to make recommendations on national health plan.
1938	American Medical Association approved in principle tax-supported health services for the poor and voluntary health insurance for others.

(continued)

TABLE 5.1 (*continued*)
Historical Highlights of Social Security

1939	51 jurisdictions began providing unemployment benefits.
1939	National Health Act of 1939 introduced by Sen. R. Wagner— provided national compulsory health insurance and their employees; funded by contributions of employers and employees to a health insurance fund. Bill died in committee.
1939	American Medical Association developed committee to fight Wagner bill.
1940	All states, the District of Columbia, Alaska, Hawaii, and Puerto Rico are providing child welfare services under the Social Security Act.
1941	President Roosevelt's State of the Union message recommended that two social insurance programs (Social Security and Unemployment) be expanded.
1945	President Truman proposes, in a special message to Congress, a prepaid medical insurance plan for all people through the Social Security System.
1948	National Health Assembly met with the Federal Security Agency to develop a 10-year health plan for the nation.
1948	American Medical Association launches a "National Education Campaign" against National Health Insurance proposals.
1949	President Truman, in State of the Union message, calls for compulsory national health insurance for all Americans to be financed by a federal payroll tax.
1950	National Conference on Aging convened by Federal Security Agency, Washington, DC.
1950	Benefits paid to dependent widows and husbands, wife younger than 65 years with child, divorced wife.
1952	SSA Annual Report (1951) recommended health insurance for beneficiaries.
1953	Eisenhower in State of the Union message recommends that "old-age and survivor's Law" be extended to millions of Americans left out of Social Security.
1954	Social Security Act amended to extend coverage to self-employed farmers, certain professions, domestics, and, on a voluntary basis, to members of state and local government systems.
1955	Federal employees brought into unemployment system.
1956	Social Security Administration's new electronic system, IBM 705, began operating.
1957	First disability payments paid under OASDI.
1959	Senate Committee on Labor and Public Welfare set up special subcommittee to study problems of the aged and aging.
1960	Study unveiled: The Aged and Aging in the United States: A National Problem.
1960	Benefits become payable to disabled of any age.
1961	White House Conference on Aging convened by HEW.

(continued)

TABLE 5.1 *(continued)*
Historical Highlights of Social Security

1961	President's health message first of its kind to be exclusively devoted to the need for national health care program.
1965	Older Americans Act signed by President Johnson.
1965	Health insurance for elderly signed in Independence, MO, with Harry Truman watching; he began the fight for health care in 1945.
1968	National Health Insurance in effect for Canada residents.
1972	Nixon signs COLA provisions for automatic COLA.
1972	SSI enacted for low income, aged, blind, and disabled.
1981	Reagan convenes the National Committee on Social Security Reform.
1986	Reagan signs law requiring all children older than 5 years to be assigned a Social Security number.
1998	First White House Conference on Social Security held.

COLA, cost-of-living adjustment; HEW, Department of Health, Education, and Welfare; OASDI, Old Age, Survivors, and Disability Insurance Program; SSA, Social Security Administration; SSI, Supplemental Security Income.

Adapted from Social Security Administration (2014a).

POVERTY RATES AND THEIR CALCULATION

Prior to the 1960s there were few reliable estimates of poverty rates of older adults. In 1959, the poverty rate among elders was estimated at 35% and by 2005 this poverty rate for elders had declined to 10.8% (Martin & Weaver, 2005). The poverty rate, as discussed earlier in this chapter, is a very basic standard. Most federal and state programs for income-eligible persons rely on a minimum standard of 125% to 185% of the poverty level. In 2011, the Census Bureau began using an alternative measure of poverty. The Supplemental Poverty Measure includes cash income and noncash income as well as necessary expenses, such as taxes, child care, and work-related expenses, as well as health care insurance and out-of-pocket medical expenses (Short, 2013). The Supplemental Poverty Measure estimates of poverty among older adults is 15%—higher than the average poverty rate based on "traditional" poverty levels. In large part, this is due to the inclusion of health care expenses—both premiums for health insurance and out-of-pocket costs.

In an analysis conducted by Levinson, Damico, Cubanski, and Neuman (2013), nearly half (48%) of America's older adults live with incomes less than 200% of the poverty level using the Supplemental Measure, as compared to 34% when calculated using the traditional poverty measure. Additionally the Elder Index—a methodological approach that includes specific costs of services of importance to older adults, geographical factors that influence the cost of living in different states, and home ownership versus renting— estimates that in contrast to the standard poverty level of $11,670 for a single person and $15,730 for a couple; the minimum amount of income needed for an individual to live modestly is between $16,716 and $29,604 per year (Gerontology Institute, 2012).

In summary, poverty rates are not necessarily a good indicator of the difficulty an individual faces in making ends meet as he or she ages. The ability to live independently as a retired older adult is influenced not only by the Social Security benefit earned during a lifetime of working, but also additional income from pensions, savings and investments; and the costs of health care, housing, and living; as well as catastrophic expenses that derive from serious health care expenditures associated with long-term care of a spouse or the individual him- or herself. Ellen Bruce, one of the developers of the Elder Index, discusses the complications of managing the income needs of the growing numbers of older Americans below.

PERSPECTIVES

WHAT IS THE BEST WAY TO ENSURE A REASONABLY COMFORTABLE RETIREMENT FOR OLDER AMERICANS?

Ellen A. Bruce, JD
University of Massachusetts, Boston
Boston, MA

Having enough income and resources to support oneself in retirement is a worry for most Americans. This is not an issue that is easily resolved by an individual or a couple. The components of a secure retirement include Social Security, pension income, savings and investments, and nonliquid assets such as a house.

(continued)

It also depends on your expenses, such as housing and health care, and the cost of living in the part of the country where you reside.

Policy makers trying to address this concern must address a number of issues. How much money is necessary? What role should government play in ensuring a secure retirement for its citizens? Does private business have an obligation to be part of the solution? Should the government provide a safety net and, if so, at what level?

For years, we have used the poverty level as the benchmark for how much money is needed to live. In 2012, an elderly individual was considered above poverty if he or she had an income of $11,011/year and a couple was considered above poverty if it had an income of $13,892/year. Clearly, this level of income is too low to support an individual in almost all areas of the country. The Elder Index provides a more realistic benchmark because it considers how much it costs to live by geographical area.[1] This benchmark finds that individuals need between $16,716/year and $29,604/year to live modestly without government supports. The variation is due to whether the individual owns his or her own house and the cost of living in his or her geographical location.

Given This Large Variation, How Should Public Policy Account for the Difference in Needs?

The United States already has a number of policies aimed at ensuring that retirees have an adequate amount of income. Most important, the Social Security program provides a monthly stream of income for more than 40.2 million people 65 years and older.[2] The Social Security program began in 1948 and has expanded

---

[1] Gerontology Institute. (2012). *The National Economic Security Standard Index*. Gerontology Institute Publications. Paper 75. Boston, MA: University of Massachusetts. Retrieved from http://scholarworks.umb.edu/gerontologyinstitute_pubs/75
[2] See: http://www.ssa.gov/policy/docs/quickfacts/stat_snapshot/Approximately 94% of people 65 years and older in the United States receive Social Security.

(continued)

several times since then to provide almost universal coverage for retirees. It is a social insurance program by which workers pay a flat percentage of their pay and then are paid a benefit in retirement, which is calculated on a progressive formula. It is a mandatory system, which both workers and employers must pay into. Although this system has worked very well to reduce poverty among older retirees, its future solvency is in question. The Social Security Trustees' projection in 2013 is that the program will not be able to pay full benefits starting in 2033.[3]

What should policy makers do to ensure the future solvency of the Social Security program? Should they cut benefits? Should they increase the payroll tax or create new revenue sources for the program? Should they totally revamp the program?

Social Security has been very successful and is very popular but it does not provide a secure retirement for all retirees. From its beginning its aim was to be part of a three-legged stool that supported retirees. The other two legs were pensions and savings. Today it is difficult to separate out pensions and savings because with the advent of the defined contribution (DC) pension plan, savings and pensions have become often the same thing.

Over the last 30 years, there has been a remarkable growth in DC plans like the 401(k) plan and an equally remarkable drop in defined benefit (DB) plans, which are often referred to as a traditional pension plan. In 1980, of the workers who had a pension plan, 60% had only a DB plan, 17% had only a DC plan, and 22% had both. By 2005, only 10% of covered workers had DB plans, 65% had DC plans, and 26% had both.[4] The precipitous drop in DB plans has serious consequences for the retirement security of future retirees.

Although DB plans provide a monthly stream of income, which will last a person's lifetime and are guaranteed by the Pension Benefit Guaranty Corporation, DC plans primarily

---

[3] *The 2013 Annual Report of the Board of Trustees of the Federal Old-Age and Survivors Insurance and Federal Disability Insurance Trust* Fund. Retrieved from http://www .ssa.gov/OACT/tr/2013/tr2013.pdf

[4] FAQs About Benefits—Retirement Issues, Employee Benefit Research Institute, 2013. http://www.ebri.org/publications/benfaq/index.cfm?fa=retfaqt14a

(*continued*)

provide a lump-sum payment to the worker on retirement. It is up to the retiree to invest the money and make it last a lifetime. The lump-sum payment is not guaranteed and can be lost if invested poorly. In short, DC plans place the investment risk and the longevity risk on the individual, whereas in the DB model, the risk was held by the sponsor of the plan. Another difference between the two models is that DB plans were primarily funded by the employer but the implementation of DC plans typically requires the worker to contribute to the plan, which then may be matched up to a certain percentage by the employer. Thus, a lower-wage worker may have a harder time setting aside some wages for retirement and not take advantage of the employer match. In essence, these workers lose money, which could have been added to a retirement fund.

DC plans do have some benefits. The value of the lump-sum may increase and thereby provide some protection against inflation, which DB plans typically do not. DC plans are also typically portable, allowing workers to change employers without losing accumulated benefit.

The challenge for policy makers is to create a plan that will spread the risk beyond the individual, provide a monthly benefit that will last a lifetime and be both portable and guaranteed. Participation rates are also a challenge. Offering a pension plan is voluntary for an employer and many do not offer any plan. When they do offer a DC plan, workers may decide not to contribute.

Employers offer plans for a variety of reasons, not the least of which is that they receive a tax benefit for doing so. Individuals also receive tax benefits for contributions they make to their retirement accounts. These tax benefits are foregone tax revenue for the federal government. Is providing a tax break the most efficient way to encourage retirement savings?

How can policy makers encourage more employers to offer pension plans to their workers? Should the federal government require all employers to provide their workers with a pension or an opportunity to save for retirement? How can workers be helped to save money for their retirement either through their work or on their own?

Gender, Age, and Poverty

Whatever metric we use to measure poverty, older women are most likely to experience it. This is particularly the case for women of color. In an analysis of poverty between 2000 and 2012, Entmacher, Robbins, Vogtman, and Frohlich (2013) found that older women consistently had high rates of poverty and those older women of color, the highest. The "extreme poverty" rates actually increased for both older men and older women between 2011 and 2012—from 2.6% in 2011 to 3.1% in 2012 for women and 1.9% in 2011 to 2.3% in 2012 for men. For White, non-Hispanic women older than 65 years, the poverty rate in 2012 was 8.6%. This compares with poverty rates of 21.2% for Black older women, 21.8% for Hispanic older women, and 27.1% for Native American older women. Living alone is an additional risk factor for older women with 18.9% living in poverty in 2012. The average poverty rate for older women was 11.0% in 2012 compared with 6.6% for men.

According to the 2014 Fact Sheet of Social Security (Social Security Administration, 2013), 52% of couples and 74% of unmarried persons receive 50% or more of their income from Social Security. Twenty-two percent of couples and 47% of unmarried persons rely on Social Security for 90% or more of their income. Social Security is an essential lifeline for single, unmarried older adults and even for those who rely on Social Security, income adequacy can be problematic.

The poverty rate for elders 90+ years of age is higher than that for other elders. Between 2006 and 2008, 14.5% of those 90 years and older lived in poverty. Women represented 81% of these poor elders but also represented 74% of the population 90 years and older. Poverty rates for women was 16.5% and for men 9.6%.

Blacks who were 90+ had the highest rate of poverty with about a fourth of this group living in poverty, with 21% of Hispanic elders living in poverty (He & Muenchrath, 2011).

For some older adults, their only income option is Supplemental Security Income (SSI), which provides income to those who have very low income, and/or are blind or disabled. SSI is administered by the Social Security Administration, but the funding for SSI comes from the U.S. Treasury, not the Social Security funds. The older adults most at risk for poverty are those who have experienced cumulative disadvantage as a result of low educational attainment, entering the workforce for the first time during an economic recession, health problems that limit their ability to work over long periods of time and involve extraordinary expenses for either themselves or family members, and other vagaries of life.

PERSPECTIVES

THE WORK LIVES AND RETIREMENT PLANS OF WOMEN AGED 50 YEARS AND OLDER

Barbara A. Hirshorn, PhD
University of South Carolina
Institute for Families in Society
Columbia, South Carolina

For midlife and older women—say 50 to 75 years of age—the experience and the planning of their work lives and postwork lives involve both deliberately made choices and the need to respond to circumstances—"to play the hand one has been dealt." An array of issues is involved here. For one thing, over much of their lives, women, in particular, have "interlocking roles" regarding work, family life, and community life. These roles are interdependent, with the tasks, timing, and relationships involved in one role likely to impact the others considerably.[1-3]   Therefore, the paths women take and choices that they make at *earlier* points along the life course impact their work and retirement plans in midlife and old age.

Furthermore, a range of larger structural and contextual factors impact the capacity of women in their 50s and older to work and to retire. For many women, maintaining themselves financially in midlife and old age remains challenging—and

---

[1] Moen, P., & Wethington, E. (1999). Midlife development in a life course context. In S. E. Willis & J. D. Reid (Eds.), *Life in the middle, psychological and social development in middle age* (pp. 3–23). San Diego, CA: Academic Press.
[2] Settersten, R. A., Jr. (2003). Propositions and controversies in life-course scholarship. In R. A. Settersten, Jr. (Ed.), *Invitation to the life course: Toward new understandings of later life* (pp. 15–45). Amityville, NY: Baywood Publishing Company.
[3] Harrington Meyer, M., & Parker, W. M. (2011). The changing worlds of family and work. In R. A. Settersten, Jr. & J. A. Angel (Eds.), *Handbook of sociology of aging* (pp. 263–278). New York, NY: Springer Publishing Company.

(continued)

even daunting. Although the national economy has added jobs in recent years, older unemployed adults continue to take longer than their younger counterparts to find work in the post–Great Recession world. In December 2012, for example, 54.4% of unemployed women 55 years to 64 years and 48.2% of those 65 years and older had been out of work for more than 6 months.[4] Also, the economic restructuring marking a globalized economy—from the permanent or long-term, core-economy job with a DB pension and health care structure to flexible and often marginalized employment—has meant that many midlife and older women have been forced to make "career changes," to take advantage of what jobs are available. In the process, they find themselves in "new careers" with substantially lower wages.[5] Or, many who sought full-time work have been forced into part-time positions because of inadequate opportunity or business conditions.[6] The restructured economy also has left many midlife and older women as "free agents" in the marketplace, whether they are ready for that role or not.[7] By force or by choice, this new personal status requires women to undertake new personal strategies and tactics, such as training for a different line of work, job searches in different industrial sectors, and part-time work or phased retirement.[8,9]

Geographical location and place attachment also impact work and retirement. In the United States today, such factors as distribution by income in the neighborhoods where people live

[4] Johnson, R. W., & Park, J. S. (2013, January). *Labor force statistics on older Americans, 2012.* Retirement security data brief no. 8. Washington, DC: Urban Institute Program on Retirement Policy.

[5] Johnson, R. W., Kawachi, J., & Lewis, E. K. (2009). *Older workers on the move: Recareering in later life.* Research report no. 2009–08. Washington, DC: AARP Public Policy Institute.

[6] United States Government Accountability Office. (2011). *Income security: Older Adults and the 2007–2009 recession.* Washington, DC: Author.

[7] Elman, C. (2011). The midlife years: Human capital and job mobility. In R. A. Settersten, Jr. & J. A. Angel (Eds.), *Handbook of sociology of aging* (pp. 245–261). New York, NY: Springer Publishing Company.

[8] Elman, C. (2011).

[9] Elman, C., & O'Rand, A. (2002). Perceived job insecurity and entry into work-related education and training among adult workers. *Social Science Research, 31,* 49–76.

(continued)

in relation to where the jobs actually are and the availability of public transportation mean that the capacity to make a living, especially for lower income individuals and households, varies considerably according to locale.[10] Additionally, living in a rural or small-town environment often includes other challenges (e.g., scant or nonexistent public transportation, few or only poorly remunerative opportunities for work).

As some analysts have put it, when it comes to planning for later life, it is important "to distinguish which process is in play, what matters most (luck or planning, structure or agency) and when."[11] This is certainly true regarding the decision to leave the labor force entirely, with the intention of not returning. For women now in their 50s and older, a range of macro factors, such as current economic conditions, local labor markets, social and economic policy[12-14] and personal factors, such as personal health status, family caregiving considerations, and, of course, personal and household financial resources[15, 16] must be considered.

Certainly, personal wealth strongly impacts one's capacity to retire from wage-generating work, and the Great Recession increased the amount of debt of near-retirees as many workers found themselves with decreased or tapped-out savings.[17]

---

[10] Chetty, R., Hendren, N., Kline, P., & Saez, E. (2013). The economic impact of tax expenditures: Evidence from spatial variation across the US. *Summary of Project Findings*. Retrieved November 17, 2013, from http://www.atlantamagazine.com/Other/PDFs/Executive%20Summary.pdf

[11] Street, D., & Desai, S. (2011). Planning for old age. In R. A. Settersten, Jr. & J. A. Angel (Eds.), *Handbook of sociology of aging* (pp. 379–397, 391). New York, NY: Springer Publishing Company.

[12] Han, S., & Moen, P. (1999). Clocking out: Temporal patterning of retirement. *American Journal of Sociology, 105*(1),191–236.

[13] Hardy, M., & Shuey, K. (2000). Pension decisions in a changing economy: Gender, structure, and choice. *Journal of Gerontology: Social Sciences, 55*, S271–S277.

[14] Wong, J., & Hardy, M. (2009). Women's retirement expectations: How stable are they? *Journal of Gerontology: Social Sciences, 64B*(1), 77–86.

[15] Chesley, N., & Moen, P. (2006). When workers care: Dual-earner couples' caregiving strategies, benefit use, and psychological well-being. *American Behavioral Scientist, 49*(9), 1248–1269.

[16] Pavalko, E. K., & Henderson, K. (2006). Combining care work and paid work: Do workplace policies make a difference? *Research on Aging, 28*(3), 359–374.

[17] Anguelov, C. E., & Tamborini, C. R. (2009). Retiring in debt? Differences between the 1995 and 2004 near-retiree cohorts. *Social Security Bulletin, 69*(2), 13–34.

(continued)

Moreover, heterogeneity in life events, choices, resources, and decisions *among* women (and compared with the lives of men) also make for different retirement choices and experiences. For example, across the United States, the capacity to save for retirement is unequally distributed—with women and minorities more likely than others to face a lifetime of inequality in the capacity to save for retirement. Also, compared with their male counterparts, women who are single or divorced are more likely to *need to* work during their 60s and older, and the recent economic downturn has only exacerbated the negative impact on any savings.[18, 19]

Interrupted labor force participation, particularly for women who took time off from full-time employment to raise children or provide elder care, reduces potential retirement wealth because of income not earned during that time-out period.[20] Indeed, although the gender gap has narrowed some, over their lifetimes, women continue to perform about twice as much care work for frail or disabled family members, often reducing or eliminating paid work for the duration. This leads not only to sporadic work patterns over the life course[21] and reductions to income while still working but also to reduced income in old age from public and private pensions and savings.[22]

Yet, in the wake of the Great Recession and continued economic instability, for so many women, the very notion of making a deliberate, premeditated effort to "plan for" one's old age must be tempered by the ongoing need to accommodate to the

[18] DeLong, D. (2006). *Living longer, working longer: The changing landscape of the aging workforce, a MetLife study.* New York, NY: MetLife Mature Market Institute.
[19] Thayer, C. (2008). *Retirement security or insecurity? The experience of workers aged 45 and older.* Washington, DC: AARP Knowledge Management.
[20] Cahill, K. E., Giandrea, M. D., & Quinn, J. F. (2007). *Down shifting: The role of bridge jobs after career employment. Issue brief no. 6.* Chestnut Hill, MA: Boston College Center on Aging & Work.
[21] Mutchler, J. E., Burr, J. A., Pienta, A. M., & Massagli, M. P. (1997). Pathways to labor force exit: Work transitions and work instability. *Journal of Gerontology: Social Sciences, 52*(1), S4–S12.
[22] Harrington Meyer, M., & Parker, W. M. (2011). The changing worlds of family and work. In R. A. Settersten, Jr. & J. A. Angel (Eds.), *Handbook of sociology of aging* (pp. 263–278). New York, NY: Springer Publishing Company.

(continued)

range of structural constraints in the economy that may impact personal financial realities. And, if advantages *or* disadvantages (e.g., in income, education, health care resources) amass over the life course, challenges to one's well-being in old age will mark the lives of some women—but not as much the lives of others.[23, 24]

In sum, what may be widely different work and retirement experiences in midlife and old age are the result of not only the impact on women of the times and places that they live in and larger economic and social structures but also—for any particular woman—by the timing and sequencing of personal decisions, interdependencies with family members and others in her social network, and opportunities and constraints that play out across the course of her life.[25-27] These have immediate as well as long-term implications for her decisions regarding work and retirement, her capacity to plan, and her well-being in her later years.

Some critical thinking questions exemplifying the varying roles of luck or planning, structure or agency:

1. *What happens to the work-life trajectories of women aged 50 years and older when the available jobs in their community force them into "new careers" with substantially lower wages? What are some of the possible action steps for them to take?*

---

[23] Dannefer, D. (2003). Cumulative advantage/disadvantage and the life course: Cross-fertilizing age and social science theory. *Journal of Gerontology: Social Sciences, 58*, S337.

[24] O'Rand, A., & Henretta, J. C. (1999). *Age and inequality: Diverse pathways through later life.* Boulder, CO: Westview Press.

[25] Elder, G. H. Jr., Kirkpatrick Johnson, M., & Crosnoe, R. (2003). The emergence and development of the life course. In J. T. Mortimer & M. J. Shanahan (Eds.), *Handbook of the life course* (pp. 3–19). New York, NY: Plenum Press.

[26] Hagestad, G. O. (2003). Interdependent lives and relationships in changing times: A life-course view of families and aging. In R. A. Settersten, Jr. (Ed.), *Invitation to the life course: Toward new understandings of later life* (pp. 135–160). Amityville, NY: Baywood Publishing Company.

[27] Henretta, J. C. (2003). The life-course perspective on work and retirement. In R. A. Settersten, Jr. (Ed.), *Invitation to the life course: Toward new understandings of later life* (pp. 85–105). Amityville, NY: Baywood Publishing Company.

(continued)

> **2.** *For nonwealthy working women aged 50 years and older, what are some of the likely impacts on "retirement planning" of having spent your 20s and 30s entirely out of the labor force and raising children?*
>
> **3.** *What are some of the immediate impacts of the Great Recession and continued economic instability on the capacity of women currently aged 50 years and older to "plan for" their old age? What are some likely impacts of this economic instability on the midlife and later financial well-being of women who are currently in their 20s?*

OLDER WOMEN AND SOCIAL SECURITY: A SNAPSHOT FROM HISTORY

Social Security is an important program for Americans as they grow old. It not only has kept millions of Americans out of poverty but it has increased the possibility of continuing to live independently in late life. A study conducted by McGarry and Schoeni (2000) examined the role of Social Security in widows' independence. They found that only 15% of the widows lived alone at the turn of the 20th century and by 1990, 62% were living alone. Concomitant with this increase in widows living alone was a linear decrease in widows living with their adult children (71% to 20%). Their analysis suggests that the increases in Social Security explain 47% of the change in living with adult children by widows between 1940 and 1990.

Growing up in the 1950s and 1960s it was commonplace to have a grandparent living in the household. As children, we thought it was great fun to have another adult around—particularly one who would give you anything you wanted and, when they were in charge because the parents were out, let you do things you normally were not allowed to do. I knew my grandmother received a check from the state government for $10.00 each month but did not realize it was a welfare check. Nor did we, as children, realize that our grandmother was not there because she necessarily wanted to live with her adult son and daughter-in-law and four children. She was there because she could not afford to live independently.

SOCIAL SECURITY IS NOT JUST FOR RETIRED ELDERS

Social Security is a program that is designed to support Americans with retirement income and is primarily associated with this function for many

Americans. However, the program also supports survivors after the death of a parent or spouse and individuals who become disabled. Social Security is a program for American families and for people of all ages when they need it the most. Nancy J. Altman and Eric R. Kingson, two nationally recognized experts, discuss the range of Social Security programming and what they hope will happen in the future to expand Social Security. The two are founding codirectors of *Social Security Works* and cochair the Strengthen Social Security Coalition. Their new book *Social Security Works! Why Social Security Isn't Going Broke and Why Expanding It Will Help Us All* (2015) makes the case for expanding Social Security protections.

PERSPECTIVES

SOCIAL SECURITY WORKS FOR ALL GENERATIONS

Nancy J. Altman
Codirector
Social Security Works
Washington, DC

Eric R. Kingson
Syracuse University
School of Social Work
Syracuse, New York

Generations of Americans built our Social Security system, and they constructed it well. Designed to last, Social Security has worked efficiently for nearly 80 years, never failing to meet its obligations, even during the deep recession that followed the near-collapse of the economy in 2008. And, if the public wants, it will be with us as long as there is a United States.

Social Security reflects solidarity across generations integral to a well-functioning society. It puts widely held moral and religious values into action. It is a trust based on those broadly shared

(continued)

civic and religiously based principles—concern for our parents, for our neighbors, personal responsibility, hard work, and dignity.

Each month of 2014, 165 million workers make Social Security contributions and 58 million receive earned benefits, a combined total of $864 billion in 2014.[1] Nearly two thirds of today's elderly receive at least half of their income from Social Security. More than 75% of the income going to the bottom 60% of senior households, those with less than $35,493 in income in 2012, comes from Social Security. Furthermore, Social Security is also by far the most important income source going to the 20% of senior households with incomes between $35,493 and $63,648.[2] It is also the primary disability and life insurance protection for the vast majority of Americans, including the nation's children.

Even so, it is important to recognize that:

■ Social Security's benefits are modest, averaging around $15,600 a year for retired worker beneficiaries.

■ At any one point in time, nearly half of Americans aged 65 years or older are either already unable to meet basic needs of food, clothing, and shelter, or are just one serious economic setback away from not being able to meet those most basic subsistence needs.[3]

■ By virtually all measures, the harsh reality is that the majority of today's workforce—probably the large majority—are heading toward very difficult, and in some cases, financially disastrous retirements.

Expanding Social Security is the single most effective and only widespread solution to the economic insecurity of a large number

---

[1] Social Security Trustees. (2013, May). *The 2013 annual report of the Board of Trustees of the Federal Old-Age and Survivors Insurance and Federal Disability Insurance Trust Funds,* (Table IV.A3). Retrieved from http://www.ssa.gov/oact/TR/2013/tr2013.pdf
[2] Social Security Administration. (2014, April). *Income of the population 55 and older, 2012* (Table 9.A1). Retrieved from http://www.ssa.gov/policy/docs/statcomps/income_pop55/2012/sect09.html#table9.a1
[3] Twice the poverty line is a measure of economic deprivation used routinely by researchers and government programs. This estimate uses 200% of the U.S. Census Bureau's Supplemental Poverty measure as the cutoff.

(continued)

of today's elderly and to the retirement income crisis facing workers. That is why a growing number of Congressional representatives and senators support expanding Social Security, including an across-the-board benefit increase and an inflation adjustment measure that would do a better job of maintaining the purchasing power of benefits than is currently the case. The policy makers support paying for the improvements by requiring the well-off—including millionaires and billionaires—to pay their fair share by making Social Security contributions on all their earnings, just like everyone else.

It is important to note that these expansions will go mainly to today's young and middle-class workers and their families, when they become old or become totally and permanently disabled or die leaving behind dependent children. Indeed, Social Security is best thought of as a family protection program. In our book, *Social Security Works! Why Social Security Isn't Going Broke and Why Expanding It Will Help All* (Altman & Kingson, 2015), we put forward the "Social Security works all generations plan." In addition to addressing the financial stress of today's and tomorrow's old, the plan also helps, to a small extent, family caregivers, whose essential work is financially uncompensated, college students whose parent died or became disabled, and workers who must take time off from work as the result of illness or the birth or adoption of a child. It also helps to slow the growth of the nation's perilous levels of income and wealth inequality.

Although not often understood as such, Social Security is a solution, not a problem.

CRITICAL THINKING QUESTIONS

1. *The media often reports that Social Security is going bankrupt. Why is that an impossibility?*

2. *Why do we say that Social Security is a solution, not a problem?*

3. *How does Social Security, which provides life insurance, disability insurance, and old-age annuities, measure up*

(continued)

> *against private sector arrangements in terms of efficiency,*
> *universality, security, and distributional fairness?*

Nancy Altman, author of *The Battle for Social Security*, and Eric Kingson, Professor of Social Work at Syracuse University, are founding codirectors of Social Security Works and cochair the Strengthen Social Security Coalition. The authors served as staff for the 1982 National Commission on Social Security Reform. Their new book, *Social Security Works! Why Social Security Isn't Going Broke and Why Expanding It Will Help Us All* (Altman & Kingson 2015), makes the case for expanding Social Security protections. Portions excerpted from *Social Security Works! Why Social Security Isn't Going Broke and Why Expanding It Will Help Us All*. Copyright © 2015 by The New Press. Reprinted by permission of The New Press. www.thenewpress.com.

HOW SOCIAL SECURITY WORKS

Social Security benefits are calculated on the amount of income you have earned during your work life. You are eligible to receive Social Security benefits after working at least 10 years and reaching the age of 66 years or above. In the past, Social Security retirement benefits were available to those 65 years and older. The age was increased shown in Table 5.2.

Early retirement starts at age 62 years with reduced benefits. If a worker retires at 62 years of age, his or her benefits will be 25% less than what he or she would have received by waiting until the full retirement age. This reduction is permanent. Conversely, if a worker waits to retire until age 70 years, the benefit will be increased from that offered at full retirement

TABLE 5.2
Social Security Retirement Benefits by Birth Year

Birth Year	Full Retirement Age
1943–1954	66 years
1955	66 years and 2 months
1956	66 years and 4 months
1957	66 years and 6 months
1958	66 years and 8 months
1959	66 years and 10 months
1960 and later	67 years

Adapted from Social Security Administration (2014c).

age. For those workers who were born in 1943 or later, Social Security payments will be 8% higher for life if they delay retirement until age 70 years.

Social Security replaces only about 40% of the income a worker earns while working. Most financial planners suggest that between 70% and 80% of the income earned during working years is required during the retirement years. Social Security was not designed to provide all of the income needed in old age. However, most older beneficiaries rely on Social Security. According to the Center on Budget and Policy Priorities (2012), 24% of Social Security beneficiaries receive all of their income from Social Security. Benefits from Social Security are of particular importance to minority beneficiaries, with Social Security representing 90% or more of the income of 42% of Asian Americans, 49% of Blacks, and 55% of Hispanics compared with 35% of Whites. Advanced age is also a factor in the relative importance of the Social Security benefit. Among beneficiaries who are 80+, Social Security provides the majority of income for 76% of the beneficiaries and nearly all of the income for 45% of older beneficiaries.

Widows and widowers are eligible to receive benefits at 60 years or, if disabled, at 50 years. A widow can receive her widow benefit at 60 years and move to a higher full benefit when she reaches full retirement age. Family benefits, based on the fully retired individual, are available to spouses who are 62 years of age or older or spouses who are younger if they are taking care of a child who is entitled to the retired individual's benefits who is younger than 16 years or is disabled. Benefits can also be claimed by a divorced spouse at age 65 years if the marriage lasted for 10 years and the ex-spouse is unmarried.

For Social Security beneficiaries, any wages you receive after you reach full retirement age will not affect your benefit. If you began receiving benefits before full retirement age, you will have benefits deducted for wages earned until you reach full retirement age.

SAME-SEX COUPLES

Since the Supreme Court ruling in 2013 that the Defense of Marriage Act is unconstitutional, Social Security is now able to pay benefits to eligible survivors and partners who are married. The Department of Justice is working with Social Security personnel to determine policy for civil unions. This new approach to same-sex couples affects not only Social Security benefits, but SSI benefits as well. SSI is the federal program for low-income individuals who may not have access to Social Security or who are determined to be "dual eligible" due to very low income and disability.

HOW MEDICARE WORKS

Medicare is the health insurance program for people aged 65 years or older, and those with permanent kidney failure or who have a disability at any age. There are four parts to Medicare: Part A, which covers hospitalization; Part B, which covers outpatient care and physician services; Part C, which covers an optional "Medicare Advantage" Plan that covers Part A and Part C services as well as other services; and Part D, which covers prescription drugs. If an individual is 65 years of age or older and is working with employer-provided health insurance, Medicare Part A becomes the primary hospital coverage. Part A has no fees. The employer-provided health insurance continues to cover other health-related expenses that are included in the employer policy.

Medicare was enacted into law in 1965 after many years of attempts by members of Congress and/or the president. See the timeline earlier in this chapter for an overview of efforts to get health care coverage for all. The first compulsory health insurance program was enacted in 1888 in Austria. Despite the efforts of many public leaders, the United States did not get a national health care system until the Affordable Care Act was passed in 2010. Today the only social insurance-based health care is for individuals who are eligible for Medicare by virtue of their age or specific conditions.

Medicare covers most of the "usual" health care services needed by beneficiaries, including physician visits, lab tests, hospital services, and now, as a result of the passage of the Affordable Care Act, prevention services at no charge. Medicare does not, however, cover long-term supports or services. The only nursing home service that is covered by Medicare is a 100-day maximum stay at a long-term care facility for rehabilitation after a hospitalization. There are also limited home health care services and hospice services eligible for Medicare coverage.

Medicare coverage does not cover all medical services completely and those beneficiaries who can afford it purchase "Medi-gap" services or participate in Medicare Advantage programs, which cost more to purchase, but provide more comprehensive coverage.

In Figure 5.3, President Lyndon Johnson (*right*); secretary of Health, Education, and Welfare (HEW), John Gardner (*second from left*); and Social Security Administration (SSA) Commissioner Bob Ball (*left*) received the first Medicare Part B application form from a member of the general public, Mr. Tony Palcaorolla, of Baltimore, Maryland (*next to President Johnson*). Shortly after enactment of the legislation, SSA sent a mass mailing of application forms to all Social Security beneficiaries near or older than 65 years. Mr. Palcaorolla's completed and returned form was the symbolic first received from this mailing. September 1, 1965.

FIGURE 5.3 First Part-B Medicare application returned by a member of the public.

Source: Social Security Adminstration (2014).

MEDICAID

Medicaid is an entitlement program that provides medical coverage for low-income Americans. Medicaid is not an age-based program. Medicaid is the largest payer of health insurance for children. In 2008, Medicaid covered 31 million children (The Kaiser Commission on Medicaid and the Uninsured, 2013).Under the Affordable Care Act, Medicaid will be expanded in 2014 to include many Americans who were not included in the original eligibility standards for Medicaid.

Medicaid is supported by federal dollars and state dollars. The federal match is at least 50% but in states with lower incomes, the federal match may exceed 50%. Waivers can be approved by the federal government to support benefits and eligibility requirements not generally covered through the Medicaid program. These waivers have been used to support community-based programs for older adults and persons with disabilities as an alternative to nursing home care and are generally viewed as a cost-effective approach to long-term care. Program waivers have also been used by states to provide managed care for certain beneficiaries.

Medicaid is the primary source of funding for LTSS, covering almost 10 million Americans of all ages. It covers nursing home care and finances 40% of all long-term care spending. More than half of the Medicaid spending for long-term care is for nursing homes. However, this is shifting and

TABLE 5.3
Nursing Home Room Rates by State

California	Semiprivate room	$86,815	Private room	$104,025
New Mexico	Semiprivate room	$73,263	Private room	$ 82,837
Pennsylvania	Semiprivate room	$99,196	Private room	$107,493

LTSS spending is moving to home- and community-based care that is more cost-effective and, for many older Americans, supports their preference for remaining in the community rather than receiving care in an institutional setting. Medicaid covers approximately one out of five Americans of all ages.

Individuals who are eligible for Medicaid may also be eligible for other programs designed to assist very poor individuals. For example, low-income elders may be eligible for food stamps or the SNAP program as it is currently called as well as other income-eligible programs and services. Medicaid also provides coverage for low-income elders—also referred to as dual-eligible elders. One in every five Medicare beneficiaries is a dual-eligible elder.

An individual who requires 24-hour care can receive this care at a nursing home. The average annual cost of nursing home care is determined on a state level. Table 5.3 lists the states that the authors have lived in or are currently living in. The costs are derived from the annual survey conducted by the Centers for Medicare and Medicaid Services (2014).

THE THREE- OR FOUR-LEGGED STOOL

Social Security has often been referred to as one leg of a three-legged stool. The other two legs, savings and retirement benefits as a result of employment (DC or DB plans), are as important as Social Security. As mentioned earlier, Social Security benefits are relatively small and, for most retired Americans, not sufficient to maintain a lifestyle consistent with preretirement lifestyles. In the 1960s, 1970s, and 1980s it was assumed that most people would retire at 65 years or earlier. During those decades there were still pensions available from many employers that added value to the Social Security benefit. There were also "mandatory" retirement policies and laws in place for certain occupations. Today, in 2014, those mandatory retirement policies and practices have just about all disappeared. Today older workers are remaining in the workforce longer and, in some cases, have no plans to retire at all. In a recent survey of college professors conducted by Fidelity Investments (2013), 74% of faculty surveyed between the age of 49 years and 67 years reported that they were planning on delaying retirement past age 65 years or to never retire at all. Higher education is not the only workforce that is experiencing delayed retirement. The percentage of Americans older than 65 years who continue working has been steadily increasing. Between 1977 and 2007, the number of workers older than 65 years increased by 101%. The number of male workers older than 65 years increased 75% during that time period, whereas female workers older than 65 years increased by 147% (U.S. Bureau of Labor Statistics, 2008).

According to the Government Accountability Office, the number of workers older than 55 years is projected to make up 20% of the country's workforce by 2015 (Tishman, Van Looy, & Bruyere, 2012). In order to assist employers to better manage the increasing number of older workers, the National Technical Assistance and Research Center to Promote Leadership for Increasing the Employment and Economic Independence of Adults with Disabilities (Johnson, 2012) conducted research to develop recommendations to the nation's employers regarding the management and retention of older workers. The "best practices" identified by the study included developing a "brand" that attracts and retains the best older workers, engaging them fully in the decision making, and developing strategies to retain the workers. Of particular importance, the researchers point out the importance of ongoing training of older workers, flexibility in workplace hours and career options, and the avoidance of discriminatory practices.

There are many reasons that older Americans are staying in the workplace or returning to work. These include better health and higher educational attainment levels of this cohort as well as financial considerations. The decision to continue working is an individual one: One worker might choose to leave a job or career in order to take care of a spouse in failing health; another might continue working while providing care to the spouse in order to have a "respite" from the stress and responsibilities of full-time caregiving. And, there are those elders who have lost a job and must find another one in order to support their families and themselves, or are older adults who have had a lifetime of low-paying jobs and have few retirement choices due to low income.

As a result of the increasing popularity of continuing work in late life, there are a growing number of organizations emerging to provide training, support, and job-search services to this sector of the population. These organizations are both for-profit and nonprofit. And, there is an Older Americans Act (OAA) program designed to support low-income elders with subsidized employment. The Senior Community Service Employment (SCSEP) for older Americans, Title V of the OAA, is designed to provide meaningful employment to older adults with low income (125% of the poverty level) and poor employment options (Napili & Colello, 2013). SCSEP participants are employed in community service jobs on a part-time basis and paid with OAA funds through the states and nonprofit organizations that receive Title V funding. The goal of the program is to provide on-the-job training opportunities to the participants in order to improve their ability to compete in the job market, meet a community service need, and provide paid employment while they are employed in jobs that will improve their skills. This is the only OAA program that is not managed by the AoA. The Department of Labor manages this program and subcontracts with states and nonprofits to manage the program. Participants must be 55 years and older and of low income. These participants can continue in subsidized position for up to 48 months, but the program goals include moving them into unsubsidized positions as soon as possible. In reality, some of the older Americans participating in the SCSEP program are not likely to be competitive in the job marketplace and will rely on this program to supplement their Social Security payments as long as possible.

CRITICAL THINKING QUESTIONS

1. *What is the role of society for a group of young adults who are delayed in their career aspirations as a result of an economic recession? Should the nation do something to ensure that these Americans do not continue being unemployed or underemployed over time? How will they fare later in life if their career has been stalled for a decade or so?*

2. *How can the nation better manage the range of services needed by people with long-term care needs so they have more options about where they live and how they live?*

3. *Should older people be required to spend all of their money in order to get Medicaid support for either LTSS or nursing home care? Why or why not?*

REFERENCES

Altman, N. (2008). *The battle for Social Security.* Hoboken, NJ: Wiley.

Altman, N. J., & Kingson, E. K. (2015). *Social Security works! Why Social Security isn't going broke and why expanding it will help us all.* New York, NY: The New Press.

Assistant Secretary for Planning and Evaluation (ASPE). (2014). *2014 poverty guidelines.* Retrieved October 10, 2014, from http://aspe.hhs.gov/poverty/14poverty.cfm

Center on Budget and Policy Priorities. (2012). *Policy basics: Top ten facts about Social Security.* Washington, DC: Author. Retrieved June 1, 2014, from http://www.cbpp.org

Centers for Medicare and Medicaid Services. (2014). *Nursing home compare.* Retrieved from http://medicare.gov/nursinghomecompare/search.html

Desilver, D. (2014). *Who's poor in America? 50 years into the 'war on poverty', a Data Portrait.* Washington, DC: Pew Research Center. Retrieved from http://www.pewresearch.org/fact-tank/2014/01/13

Entmacher, J., Robbins, K.G., Vogtman, J., and Frohlich, L. (2013). *Insecure and unequal poverty and income among women and families, 2000–2012*. Washington, DC: National Women's Law Center.

Fidelity Investments. (2013). *Three fourths of higher education baby boomer faculty members plan to delay retirement, or never retire at all. Inside fidelity*. Retrieved from http://www.fidelity.com/inside-fidelity/employer-services.

Gerontology Institute. (2012). *The National Economic Security Standard Index*. Gerontology Institute Publications, Paper 75. Retrieved from http://scholarworks.umb.edu/gerontologyinstitute_pubs/75

He, W., & Muenchrath, M. (2011). *90+ in the United States: 2006–2008, American Community Survey Reports*. U.S. Census Bureau, ACS-17. Washington, DC: U.S. Government Printing Office.

Johnson, R.W. (2012). *Impact of federal policies on an aging workforce with disabilities*. New Brunswick, NJ: National Technical Assistance and Research Center. Retrieved from http://www.dol.gov/odep/pdf/NTAR_Impact_Federal_Policies_Report.pdf

The Kaiser Commission on Medicaid and the Uninsured. (2013). *Medicaid: A primer*. Menlo Park, CA: Author. Retrieved from http://kff.org/medicaid/issue-breif/medicaid-a-primer/

Levinson, Z., Damico, A., Cubanski, J., & Neuman, T. (2013). *Issue brief: A state-by-state snapshot of poverty among seniors: Findings from analysis of the supplemental poverty measure*. Menlo Park, CA: The Henry Kaiser Family Foundation. Retrieved from http:// www.kff.org

Marmor, T.R., & Marshaw, J.L. (2002). The case for universal social insurance. In S.H. Altman & D. Shactman (Eds.), *Policies for an aging society*. Baltimore: MD: Johns Hopkins University Press.

Martin, P., & Weaver, D. (2005). Social Security: A program and policy history. *Social Security Bulletin, 66*(1). Retrieved from http://www.socialsecurity.gov/policy/docs/ssb/v66n1/v66n1p1.html

McGarry, K., & Schoeni, R. (2000). Social Security, economic growth, and the rise in elderly widows' independence in the twentieth century. *Demography, 37*(2), 221–236.

Napili, A., & Colello, K. (2013). *Funding for the Older Americans Act and other aging services program*. Congressional Research Service, 7–5700. Washington, DC: U.S. Government Printing Office. Retrieved from http://www.crs.gov

Short, K. (2013). *The research: Supplemental poverty measure: 2012*. Washington, DC: U.S. Department of Commerce, Economics, and Statistics Administration, U.S. Census Bureau. Retrieved June 10, 2014, from http://www.census.gov

Social Security Administration. (2014a). *Social Security history*. Retrieved from http://www.ssa.gov/history

Social Security Administration. (2014b). *Fact sheet on the old-age, survivors, and disability insurance program*. Retrieved from http://www.ssa.gov/OACT/FACTS/

Social Security Administration (2014c). *Retirement planner: Benefits by year of birth*. Retrieved from http://www.ssa.gov/retire2/agereduction.htm

Tishman, F., Van Looy, S., & Bruyere, S. (2012). *Employer strategies for responding to an aging workforce*. New Brunswick, NJ: The NTAR Leadership Center. Retrieved July 1, 2014, from http://www.ntarcenter.org

U.S. Bureau of Labor Statistics. (2008). *BLS spotlight on statistics: Older workers*. Washington, DC: Author Retrieved July 1, 2014, from http://www.bls.gov/spotlight

Protecting the Rights and Well-Being of Older Americans: Elder Justice and Disaster Preparedness

In this chapter, we will cover a broad array of topics related to the protection of the rights of older adults, including elder justice, the Ombudsman program, and legal assistance. Although disaster preparedness is not necessarily viewed as something to be protected from and is not specifically mentioned in the Older Americans Act (OAA) objectives, we feel that it is an absolutely critical issue. The OAA, as described in Chapter 2 of this book, begins with a list of objectives framed as the "rights" of older adults. Today, 50 years after the passage of the OAA, these objectives have remained elusive for many older Americans. Elders are victims of scams, fraud, abuse, and exploitation on an alarmingly regular basis. Vulnerable, frail elders are often easy targets for unsavory and exploitative activities. Also, many older adults do not have adequate information to make informed decisions about guardianship, living wills, housing contracts, managing home health care arrangements, or housing modification contracts. Additionally, the weather is not always on our side and if you are an older adult with little access to a social network, limited financial resources, and faced with challenges related to functional status, the extreme weather can pose a serious threat.

After reading this chapter, we hope you are curious about:

(a) *Why protecting the rights of older adults is so important*

(b) *Why some forms of elder abuse are treated differently from domestic violence*

(c) *The role of the aging networks in protecting vulnerable older adults*

(d) *The objectives of the OAA and the view that they are the rights of older adults*

The protection of the rights of older adults is an ongoing challenge for aging advocates but there has been some promising movement in the area of elder justice. In the OAA, Title VII was modified in 1992 to create a unified title dedicated to the protection of the rights of older Americans and to carry out programs and services that would prevent elder abuse, neglect, and exploitation. In 2009, the Elder Justice Act (EJA) was signed into law as part of the Affordable Care Act. This is the first comprehensive national legislation addressing elder abuse and the hope is that it will dramatically increase the protection available to older Americans.

ELDER ABUSE

Elder abuse includes physical, emotional, and sexual abuse; exploitation, neglect, and abandonment; and self-neglect. Elder abuse encompasses both domestic and institutional abuse. Domestic abuse occurs when the abuse is committed by someone with whom the older adult has a trusted relationship, including a spouse, child, caregiver, or friend. Institutional abuse occurs within the context of an institutional setting (nursing home, assisted-living or personal care home, etc). According to the National Center on Elder Abuse (NCEA, 2006) the categories include the following:

- *Physical abuse*—Inflicting, or threatening to inflict, physical pain or injury on vulnerable elders, or depriving them of a basic need.

- *Emotional abuse*—Inflicting mental pain, anguish, or distress on an elder person through verbal or nonverbal acts.

- *Sexual abuse*—Nonconsensual sexual contact of any kind, coercing an elder to witness sexual behaviors.

- *Exploitation*—Illegal taking, misuse, or concealment of funds, property, or assets of a vulnerable elder.

- *Neglect*—Refusal or failure by those responsible to provide food, shelter, health care, or protection for a vulnerable elder.

■ *Abandonment*—The desertion of a vulnerable elder by anyone who has assumed the responsibility for care or custody of that person.

Prevalence estimates suggest that between 1 and 2 million older Americans experience some form of abuse (NCEA, 2005). According to the National Elder Mistreatment Study and the Elder Justice Roadmap, approximately 1 out of 10 noninstitutionalized older adults (60+) experiences some form of abuse. However, research suggests that the majority of elder abuse cases go unreported. In fact, research shows that "for every 1 case of elder abuse that comes to light, another 23 remain hidden" (Connolly, Brandl, & Breckman, 2014, p. 3). In the 2004 Survey of State Adult Protective Services (APS), the majority of cases reported to APS (89%) occurred at home. Adult children were most likely to be the perpetrators of abuse; older women were most likely to be the victims. Fisher and Regan (2006) conducted a community-based survey to examine the extent to which older women had been involved in abuse situations. They found that nearly half (47%) had experienced abuse since they were 55 years of age and many had experienced repeated abuse. The study found that those who had experienced abuse, regardless of the type of abuse, reported more health problems than other women.

According to Frazer (2009), acceptance of lesbian, gay, bisexual, and transgender (LGBT) older adults is an issue for many caregivers. In a survey of 3,500 LGBT elders aged 55 years and older, 8.3% of the respondents reported being abused or neglected by a caregiver because of homophobia and 8.9% actually experienced some form of blackmail or financial exploitation. Additionally, in a survey of 416 LGBT older adults aged 60 years or older, 65% of respondents reported that they had experienced abuse as a result of their sexual orientation and 29% had been physically attacked. Gender differences exist, with men reporting that they were physically attacked nearly three times more often than women (D'Augelli & Grossman, 2001).

Like domestic violence, elder abuse is often about control and power relationships. Whether it is an adult child or grandchild or a spouse, abuse is often correlated with the dependence of the victim. In an issue brief prepared for the aging network by the National Association of State Units on Aging (NASUA), the authors encourage aging network professionals to support the older victims by any means possible and not be concerned about whether they are a victim of domestic violence of elder abuse. Domestic violence organizations are available to support an older abuse victim and "efforts should be made to maximize the capacity of both systems by partnering to meet older victim's unique needs" (Aravanis, 2006,

p. 2). Elder abuse is also not necessarily a result of a stressful family caregiving situation. There is no clear linear relationship between the stress of family caregiving and an abusive response. Most research suggests that caregivers who abuse the care recipient have poor emotional or psychological coping skills and/or alcohol or drug use problems. Abandonment, another form of abuse, is sometimes a result of stressful caregiving situations. "Granny dumping" has received media attention when an elder is left sitting in an airport, bus station, or mall with his or her luggage. There is no evidence that this is a common form of abuse or that the incidence of this form of abuse is increasing.

According to the 2004 APS survey, self-neglect is the most commonly reported "abuse," with caregiver neglect being the second most common. Self-neglect is a complicated situation. Older adults who are reported to APS for self-neglect are 50% more likely to die within 3 years than those reported for other forms of abuse. The primary symptoms of self-neglect are poor hygiene, living alone, hoarding, and "domestic squalor" (Poythress, Burnett, Naik, Pickens, & Dyer, 2006).

Financial abuse is a growing form of abuse and costs older Americans an estimated $2.6 billion a year (MetLife Mature Market Institute, 2009). A perpetrator of financial abuse can be a stranger, a trusted friend or adviser, or a family member. Hounsel (2009) points out that telemarketers, predatory lenders, and home improvement contractors often exploit the older adult. In one common scam described as the "senior seminar," predators offer older adults expert advice on financial planning with an alternative agenda in mind. These seminars may occur at senior centers or other places where older adults congregate. Another example of elder abuse closer to home is the abuse of durable power of attorney (Stiegel, 2008). This is when an individual becomes an agent under the durable power of the attorney process and exploits his or her status as the agent of the elder by going against the wishes of the elder for his or her own personal gain.

Elder abuse is a sad fact of life for too many older Americans; it has negative outcomes, regardless of the type of abuse involved. Often the signs of elder abuse are not obvious, and as the majority of abuse occurs in the privacy of the home, may not be noticed by people outside the family. Training health care providers and personal care attendants to look for the signs of elder abuse is an important first step in addressing the problems associated with elder abuse. Making sure that the intervention system is effective and easily accessible is of equal importance, as is encouraging people to report suspicious activities when they become aware of them.

The Elder Justice Act

The Elder Justice Act (EJA) was passed as part of the Affordable Care Act. The EJA is the most comprehensive federal initiative to address elder abuse ever passed. However, advocates and partners in the Elder Justice Coalition point out that some key elements were not included in the bill, such as the justice provisions that would support criminal and justice systems' involvement in elder abuse issues. Bob Blancato, the national coordinator of the Elder Justice Coalition who championed the EJA, prepared a supplement to his testimony on hearings conducted on March 25, 2014, after the bill was passed in March. In these remarks, he urged that the 2011 reauthorization of the OAA include strengthening of Title VII and the integration of the Elder Justice goals into other titles and the programs they support. Stiegel (2010) also argues that advocates and members of the Elder Justice Coalition need to focus their efforts to gain funding for the Act and work toward passage of the Elder Abuse Victims Act of 2009. This act would link justice-related activities to support the EJA, including the creation of a Center for the Prosecution of Elder Abuse, Neglect, and Exploitation to advise prosecutors and courts.

Provisions of the EJA include the development of an Elder Justice Coordinating Council to make recommendations to the secretary of Health and Human Services (HHS) within 2 years. There would also be $400 million of dedicated funding for APS, money needed to set up Elder Abuse, Neglect, and Exploitation Forensic Centers and additional funding for the Ombudsman Program and training programs for Ombudsmen activities.

The EJA of 2009 established many programs, services, and grants, for example, the Elder Justice Coordinating Council, a council charged with organizing related activities and programs across the federal government. According to the Administration on Community Living/Administration on Aging (AoA), the Council is directed by the secretary of HHS who serves as the chair of the Council. Additionally, the attorney general is a permanent member of the Council.

The Elder Justice Interagency Working Group has developed several projects since the creation of the Elder Justice Coordinating Council to bring together a myriad of agencies in the interest of protecting older adults. An example of their projects can be accessed at: www.aoa.gov/AoARoot/AoA_Programs/Elder_Rights/EJCC/docs/AgencyDescriptions.pdf/.

This includes Elder Abuse Intervention Grants, The National Adult Protective Services Resource Center, and Late Life Domestic Violence projects.

According to the Elder Justice Roadmap (2014, p. 1) the priorities for addressing the elder abuse crisis include the following:

1. **Awareness:** Increase public awareness of elder abuse, a multifaceted problem that requires a holistic, well-coordinated response in services, education, policy, and research.

2. **Brain health:** Conduct research and enhance focus on cognitive (in)capacity and mental health—critical factors both for victims and perpetrators.

3. **Caregiving:** Provide better support and training for the tens of millions of paid and unpaid caregivers who play a critical role in preventing elder abuse.

4. **Economics:** Quantify the costs of elder abuse, which is often entwined with financial incentives and comes with huge fiscal costs to victims, families, and society.

5. **Resources:** Strategically invest more resources in services, education, research, and expanding knowledge to reduce elder abuse.

The National Center on Elder Abuse

The National Center on Elder Abuse (NCEA) is authorized under Title II and is a national resource center focused on the prevention of elder abuse. The Center conducted a public awareness campaign in conjunction with the University of Delaware Center for Community Research and Service (CANE-UD) that involved broadcast messages; voices of seniors speaking about elder abuse, neglect, exploitation, and ageism; a public awareness inventory to provide materials for local and state organizations to use in their public awareness campaigns; and a "youth movement" to involve young people in elder abuse prevention (Clearinghouse on Abuse and Neglect of the Elderly, 2014). The Center is also involved in supporting Elder Justice Local Development Networks and providing training and technical assistance to the aging network. Finally, the National Adult Protective Service Association (NAPSA) partnered with the Center to assess the training needs within criminal justice, health care, the aging network, victim's services, and the financial industry, and to expand the training materials available to address these needs.

In 2011, AoA awarded two new grants totaling $761,000 for the NCEA, including first-time funding specifically dedicated to elder abuse prevention in Indian country. A $561,000 award for the NCEA Information Clearinghouse went to the University of California, Irvine (UCI), and the

Center of Excellence on Elder Abuse and Neglect. The NCEA Clearinghouse will provide a national source of practical information to support federal, state, and local efforts to prevent, identify, and effectively respond to elder abuse. The Clearinghouse will provide information and technical support; translate the latest research in the field; and disseminate best practices for state, local, and tribal practitioners. The NCEA also provides technical assistance on developing effective prevention, intervention, and response efforts to address elder abuse (AoA, 2014a).

A $200,000 award for the NCEA National Indigenous Elder Justice Initiative (NIEJI) was made to the University of North Dakota (UND). The NCEA NIEJI will begin to address the lack of culturally appropriate information and community education materials on elder abuse, neglect, and exploitation in American Indians. Some of the undertakings of the initiative will include establishing a resource center on elder abuse to assist tribes in addressing elder abuse, neglect, and exploitation; identifying and making available existing literature, resources, and tribal codes that address elder abuse; and developing and disseminating culturally appropriate and responsive resources for use by tribes, care providers, and law enforcement and other stakeholders (AoA, 2014a).

Funding for the NCEA has remained relatively flat despite new initiatives and the passage of the EJA. The values of a society are reflected not only in the passage of public policy that addresses issues of societal importance but in the funding of those programs. When it comes to programs for older adults it is clear where we stand as a society when we examine the funding allocated in recent fiscal years (FY):

FY 2006 $815,250

FY 2007 $814,473

FY 2008 $796,832

FY 2009 $811,000

FY 2010 $811,000

Similarly, funding for the Prevention of Elder Abuse, Neglect, and Exploitation program has also remained flat and even decreased:

FY 2006 $5,142,000

FY 2007 $5,094,540

FY 2008 $5,005,538

FY 2009 $5,005,440

FY 2010 $5,005,440

FY 2011 $5,032,634

FY 2012 $4,986,098

(AoA, 2014)

THE OMBUDSMAN PROGRAM

The Long-Term Care Ombudsman program is a national program that is authorized by the OAA. Ombudsmen provide advocacy services for residents of nursing homes and other residential settings. Each state in the country has a state ombudsman who is supported by local ombudsmen and volunteers. This ombudsmen network is supported by the National Long-Term Care Ombudsman Resource Center, which is operated by the National Consumer's Voice for Quality Long-Term Care (formerly the National Citizens' Coalition for Nursing Home Reform), which provides services in partnership with NASUA. The Resource Center provides print material, training, and technical assistance to all of the state and local ombudsmen. According to the data collected by AoA, there were 9,000 certified ombudsmen in 2011 and more than 1,100 full-time staff. These ombudsmen resolved more than 204,000 complaints and opened 134,775 new cases (some may originate from the same individual). Ombudsmen also provided information about long-term care to 289,668 people in 2011 and conducted 5,144 training sessions in facilities on a variety of topics, including residents' rights. According to the AoA, the five most frequent nursing facility complaints in 2011 were:

■   Improper eviction or inadequate discharge planning

■   Lack of respect for residents and poor staff attitudes

■   Medications—administration, organization

■   Resident conflict, including roommate to roommate.

The five most frequent board and care and similar facility complaints were:

■   Quality, quantity, variation, and choice of food

■   Medications—administration and organization

■   Inadequate or no discharge/eviction notice or planning

- Equipment or building hazards
- Lack of respect for residents and poor staff attitudes

(AoA, 2014b)

LEGAL ASSISTANCE

Legal assistance is supported by OAA as a way to empower older Americans to remain independent and autonomous. Three titles of the OAA support this type of assistance. Title III-B provides funds for attorneys to help those with social and economic needs. These attorneys provide consultation and assistance on income security, health care, long-term care, nutrition, housing, utilities, protective services, guardianship, abuse, neglect, and exploitation. Title IV provides funds for a National Legal Resource Center that includes case consultation through the National Senior Citizens Law Center for professionals and advocates, and training for professionals and advocates in the area of legal and elder rights is provided by the National Consumer Law Center. The American Bar Association Commission on Law on Aging provides information and resources to professionals and advo-cates working in the aging network and the legal services fields. And two organizations—The Center for Social Gerontology (TCSG) and the Center for Elder Rights Advocacy (CERA) provide technical assistance in service systems and legal helplines. Title IV also provides discretionary grants to help states develop senior legal helplines and integrate them into the larger legal service system. Twenty-four states have been funded under the Model Approaches to Statewide Legal Assistance systems. Finally, Title VII funds are used for the Legal Assistance Developer program. This program requires every state to have a legal assistance developer who is responsible for developing and coordinating the state's legal services and elder rights programs. Each state is required to develop a plan to address elder rights and ways in which the legal assistance developer can work to improve access to legal services for those with the most social and economic needs.

DISASTER PREPAREDNESS AND EMERGENCY ASSISTANCE

The headlines for a short article found in the weather section of the *Washington Post* on June 26, 2010, reads: "3 Heat-Related Deaths and a Record Breaker." The 108°F heat that broke a 116-year-old record was the lead paragraph, followed by the information that "Each of the people who died in Maryland was 65 or older and all had underlying health conditions. In at least two residences air conditioning was not in use" (Weil, 2010). The article went on to describe in detail the record-breaking weather and ended with this admonition: "officials urged people to look out for those needing help" (Weil, 2010).

Was there something that could have been done to prevent these deaths? Were the two casualties of the heat not using air conditioning because they did not have an air conditioner or were worried about the expense of running it? And, the bigger question: Are we as a society prepared to accept the deaths of older people during a heat emergency without asking questions about the underlying causes and ways in which we might have ensured their safety? Preparing for a disaster such as a hurricane, flood, or earthquake or a weather emergency like snow or heat is a responsibility that falls not only on governments and their designated "first responders" but also on the aging network as well. There is widespread consensus that older Americans are too often overlooked in the detailed planning and response and therefore are more likely casualties of emergency situations.

In 1960, Hiram Friedsam, a pioneer in the field of gerontology, prepared an article for the *Journal of Health and Human Behavior* entitled "Older Persons as Disaster Casualties." He lamented the fact that there had been very little research on or attention given to casualties of disasters. The article was based on his work as a member of the Disaster Research Group of the National Academy of Sciences—National Research Council in which he conducted an analysis of demographic characteristics of disaster casualties. He hypothesized that, based on anecdotal evidence and limited data, "casualties do not occur at random in age terms, but that the young and the old, particularly the latter, become casualties with far greater frequency than their numbers... would lead one to expect" (Friedsam, 1960, p. 269). Using data collected on casualties from Hurricane Audrey (1957) in Cameron Parish, Louisiana, he developed an index based on the age and sex of casualties and found that both groups—the young (less than 10 years of age) and the old (more than 60 years of age)—were much more likely to be in either the "missing" or the "dead" casualty categories after this hurricane than did those between 10 and 59 years of age. This "relative vulnerability" observed 57 years ago appears to be relevant to our discussion of the state of disaster effects. In this section, we will review the planning for emergencies, the extent to which this planning has adequately included older adults, the response to emergencies and the adequacy of the response for older adults, the role of the aging network, and future challenges.

PERSPECTIVES

ELDERS DYING ALONE, A CASE FOR INTEGRATION: THE INTERSECTION OF GERONTOLOGY, COMMUNITY, AND THE AGING NETWORKS

Kelly Niles-Yokum, PhD, MPA
University of La Verne
La Verne, California

Donna L. Wagner, PhD
Las Cruces, New Mexico

Woman puts 73-year old Johnny Davis in suitcase and wheeled it on a borrowed dolly to abandoned building in the Bronx. She had called a family member who hung up on her when she reported Davis was dead. She called a friend who told her if someone dies in your apartment "you go to jail"
—*Newman, 2011*

Elderly Rockwood man froze to death in his home: An elderly Roane County man was found dead in his home Tuesday. Officials said he'd fallen through the floor and froze to death. According to Chief Danny Wright of Rockwood Police, Ray Knight, 85, lived alone in his home on Elm Street. He was reclusive, and never wanted anyone to help him. Someone checked on him on Sunday and Monday during the unusually cold weather, and he was fine. But on Tuesday, it was discovered that Knight was trapped up to his armpits in the floor, which was in bad shape. The coroner said he died of hypothermia.
—*WBIR Staff, 2014*

We are an aging society. By the year 2030, nearly a quarter of the population will be aged 65 years or older. We face many challenges, but most important, many opportunities as well. Although there is abundant research on topics ranging from meeting the long-term care needs of older adults, financing health care, aging in place, to an evolving aging network, we have yet to face one aspect that most do not want to think about, dying alone. We are not only an aging society but a society with fewer available family caregivers

(continued)

and a strong desire to remain in our own homes as we grow old. We need to begin to explore ways that allow all of us to experience a death that is dignified and fears of dying alone no longer exist.

According to the AoA (AoA, 2012) approximately 28% (11.8 million) of noninstitutionalized older persons live alone; this includes 8.4 million women and 3.5 million men. Additionally, almost half of older women (46%) aged 75+ live alone. As many in the field of aging know, living alone in late life can be an indicator of a variety of issues for older adults who have few resources and small social networks. For LGBT older adults, living alone becomes even more of an issue because of a variety of factors that can serve to further isolate these adults in different ways, including a reluctance to access aging networks programs and services for fear of discrimination. Brennan-Ing, Seidel, Larson, and Karpiak (2014) report that for LGBT older adults "limited social networks that may not be able to meet their needs, and continued barriers to service such as discrimination, heterosexist attitudes, and a lack of cultural competence on the part of providers" (p. 4). The complicated and multifaceted issue of elders dying alone is not just a gerontological concern, it is and should be a concern for all of us.

The Japanese call it Kodokushi, or lonely/solitary death. It is not unique to the United States. But what is unique is that we have not yet begun to explore the concept or the very real implications related to elders dying alone in the United States. The field of gerontology is a good home for the issue but it cross-cuts many disciplines for a myriad of reasons. For example, elders dying alone has aspects that are rooted in public health, public administration, psychology, sociology, and political science. The only surveys on dying alone in the United States (Niles-Yokum, Wagner, & de Medeiros, 2011; Niles-Yokum, Brennan-Ing, Wagner, & de Medeiros, 2014) reveal limited understanding of this phenomenon, little consideration of future trends based on an aging population, a wide range of record-keeping practices related to individuals who die alone in their homes, and concerns of LGBT older adults regarding their own dying alone and that of others in their network. Findings indicate that risk factors for dying alone include living alone, limited social networks, and increased risk for falls. Overall, our findings highlight an overlooked yet important social phenomenon that carries great implications for policies and programs.

Given the demographic reality of our aging society and the way in which death is viewed in the United States, older adults

(continued)

may instead face what they fear the most, dying alone. Although Cicerelli (2006) found that attitudes about the dying process varied based on socioeconomic status (SES), race, gender, and age, much of the research points to the fear of dying alone being common among older adults in general. For example, Johnson and Barer (1997) found that most older adults not only feared dying alone, but also were concerned about who would find them after they died. We feel that the networks of programs and services for older adults are well suited to address this issue. A proactive approach rather than a reactive one would serve to not only protect older adults but would help to alleviate the fears that many people have about the issue of dying alone. The United Kingdom, Japan, Australia, Korea, and New Zealand are currently putting the issue of elders dying alone on their respective radars. Many of these countries are conducting research and implementing programs to protect the older adults in their communities. It is time for us to do the same.

CRITICAL THINKING QUESTIONS

1. *If dying alone is an issue for other countries why do you think we have not made it a priority in this country, particularly given the demographic reality of population aging?*

2. *If you were the director of an Area Agency on Aging, what might you do to begin to address the issue of dying alone in your community?*

3. *Why should we care about dying alone and what are the ethical issues related to this issue?*

REFERENCES

Administration on Aging (AoA), Administration for Community Living. (2012). *A profile of older Americans: 2012*. Washington, DC: U.S. Department of Health and Human Services.

Brennan-Ing, M., Seidel, L., Larson, B., & Karpiak, S. (2014). Social care networks and older LGBT adults: Challenges for the future. *Journal of Homosexuality, 61*(1), 21–52.

Cicerelli, V. G. (2006). *Older adults views on death* (p. 181). New York, NY: Springer Publishing Company.

Johnson, C. L., & Barer, B. M. (1997). *Life beyond 85 years: The aura of survivorship*. New York, NY: Springer Publishing Company.

EMERGENCIES AND DISASTERS: PLANNING AND RESEARCH

Planning and community response in an emergency or disaster is conducted on national, statewide, and local levels. Key federal agencies, including the Federal Emergency Management Association (FEMA), Centers for Disease Control and Prevention (CDC), and the U.S. Department of Homeland Security, play pivotal roles in not only planning but also responses, depending on the nature of the problem. Websites of these three agencies include consumer information about emergency planning, as does those of the Department of Health and Human Services (HSS) and the Administration of Aging. Each state has its own Office of Emergency Planning, which plans, monitors risks, and oversees community-level efforts. The Red Cross is the primary nongovernmental organization to be involved in all aspects of an emergency or disaster from planning to playing an important role in seeing to the well-being of the casualties after an event has occurred.

The "disaster cycle" can be viewed as having four different phases: the mitigation phase, preparedness, response during the disaster, and recovery (Jenkins, Laska, & Williamson, 2007–2008). The mitigation phase describes the work that needs to be done to minimize the effects of a disaster before it occurs. Iverson and Armstrong (2008) point out that disaster is more than an event and requires careful analysis of the vulnerability of the community and its social strength. Community planning that involves the community and addresses the relative vulnerability along social and economic dimensions could ideally be conducted during this phase.

Preparedness is an important part of emergency planning and involves providing education and information to residents to help them prepare for emergencies: having gas in the car; food and water in the pantry; and contact information of family, friends, and medical services, for example. Preparedness for an emergency is an individual responsibility as well as a community responsibility. The response phase refers to the actions of first responders, as well as community and governmental agencies. During this phase, the adequacy of both mitigation and preparedness are put to the test and, as we shall see later in this chapter, does not always work for the older residents. Finally, during the recovery phase, a range of resources is needed, including both long-term and short-term resources, such as food and shelter, health and mental health interventions, and rebuilding efforts.

Disasters

The recent experience of older persons during disasters such as Hurricane Katrina suggests that the vulnerability of older persons persists in emergency situations. Glass (2006) reports that, based on the Knight Ridder analysis of mortality data, although people older than 60 years represented only 15% of the population in New Orleans, 74% of the dead as a result of Hurricane Katrina were 60 years of age and older. Age is not the only vulnerability factor, however. The most vulnerable groups in any emergency situation are people with low income, health problems, and mobility limitations, and those who are living alone (Wilson, 2006). Unfortunately, advanced age is often closely associated with low income, health and mobility limitations, living alone, and being a woman.

In Hurricane Katrina, older people living in the community were at risk and those who were living in skilled care facilities were also at risk. Laditka et al. (2008) analyzed the extent to which nursing homes were prepared for the disaster. They reported that 70 nursing home residents died in 13 nursing homes in the New Orleans area. In their analysis, they observed that although most facilities were prepared for "treatment and triage," there were many shortcomings, including inadequate supplies and medication, limited record keeping about transfers, staffing issues, and support. Their recommendations suggest the incorporation of nursing homes in the community disaster plan and including them on the priority list along with hospitals.

Friedsam (1960) posed two levels of effects of a disaster or large-scale emergency: direct effects that occur as a result of the event and indirect effects that occur later as a result of cascading events that begin during the initial event. Indirect effects could include the deaths of nursing home residents, such as those in New Orleans who died as a result of being evacuated and those whose care was diminished during the event and who died later. Mental health issues could also be described as indirect effects. During the event, people are busy managing their own survival in some cases and escaping in others. Only later do the mental health issues begin to take center stage in the form of posttraumatic stress disorder (PTSD), depression, anxiety, and other manifestations. These issues can be extremely difficult to handle after a disaster. Research suggests that older adults actually do better after a disaster than younger persons. In one study of adults after the September 11, 2001, terrorist attack (Tracy & Galea, 2006), the highest prevalence of PTSD was found among 18- to 34-year-olds, observed in 13.8%, whereas only 12.2% of those 55+ had

PTSD symptoms. Similarly, the rate of depression was lowest among the respondents who were 55+. The researchers found an association between ongoing stressors and PTSD among the older respondents and pointed out that a previous history of psychopathology had also been associated with depression after a traumatic event. The research team led by Lattice also recommended ongoing post-event mental health services for residents and staff after a disaster or traumatic event. Their interviews revealed ongoing mental health needs for 5 months after the event.

Emergencies

Emergencies are not a disaster, but they can have disastrous effects on those involved. According to Glass (2006), disasters are events that stretch the professional response options beyond their limit, whereas emergencies are events that require professional response, but this response is sufficient for the task. Heat waves are emergencies that are actually more deadly than all other weather-related events, such as hurricanes and earthquakes. The 1995 heat wave in Chicago, for example, killed 700 residents, most of them older than 65 years (Klinenberg, 2006). As described earlier, the people who died in the heat wave were often old (73%), poor, and living alone. The CDC reports that older adults are more likely to suffer from heat stress because their bodies have a difficult time adjusting to changes in temperature; they are more likely to have a chronic condition and to take prescription medications that further affect the ability to respond to heat. The 1995 heat wave revealed to Chicago residents and policy makers the need to develop a better approach and plan.

Other emergencies are more personal in nature but often require the assistance of first responders. An elder with dementia who wanders off and is lost to his or her family, an elder with early-stage Alzheimer's disease (AD) who drives his car away and cannot remember where he is or how to get home are variations on the same theme that will become more common as the number of older Americans with dementia increases as predicted in the future. Some states have begun Silver Alerts to mobilize the public to help with these cases. The Silver Alerts are modeled after the Amber Alerts issued when a child goes missing. Several states have begun Silver Alerts or related programs. Maryland passed legislation to allow Silver Alerts in October 2009 and issued its first Silver Alert in November 2009. Over the years, the Silver Alerts in many states have been used for individuals with a variety of cognitive impairments, including traumatic brain injury. For example, the North Carolina Department of Public Safety has a Silver Alert page on its website that lists the details of individuals for whom a Silver Alert was implemented. Many of these individuals are younger than 65 years but suffer from some kind of cognitive impairment. This speaks to the broad scope of this program and the ability to help those of any age and reminds us that it is not just older adults who are impacted by cognitive impairment issues. Activation criteria vary by state, and some states only implement the alert for older adults with a medical diagnosis of impairment, whereas other states have expanded these criteria to include other diagnoses and ages.

PLANNING FOR THE FUTURE

The majority of older adults reside in the community, and both the aging network and public policy support continued independence in the community for all persons, including those with health and mobility limitations. Ironically, this public policy focus on community living can have disastrous effects when a disaster comes along. Research on recent disaster response suggests that there continues to be a disconnect among public health, emergency planning/management efforts, and the aging network.

Nursing homes are not included in community planning strategies. FEMA recommends that persons with disabilities create an informal support network to help them in case of an emergency and the AoA has checklists and suggestions for the family caregiver to use when planning for emergencies affecting the care recipient. However, there is little evidence to suggest that people use these tools to protect their well-being during an emergency or a disaster.

There is also evidence that elders are less likely than others to have needs met after a natural disaster and that isolation after an event occurs increases the negative effects for older adults. Pekovic, Seff, and Rothman (2007–2008) suggest that there needs to be a coordination of efforts in the planning phase; flexibility in planning to accommodate different contingencies; and clear understanding about the roles of various agencies at the local, state, and federal levels. McGuire and colleagues (2007) suggest that some form of surveillance mechanism to articulate the special situations in a community would be helpful in ensuring community residents with mobility limitations. Using databases to identify the location of people with special needs or compiling a registry of people who would need special help during an emergency are two strategies that are in use in some communities.

In the examination of the nursing homes during Hurricane Katrina, Laditka et al. (2008, p. 1291) identified eight preparedness domains, including:

1. Integrating the needs of nursing homes into disaster planning

2. Using nursing homes as a community resource during a disaster (particularly important in rural areas)

3. Ensuring that materials and supplies are on hand to maintain the operation during a disaster

4. Attending to the diverse needs of patients, visitors, and staff

5. Preparing geriatric protocols for a range of care

6. Preparing mental health strategies

7. Coordinating and planning for transportation

8. Ensuring communications

THE ROLE OF THE AGING NETWORKS

Diverse components of the aging networks have been involved in research, education, and practice in the area of emergency and disaster planning. The Geriatric Education Centers have collaborated to prepare curricula and training—Bioterrorism and Emergency Preparedness in Aging (BTEPA; Johnson et al., 2006). Area agencies have developed local responses to emergency situations and participated in planning, and the state units on aging all have plans and information addressing emergencies and disasters. Nonetheless, there continue to be disconnects in the system that will likely predict that in the next disaster, the oldest-old and those with mobility limitations are the most vulnerable. Professor Nelson, our expert commentator, suggests why this problem might continue in the future.

We started this section by talking about one of the aged's most powerful enemies—hot weather. We will end with the other extreme—a powerful snowstorm that keeps people inside their homes. As part of a project conducted among Montgomery County, Maryland, residents to develop a plan for the aging of the county, we heard from elders about their needs in the community during a series of focus groups. (Wagner et al., 2007). Many of their concerns had to do with small, yet important, aspects of trying to manage weather-related emergencies. One participant asked whether there could be a system in place to check on her well-being after a storm and the loss of power or phone service. Others spoke of the importance of getting help with snow removal, removal of debris after a windstorm, and getting food and other provisions during and after a blizzard. In 2010, Washington, DC, was hit with record-breaking snow that kept businesses closed and residential streets nearly impassable for days. Telephone service was uninterrupted in most areas, and so it was possible to communicate with an older parent or have a friend check on the parent's well-being. Many older residents were literally held captive in their homes, with unplowed sidewalks making it impossible for them to even walk to a corner grocery. Hospitals were asking for volunteers with four-wheel-drive vehicles to help transport sick and injured people to medical services.

CONCLUSION

As our population continues to age in place, it will become even more important that the aging network take an advocacy position on this issue and remind planners and community leaders of the importance of not only including issues related to the aged and disabled residents in their planning but also listening to the voices and opinions of those with special needs. Planning for emergencies and disasters is planning for the safety of a community, and involvement of the entire community is a necessary prerequisite for a safe community.

CRITICAL THINKING QUESTIONS—ELDER JUSTICE

1. *Where does the right to make poor personal choices end and the state's right to intervene begin? For example, does a 75-year-old alcoholic have the right to drink himself to death? Does your answer differ if he:*

   a. *Has a 72-year-old demented wife who cares for him?*

   b. *Has a 50-year-old disabled son living with him?*

2. *How might we increase the engagement of more citizens in the issues of elder abuse so that they understand the problem and are willing to report it?*

3. *Ensuring that elders are safe in their communities requires vigilance on the part of professionals and the public alike. What safeguards can you promote in your work or home setting?*

4. *Explore the funding differences for Administration for Children and Families (ACF) and the Administration for Community Living/ Administration on Aging programs. What do you notice about the differences? Are there changes over the last 5 fiscal years? What story does this tell?*

CRITICAL THINKING QUESTIONS— DISASTER PREPAREDNESS

1. *Search the Internet for an agency that has a site dedicated to emergency/disaster preparedness initiatives for the elderly. Describe these roles and initiatives. Do they seem effective, and do you think they will continue to provide protection?*

2. *What are the unique disaster-related needs and risks facing the frail elderly (especially isolates or the institutionalized) in your community? Do you think that these needs will be met in a major public disaster? Give an example of which agency, organization, or individuals will do what?*

REFERENCES

Administration on Aging (AoA). (2012). *A profile of older Americans: 2012* (p. 5). Retrieved from http://www.aoa.gov/Aging_Statistics/Profile/2012/docs/2012profile.pdf

Administration on Aging (AoA). (2014a). *National Center for Elder Abuse (Title II).* Retrieved from www.aoa.gov/AoA_programs/Elder_Rights/NCEA/Index.aspx

Administration on Aging (AoA). (2014b). *Long-term care ombudsman program.* Retrieved from http://www.aoa.gov/AoA_Programs/Elder_Rights/Ombudsman/index.aspx

Aravanis, S. (2006). *Late life domestic violence: What the aging network needs to know.* National Center on Elder Abuse Issue Brief. Washington, DC: National Center on Elder Abuse. Retrieved May 10, 2010, from http://www.aoa.gov

Clearinghouse on Abuse and Neglect of the Elderly (CANE). (2014). Retrieved from http://www.cane.udel.edu

Connolly, M. T., Brandl, B., and Breckman, R. (2014). *The Elder Justice Roadmap* (p. 3). Retrieved from http://appleseednetwork.org/wp-content/uploads/2014/07/The-Elder-Justice-Report-07.07.14.pdf

D'Augelli, A., & Grossman, A. (2001). Disclosure of sexual orientation, victimization, and mental health among lesbian, gay, and bisexual older adults. *Journal of Interpersonal Violence, 16*(10), 1008–1027. Retrieved from http://jiv.sagepub .com/content/16/10/1008

Fisher, B., & Regan, S. (2006). The extent and frequency of abuse in the lives of older women and their relationship with health outcomes. *The Gerontologist, 46*(2), 200–209.

Frazer, S. (2009). *LGBT health and human services needs in New York state.* Albany, NY: Empire State Pride Agenda Foundation. Retrieved from http://www .prideagenda.org/Portals/0/pdfs/LGBT%20Health%20and%20Human%20 Services%20Needs%20in%20New%20York%20State.pdf

Friedsam, H. J. (1960). Older persons as disaster casualties. *Journal of Health and Human Behavior, 4,* 269–273

Glass, T. (2006). Disasters and older adults: Bring in a policy blind spot into the light. *Public Policy and Aging Report, 16*(2), 1, 3–7.

Hounsell, C. (2009). Protecting your mother from financial fraud and abuse. In *Elder abuse: A women's issue. OWL Mother's Day Report.* Retrieved from http:// www.owl-national.org/Mothers_Day_Reports_files/OWL_MothersDay_ Report_09_Final_2.pdf

Iverson, R., & Armstrong, A. (2008). Hurricane Katrina and New Orleans: What might a sociological embeddedness perspective offer disaster research and planning? *Analyses of Social Issues and Public Policy, 8*(1), 183–209.

Jenkins, P., Laska, S., & Williamson, G. (2007–2008). Connecting future evacuation to current recovery: Saving the lives of older people in the next catastrophe. *Generations, 31,* 49–52.

Johnson, A., Howe, J. L., McBride, M. R., Palmisano, B. R., Perweiler, E. A., Roush, R. E.,... Weiss, J. (2006). Bioterrorism and emergency preparedness in aging (BTEPA): HRSA funded GEC collaboration for curricula and training. *Gerontology and Geriatrics Education, 26*(4), 63–86.

Klinenberg, E. (2006). Before the flood: What policymakers can learn from the Great Chicago Heat Wave. *Public Policy and Aging Report, 16*(2), 1, 20–21.

Laditka, S., Laditka, J., Xirasagar, S., Cornman, C., Davis, C., & Richter, J. (2008). Providing shelter to nursing home evacuees in disasters: Lessons from Hurricane Katrina. *American Journal of Public Health, 98*(7), 1288–1293.

McGuire, L. C., Ford, E. S., & Okoro, C. A. (2007). Natural disasters and older US adults with disabilities: Implications for evacuation. *Disasters, 31*(1), 49–56.

MetLife Mature Market Institute. (2009). *Broker trust: Elders, family and finances.* Westport, CT: Author.

National Center on Elder Abuse (NCEA). (2005). *Fact sheet: Elder abuse prevalence and incidence.* Retrieved from http://www.ncea.org.

Newman, A. (2011, September 7). "Rest in Peace," in a suitcase in the Bronx. *New York Times.* City Room Blog. Retrieved from http://cityroom .blogs.nytimes.com/2011/09/07/rest-in-peace-in-a-suitcase-in-the- bronx/?_php=true&_type=blogs&_r=0

Niles-Yokum, K., Wagner, D.L., & de Medeiros, K. (2011, November). *Elders dying alone: A survey of professionals in the death system.* Presented at the 64th Annual Meeting of the Gerontological Society of America, Boston, MA.

Niles-Yokum, K., Brennan-Ing, M., Wagner, D.L., & de Medeiros, K. (2014, November). *Dying alone and end-of-life planning: Older LGBT adults' perspectives and perceptions.* Presented at the 67th Annual Meeting of the Gerontological Society of America, Washington, DC.

Pekovic, V., Seff, L., & Rothman, M. (2007–2008). Planning for and responding to special needs of elder in natural disasters. *Generations, 31,* 37–41.

Poythress, E., Burnett, J., Naik, A., Pickens, S., & Dyer, C. (2006). Severe self-neglect: An epidemiological and historical perspective. *Journal of Elder Abuse & Neglect, 18*(4), 5–12.

Stiegel, L. (2008). *Durable power of attorney abuse. A National Center on Elder Abuse fact sheet for consumers.* American Bar Association. Retrieved from http://www .aba.org

Stiegel, L. (2010). Elder justice act becomes law, but victory is only partial. *BIFOCAL, 31*(4), 1–2.

Tracy, M., & Galea, S. (2006). Post-traumatic stress disorder among older adults after a disaster: The role of ongoing trauma and stressors. *Public Policy & Aging Report, 16*(2), 16–19.

U.S. Department of Justice. (2014). *The elder justice roadmap.* Washington, DC: U.S. Department of Health and Human Services.

Wagner, D., Cox, D., DeFreest, M., Nelson, W., Niles-Yokum, K., & Smith, C. (2007). *Imagining an aging future for Montgomery County, MD.* Towson, MD: Center for Productive Aging, Towson University.

WBIR, Staff (2014). Police: Elderly Rockwood man froze to death in his home. January 8, 2014. Retrieved from www.wbir.com/story/news/local/kingston-harriman-roane/2014/01/08/police-elderly-rockwood-man-froze-to-death-in-his-home/4376721/

Weil, M. (2010, June 26). 3 heat-related deaths in Maryland; temperature records broken. *Washington Post,* p. B06.

Wilson, N. (2006). Hurricane Katrina: Unequal opportunity disaster. *Public Policy and Aging Report, 16*(2), 8–13.

Our Aging Future: Collaboration, Change, and a Global Community

*T*he future is ours, and theirs. What will it look like? Who should we look to for leadership and innovation to address the persistent and emerging challenges of an aging society? What does it mean to be proactive in the face of so many challenges and a climate of uncertainty? These are but a few of the challenges we face as we look to our aging future. It is by collaborating with others—other organizations, other communities, and other countries—that we find some of the answers. It is also change and all that it brings that will help lead us to an aging future that embraces an aging society. And finally, what does it mean to be part of a global community at a time when so many of us are trying to adapt to an increasing older population? These are the questions we address in this last section and we hope that you come away with some things to consider about our aging future.

CHAPTER SEVEN

Workforce Issues
of the Aging Networks

A discussion of the aging networks would not be complete without an overview of the workforce issues associated with these networks. The aging networks span a range of settings from home- and community-based services (HCBS) that support the long-term care service and support system in the nation, to health care settings in the community, to the higher education settings that train and prepare the students who are part of the workforce of this vast range of settings, to the researchers and faculty members who, in turn, prepare the workforce for a career working with older adults and issues related to older adults. Much has been written about the condition of the workforce and the need to address projected workforce shortages, structural problems associated with each of the occupation areas contained in the workforce, and the importance of addressing these workforce issues in order to ensure that older adults have the services they need, family members are supported adequately in their caregiving, and the workers in the workforce(s) are provided with the education and training they need as well as a living wage and opportunities for advancement. There are professional associations representing each of the aging network workforce domains and we will rely on the work of these associations to define the problem and, if available, some of the solutions associated with the occupational group.

We discuss the following types of workforces: the direct care workforce, the professional aging network workforce, the health professions working within the aging networks, and finally, the educational workforce—whose job is to prepare students to work in the aging networks.

This chapter is designed to make you curious about:

(a) *Why undergraduate students are not interested in studying aging*

(b) *What factors influence a student to choose the field of gerontology*

(c) *Why we are willing to allow our older relatives to be cared for by people with only minimal training*

(d) *How society is going to manage the care of all of us when we become very old and need some help if we do not address the workforce issues now*

The workforce issues vary between the types of occupations and workplaces but they all share the same challenges. A few of these challenges include the following:

▨ *Employers do not assume that they need specialty-trained workers.*

▨ *Demand for education and training in the field of gerontology continues to lag due to a lack of understanding about the importance of gerontology/geriatric training and about the field itself.*

▨ *The majority of people now active in the field of gerontology are aging themselves.*

▨ *Salaries are not always commensurate with the education and training that would support quality care.*

▨ *Consumers of the aging networks are not informed about the "best practices" in training and education or quality indicators.*

In 2008, the Institution of Medicine (IOM) issued a report titled Retooling for an Aging America, *which addresses its concerns regarding the adequacy and quality of the workforce in the face of a rapidly expanding older population. Its work was organized along a "three-pronged approach," including the enhancement of the ability of all individuals to deliver geriatric care, the recruitment and retention of specialists and caregivers, and the redesign of care models and the roles of patients and providers to ensure greater flexibility (Institute of Medicine, 2008). This study suggests that all types of health care workers need to be trained to work with older adults and that informal caregivers (family and friends who provide care) also need training and support. Finally, they identify that the patients themselves are an important element in* the quest to improve the quality of care. Because most of the health care used by older adults manages chronic disease, patients need education and support in making sound care decisions and managing their own health. One of the important recommendations of this study was that all "licensure, certification, and maintenance of certification for all health care professionals should include demonstration of competence in the care of older adults as a criterion (IOM, 2008, p. 9).

The IOM study included the following challenges to improving care for elders:

▉ *Shortage of health care workers*

▉ *Limited training of the health care workforce in geriatrics*

▉ *Payment systems that do not foster quality care for older adults*

▉ *Limited funding*

The study points out that home health aides (HHAs) and nursing assistants who work in the community or nursing homes are required to have 75 hours of training. However, state regulations often require that cosmetologists, dog groomers, and crossing guards receive more training that direct care workers. The study concluded that the future health care workforce would not be up to the task of meeting the growing demand for geriatric health services if things remain as they are, the efforts that have been made to create geriatric leaders have been unsuccessful, the current structure of public programs is not conducive to developing an appropriate workforce, and there is an immediate need to address the status quo in order to meet the needs of older Americans in the future.

The Partnership for Health in Aging (PHA) was developed in response to the IOM study and has developed a number of strategies to address the concerns of the study. In addition, the Eldercare Workforce Alliance, a member of PHA, was formed to address the future and immediate challenges of the workforce crisis. PHA has developed, with the assistance of the American Geriatrics Society, a set of multidisciplinary competencies in the care of older adults at the completion of the entry-level health professional degree. These competencies are organized into six domains, including:

▉ *Health promotion and safety*

▉ *Evaluation and assessment*

- *Care planning and coordination across the care spectrum*

- *Interprofessional and team care*

- *Caregiver support*

- *Health care systems and benefits*

  In addition, PHA developed a position statement on interprofessional team training in geriatrics and its importance (Partnership for Health in Aging Workgroup on Interdisciplinary Team Training in Geriatrics, 2014).

  In this chapter, we first address the frontline workforce—the workers who make it possible for older adults with multiple health problems to remain independent in the community and for their caregivers to continue working at their paid jobs. Next, we move to the health care workforce, and finally, the higher education gerontological initiatives.

DIRECT-CARE WORKFORCE

In 2006, there were 2.7 million workers in the direct-care workforce (Smith & Baughman, 2007). Although estimates of the size of this workforce vary, the characteristics of the workforce are consistent in the literature. We have elected to use the estimate of Smith and Baughman because they rely on the Bureau of Labor Statistics (BLS) data for their estimates. The direct-care workers in their estimates are nurse aides and HHAs. The Paraprofessional Health Care Institute (PHI) is a national advocacy organization that represents the direct-care workforce. Their estimate of the size of the direct-care workforce is 3.3 million people because they include not only nurse aides and HHAs in their count but also personal care aides, orderlies, and attendants. PHI estimates that an additional 1.6 million positions will be required to meet the demand by 2020 (PHI, 2013). Regardless of the scope of direct-care workers and the size of this workforce, it is very large and growing. This workforce is essential to the well-being of older adults who are living in the community or living in residential care settings or nursing homes. In fact, the Long-Term Care Commission that studied long-term services and supports (LTSS) recommended that the nation adopt a national strategy to "improve and strengthen" the LTSS, reporting that direct-care workers now provide between 70% and 80% of all of the paid LTSS in the country.

Characteristics of the Direct-Care Workforce

The majority of workers in the direct-care workforce are women (90%). The average age of certified nursing assistants (CNAs) is 39 years, and that of HHAs is 46 years (Office of the Assistant Secretary for Planning and Evaluation [ASPE]/Department of Health and Human Services [HHS], 2013). These workers have demanding jobs that pay very little. According to a survey of direct-care workers, two thirds of the CNAs report household incomes of less than $30,000/year. The average hourly wage for direct-care workers was between $11 and $12 an hour. The median wage, according to Smith and Baughman (2007), is $9.26. Nearly one fourth of the direct-care workforce has received cash welfare benefits and more than 40% received food stamps. Turnover rates among direct-care workers are high. High turnover rates have a direct effect on the quality of care. In the 2007 survey of direct-care workers that the previous statistics were based on, a minority of direct-care workers were immigrants. Despite the low wages and challenging work of direct-care workers, personal care aides and HHAs are projected to be the fastest-growing professions in the nation between 2010 and 2020— 70.5% growth for personal care aides and 69.4% for HHAs (PHI, 2013).

According to Baughman and Smith (2012), the average duration of employment for a direct-care worker is 5 months. They also found that less than a third of the direct-care workers left a job to take another direct-care position. Their analysis found that there was no ladder to higher level health care positions for the workers in the direct-care workforce. More important for understanding this workforce was their observation that a worker was more likely to leave the direct-care position as a result of work-related disability than to transition to a higher level health care position. For those workers who leave and enter a new work setting, the two most common transitions were to cleaning and/or household work and retail sales. These findings bode poorly for the care recipients of the direct-care workforce. Turnover and change of caregivers are not associated with high-quality care. As the demand for home health services and HCBS grows, the direct-care workforce will not only be in more demand but be of more importance to the families that rely on this additional help to care for an elder or adult with a disability. Without the direct-care workforce, more responsibility will fall on the informal care system (read: unpaid care system) and there will be negative spillover effects on work lives, family relations, and economic well-being. We all have a stake in the well-being of the direct-care workforce and owe it to them to pay them a living wage and make sure that they have the training they need to manage the complicated jobs we are asking them to do.

PROFESSIONAL HEALTH OCCUPATIONS

The IOM (2008) report illustrates the impending health profession short-age and the consequences of this shortage in an aging society. It reminds us that 20% of the American public will be eligible for Medicare in 2030 and that older adults use a disproportionate amount of medical services. For example, older adults account for:

- 26% of physician visits

- 35% of hospital stays

- 34% of all prescription medications

- 38% of emergency medical services

- 90% of all nursing home use

The American Geriatrics Society (2012) estimates that, based on the assumption that 30% of the population older than 65 years will require the services of a geriatrician, America will need 30,000 geriatricians by 2030. In 2012, there were 7,356 certified geriatricians, which means that to meet the projected demand, 1,500 geriatricians should be trained per year for 20 years to produce 30,000 geriatricians, an ambitious estimate by all measures. In order to meet the demand for competent physicians, the American Geriatrics Society has embraced the idea proposed by the IOM study that every discipline in the American workforce needs to be compe-tent to care for older adults and recommends that:

- Geriatric medicine be recognized as a primary care discipline within the Graduate Medical Education (GME) system

- Medicare GME funding be linked to the health care workforce needs of the nation

- All health professionals supported by GME should be able to care for older adults on completing their postgraduate training. Competencies should be demonstrable in the following areas: clinical presentation, cognition, physiological changes, functional status, and medication appropriateness/safety (American Geriatrics Society, 2011).

All of the health professions are short of competent and trained geri-atric professionals. Among nurses, fewer than 1% of the registered nurses and fewer than 3% of advanced practice nurses are certified in geriatrics

(Robert Wood Johnson Foundation, 2012). Among social workers, the same trend is observed. Fewer than 5% of the social workers have a specification in gerontology or geriatrics (Stone & Bryant, 2012). Both nursing and social work have identified competencies for students pursuing professional degrees in the two fields. The Hartford Geriatric Nursing and Social Work Competencies for Practice with Family, which was designed to foster geriatric competencies, are based on the following domains (Damron-Rodriguez, 2008):

■ Diversity—clarification of attitudes and values

■ Communication

■ Assessment

■ Intervention planning and implementation

■ Family education

■ Interprofessional team work

Stone and Bryant (2012) suggest that a lack of trained faculty is a barrier to students receiving requisite training in gerontological areas. Furthermore, they point out that geriatric training is not accepted by either students or faculty as an important area of study. In their article on the Affordable Care Act (ACA) and the workforce caring for older adults, they point out that several provisions of the ACA are focused on the education of the health care workforce to better care for geriatric patients and persons with disabilities. These provisions, however, were not funded adequately to address the training and education needs of health professionals who will be called on to care for a growing number of geriatric patients.

Scholars who have investigated the barrier to geriatric study on the part of students also point out that students have a set of beliefs and attitudes that they bring into the academic program that influences their decision about specialized training in geriatrics. In reviewing medical student willingness to study geriatrics, Schigelone and Ingersoll-Dayton (2004) found that an important element was the experience the students had with older adults. The more experience a student had, regardless of whether the experience was positive or negative, the more likely the student was to have an interest in geriatrics. In addition, they found that those students who were concerned about personal gains and losses may find that a perceived stigma around aging was associated with a likelihood of a personal loss for them professionally and, thus, steer clear of geriatrics. In their study, a third element was likely to influence their interest in studying geriatrics. It was a set of beliefs about the study of medicine itself. Those with rigid attitudes about what medicine was all about were concerned about spending time trying to help an older person who might be near the end of his or her life compared with an ill child or viewed the geriatric patients as less "exciting" than other patients or care situations. In a study on dental students' perceptions of working with older patients, Fabiano, Waldrop, Nochajski, Davis, and Goldberg (2005) found that positive attitudes about older people were more predictive of an interest in working with this population than increased knowledge about aging and older adults.

THE GERONTOLOGICAL ACADEMIC WORKFORCE

Even before the passage of the Older Americans Act in 1965, there were centers of study on aging. The Duke University Longitudinal Study of Normal Aging began in 1955. In 1958, the Midwest Council on Social Research in Aging began bringing scholars together to explore aging in a systematic way. The study conducted by the Subcommittee on Problems of the Aged and Aging called for by the Senate Committee on Labor and Public Welfare was released in 1960 and called for an expansion of training that was both academic and applied as a way to improve the quality of life of older Americans. The subsequent passage of the Older Americans Act put that objective into action with funding from Title IV.

Title IV funds were used to finance the development of centers on aging around the country, to provide stipends to "leadership faculty" who, after receiving a terminal degree (PhD [doctor of philosophy], DSW [doctor of social work], etc.), would go on to educate, train, and conduct research on older persons and the community-based service network that was under construction. There were also funds to support the final dissertation through dissertation awards. In the 1970s and through the 1980s centers and institutes on aging flourished around the country and the interest in gerontology grew exponentially on the part of both faculty and students. In 1964, the Andrus Gerontology Center began; in 1969, Portland State University started the Institute on Aging; and in 1973, Penn State Center on Aging began. These centers and their faculty and graduate students competed for funding from the Administration on Aging to conduct studies on the developing aging network, the lifestyles of older adults, and the social implications of an aging society. The National Science Foundation was investing on aging at that time, as was a growing number of foundations. The field of aging was being developed and the aging network of services was being built.

In the 1980s, the first generation of gerontologically trained graduates began their university work. They taught classes in gerontology,
developed research agendas, and worked collaboratively with the Area
Agency on Aging network and community services to fine tune the work
that was going on at that level. Other graduates worked in public policy areas, business and demography, biology, and clinical fields. It was a
diverse set of graduates, all of whom had one thing in common: a love of
the field of aging. Academic programs at the undergraduate and graduate
levels were developed and students began to get degrees in gerontology
all over the country. All of the early educational training of this first class
of gerontologists was interprofessional or within a traditional discipline
(sociology, psychology, biology, health professions, etc.).

The first PhD program in gerontology was started by the University
of Southern California–Davis Gerontology Center in 1989 and followed by
University of Massachusetts–Boston. Both programs continue today and
are joined by seven other schools offering gerontology PhD degrees.

Some data suggest that we are actually losing gerontology programs
nationwide. Based on Association for Gerontology in Higher Education
(AGHE) data, between 2000 and 2010, there was an 11% drop in academic
programs—from 756 programs in 2000 to 675 in 2010 (Pelham, Schafer,
Abbott, & Estes, 2012).

Today the heyday of gerontological education is waning and many
of us are concerned about what will happen to the doctorally prepared
gerontologists if academic programs in gerontology flounder. The
AGHE represents educators and gerontology programs. Although we
are experiencing cuts in academic programs nationwide, AGHE is now
engaged in a project that it hopes will reenergize the academic field
of aging and foster new interest in the study of gerontology. AGHE is
developing competencies in the field of gerontology as a precursor to
developing an accreditation program for gerontology programs. In a
recent article (Anft, 2014), some of the more intractable issues are discussed, including the downsizing of gerontology programs and closure
of other programs.

Persistent questions exist, including: How do we attract students to
the study of gerontology? Will the growing number of older Americans
serve to remove the stigma that exists about aging or will it exacerbate
that stigma?

When our students return from their first days of internships in
the field of aging, one of their common observations is: No one in the
"center" or "program" has ever had a class in gerontology and does not
understand why a program is not working or an activity is unpopular and

that in some cases ageist attitudes are present. The research supports this observation—most professionals working in the aging network did not come out of gerontology programs. It will take a better understanding of the gerontology field for those who hire the aging network workers to value the gerontology degree. Academic gerontologists are beginning to understand that fact and associations like the American Society on Aging are working to help employers make that link.

In our aging society, we need gerontologists at all levels—higher education to train the new aging networks workforce and to conduct research into innovations in the field of aging; health care to provide competent care to a growing number of older patients and to conduct research on new models of care and well-being for an aging society; and finally, in our direct-care workforce for the benefit of older adults and their family members. Maybe it is time for another publicly funded investment in gerontology to fast track the changes that the IOM report articulated so well.

CRITICAL THINKING QUESTIONS

1. *Consider your own attitudes about old age and aging. How do you think they would translate to the workplace if you were (and if you are) working with older adults?*

2. *What can the field of gerontology do to help encourage investment and interest in working with older adults?*

3. *What competencies do you think are critical for working with older adults and why?*

REFERENCES

American Geriatrics Society. (2011). *Graduate medical education: Recommendations for addressing the nation's workforce needs.* Retrieved from http://www.american geriatrics.org

American Geriatrics Society. (2012). *Projected future need for geriatricians.* Retrieved from http://www.americangeriatrics.org

Anft, M. (2014, May). Gerontologists in demand, but degree programs languish. *The Chronicle of Higher Education.* Retrieved from http://chronicle.com/article/Gerontologists-in-Demand-but/146387

Baughman, R., & Smith, K. (2012). Labor mobility of the direct care workforce: Implications for the provision of long-term care. *Health Economics, 21*, 1402–1415.

Damron-Rodriguez, J. (2008). Developing competence for nurses and social workers. *Journal of Social Work Education, 44*(3), 27–37.

Fabiano, J., Waldrop, D., Nochajski, T., Davis, E., & Goldberg, L. (2005). Understanding dental student's knowledge and perceptions of older people: Toward a new model of geriatric dental education. *Journal of Dental Education, 69*(4), 419–433.

Institute of Medicine (IOM). (2008). *Retooling for an aging America: Building the health care workforce.* Washington, DC: National Academies of Sciences. Retrieved from http://www.nap.edu/catalog/12089.html

Office of the Assistant Secretary for Planning and Evaluation (ASPE)/Department of Health and Human Services (HHS). (2013). *Direct care workforce: An integral part of long-term services and supports: ASPE issue brief.* Retrieved from http://aspe.hhs.gov/daltcp/reports/2013/dcwIB.pdf

Paraprofessional Health Care Institute (PHI). (2013). *Occupational projections for direct-care workers 2010–2010.* Retrieved from http://www.PHInational.org

Partnership for Health in Aging Workgroup on Interdisciplinary Team Training in Geriatrics. (2014). Position statement on interdisciplinary team training in geriatrics: An essential component of quality health care for older adults. *Journal of the American Geriatrics Society, 62*(5), 961–965.

Pelham, A., Schafer, D., Abbott, P., & Estes, C. (2012). Professionalizing gerontology: Why AGHE must accredit gerontology programs. *Gerontology & Geriatrics Education, 33*(1):6–19.

Robert Wood Johnson Foundation. (2012). *United States in search of nurses with geriatrics training.* Retrieved from http://www.rwjf.org/en/about-rwjf/newsroom/newsroom-content/2012/02/

Schigelone, A. S., & Ingersoll-Dayton, B. (2004). Some of my best friends are old: A qualitative exploration of medical students' interest in geriatrics. *Educational Gerontology, 30*, 643–661.

Smith, K., & Baughman, R. (2007). Caring for America's aging population: A profile of the direct care workforce. *Monthly Labor Review 130*(9), pp. 20–26.

Stone, R. I., & Bryant, N. (2012). The impact of health care reform on the workforce caring for older adults. *Journal of Aging & Social Policy, 24*(2), 188–205.

CHAPTER EIGHT

Global Aging

Population aging is a global phenomenon. In contrast to the conventional wisdom among Americans who think about aging, the increase in an aging population is not limited to high-income nations. Although high-income nations have experienced increasing life expectancy as a consequence of better health care and healthier lifestyles, this does not mean that the size of the aging population will be the highest globally. The numbers of older adults in the world is a consequence of a complicated amalgamation of a number of factors. In low-income nations like India, the sheer size of the population is a driver of the number of older adults there who contribute to the total global aging population and its increase. In fact, the largest numbers of elders live in low-income nations. Demographers report that 65% of people 60 years and older were found in less-developed countries in 2010. By 2050, the proportion of people who are 60+ living in less-developed areas will be 85% (He, Muenchrath, & Kowal, 2012).

Why should we concern ourselves about global aging in a book that examines programs and services for older adults in the United States? There are many reasons that all of us should pay attention to world affairs regardless of the topic. The world is getting smaller due to technology and communications. Immigration patterns influence societies as a function of not only new societal members, but also as a result of what type of society the immigrants represent. As we discuss in Chapter 1 of this book, diversity of the older population is one of the changes occurring that has profound implications on policies, programs, and practice. The following list offers a few points that help one to understand global aging and the need to stay in touch with changes that affect the older population in other countries:

▨   *Social policies and practices in other countries might have important implications on our own policies as we seek to keep pace with changes.*

▨   *Understanding the culture of other societies as it pertains to expectations and treatment of older adults may help our understanding of immigrants and their adult children.*

▨   *Enhanced understanding and perspectives about the policies and practices of the United States as a result of awareness of other approaches can lead to innovative practices at home.*

▨   *An improved understanding of other cultural perspectives on aging enhances the communication and collaboration between gerontological professionals.*

▨   *The strategies used in other countries to address persistent challenges of population aging, such as age discrimination, can lead us to think differently about how we address these challenges.*

The National Institute on Aging's (NIA) 2007 report on global aging and why global aging matters also itemizes the issues of changing family structure, changing population patterns due to differentials in life expectancy, changing work patterns, and managing the increase in chronic illnesses and economic challenges. As global aging continues, there are many important changes that will occur and adaptations we will need to make to ensure that disparities are limited and a good quality of life is available to everyone on our shared planet.

This chapter is designed to make you curious about:

(a) *How other societies make adaptations to an increasing older population*

(b) *Why old patterns of social norms such as filial piety are difficult, if not impossible, to maintain in an aging world*

(c) *What we can learn from other societies about designing our own approaches to aging*

LIFE EXPECTANCY AND HEALTH AROUND THE WORLD

In 2006, there were nearly 500 million people 65 years and older. This number is expected to increase to 1 billion by 2030 (NIA, 2007). The majority of the aging population is likely to reside in less-developed nations and, as a result, lack access to the many health innovations that are increasing the life expectancy of residents of higher income nations. However, there is not necessarily a linear relationship between the income of nations and life expectancy. Olshansky et al. (2012) report that, although there has been a steady increase in the life expectancy of Americans, there is a widening gap in life expectancy as a function of educational levels and race. For example, White women who have 12 years or more of education live 10.4 years longer than those with less than 12 years' education; White men with 12 years or more of education live 12.9 years more. In 2014, the United States ranked number 26 in life expectancy, well behind our European counterparts.

Disparities in life expectancy are also dramatic when comparing people living in low-income nations with those in high-income nations. Figure 8.1 compares life expectancy at age 60 and 80 years in high- and low-income nations.

The highest life expectancy is seen in Japan, where women have a life expectancy of 87 years. In contrast, the life expectancy in sub-Saharan African countries like Angola, Chad, and Sierra Leone is less than 55 years. The majority of "premature" deaths in Africans are caused by infectious diseases. In high-income nations, chronic illness and accidents are the primary causes of death (World Health Organization [WHO], 2014).

Nations vary on a range of metrics related to income, well-being, and quality of life. The Organization for Economic Co-operation and Development (OECD, 2013) maintains data about a wide range of indicators, including indicators that pertain specifically to older adults. The OECD metrics also include metrics that compare spending on health care by different countries. The United States has the highest health expenditures among the OECD countries, the eighth lowest life expectancy (78.7 years), and the highest percentage of the population that is obese (28.6%).

Although much is known about the aging of European nations, the United States, and Canada, less information is available about nations that make up the bulk of aging individuals and will comprise the vast majority of elders by 2050. To address this lack of knowledge and understanding the WHO is conducting a study on global aging and health with six countries that represent a range of population size, four different world regions, and those at different stages of population transitions. These countries include China, Ghana, India, Mexico, Russia, and South Africa. In examining aging in the Studies on Global Aging and Adult Health (SAGE) countries, the researchers used 50 years and older as the age group for older adults due to lower life expectancies in the group of countries. The age group of those who are 50+ made up 21% of the six countries with a projection that this age group will reach 40% by 2050 or 1.3 billion people. Table 8.1 demonstrates the very wide range of life expectancies between the high- and the low-life-expectancy nations.

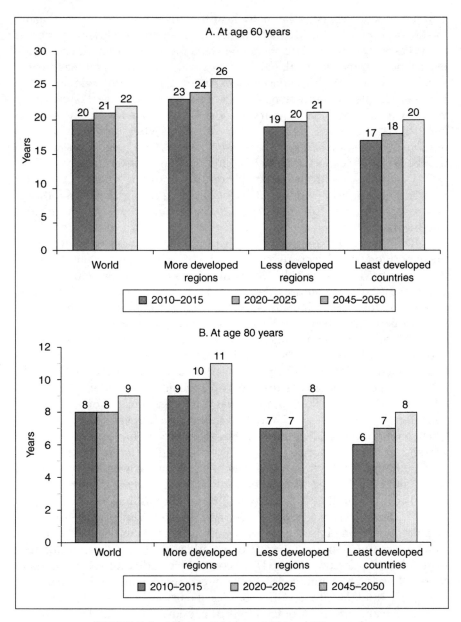

FIGURE 8.1   Life expectancy at 60 and 80 years by development status of countries.

Source: United Nations, Department of Economic and Social Affairs, Population Division (2013).

TABLE 8.1
Life Expectancy at Birth for Women
in Highest- and Lowest-Expectancy Nations

Highest-Life-Expectancy Nations	Age (Y)	Lowest-Life-Expectancy Nations	Age (Y)
Japan	87	Lesotho	48
China, Hong Kong	86	Afghanistan	49
France	85	Sierra Leone	49
Italy	85	Swaziland	49
Spain	85	Guinea-Bissau	50
Switzerland	85	Zambia	50
Australia	84	Botswana	51
Austria	84	Central African Republic	51
Cayman Islands	84	Dem. Republic of Congo	51
China, Macao	84	Chad	52
Guadeloupe	84	Mozambique	52
Iceland	84		
Israel	84		
Martinique	84		
Republic of Korea	84		
Singapore	84		
Sweden	84		
Canada	83		
United Kingdom	82		
United States of America	81		

Source: United Nations (2012).

CULTURE AND FAMILIES

According to Carstenson and Fried (2012), population aging is a cultural challenge. The rapid increase in life expectancy and the size of the older population has put stress on cultural norms and family patterns. In the United States, the absence of a publicly funded long-term care system and the increasing number of women in the workplace has created a burden of care on the family that is unprecedented. In the nations that have relied on filial piety for the care of older adults, there has been a diminution in filial support due to conflicting responsibilities.

The Indian government passed the Maintenance and Welfare of Parents and Senior Citizens Act in 2007 to address the cultural changes affecting the family's ability to treat elders as they were treated in the past. Elders have traditionally been viewed with respect and relied on for family resource management and advice (HelpAge India, 2013). As the family came under pressure, some elders were left behind by families and traditional support systems. The Act requires support for elders by children or, in the case of childless elders, other relatives if they are unable to support themselves. Relatives who are able to provide support financially but do not do so are at risk of imprisonment of 3 months and/or fines. Elders are also able to reclaim their property from children if there has been a transfer of resources. Nationwide, 23% of elders in India report abuse. Three primary types of abuse are reported, including disrespect, verbal abuse, and neglect. Perpetrators of abuse include daughters-in-law (39%) and sons (38%). In a survey conducted by HelpAge India, an estimated 70% of abuse victims did not report the abuse. Wanting to maintain the confidentiality of the family is the primary reason given for not reporting abuse, with fear of retaliation and a lack of information regarding how to report abuse being the other two reasons provided.

EXAMPLES FROM THE FIELD

We invited two researcher–educators to share with us their thoughts about countries they study and/or teach about. Our first example is provided by Dr. Emiko Tagaki and concerns Japan, the country in which she was born. She conducts research on the changing nature of family support in Japan.

PERSPECTIVES

JAPAN

Emiko Tagaki, PhD
Towson University
Towson, MD

Research on aging and families in Japan over the past several decades informs us about the critical roles families continue to

(continued)

play in older adults' lives. The research also shows that the culture and expectations surrounding intergenerational family support are not static; thus, policies and services for older adults need to be continually reevaluated for their proper roles in meeting the needs of the older population.

Japan is well known for being one of the most rapidly aging countries in the world. The country has the perfect social conditions for population aging: a life expectancy that is the longest in the world, a fertility rate that has been staggeringly low, and a strikingly low number of immigrants who, if anything, would generally supplement the numbers of younger people. At one time, the country was known as a developed nation that continued to maintain the traditional family culture rooted in the Confucian principle of filial piety. Many used to abide by the doctrine of filial piety by fully accepting the obligation of adult children to live with and care for their aging parents until the end of their lives.

However, this practice of filial piety is visibly decreasing in Japan. Increasing numbers of older adults are now living separately from their children and making their best efforts to remain independent as long as possible. Older adults' social isolation has become a serious public concern in Japan; pundits debate about ways to intervene with the rising numbers of older adults—who live alone and far away from their children—to assure their health and well-being.

In response to the aging population and the cultural changes surrounding intergenerational family support, service networks for older adults in Japan had to be restructured. The introduction of a national long-term-care policy in 2000, for example, has redefined the role of government in providing care for aging adults. Although the family still plays a role, many now accept the idea of having service providers involved in the care arrangements and sharing some of the family's caregiving responsibilities. The expansion of caregiving services through this policy has changed social perceptions toward long-term care services in Japan, from welfare services only for those in desperate need to services that everyone is entitled to as a consumer.

(continued)

The rapidly aging population in Japan has altered the dynamics of intergenerational family relationships and shifted the balance between private and public caregiving entities. Many countries will soon face a similar challenge in meeting the needs of an aging population when the traditional availability of family caregivers becomes increasingly limited. Each country will then need to reevaluate its own cultural values, norms, and ideologies regarding the roles and responsibilities that families and government should assume to meet older adults' needs. This reevaluation then needs to create a new network of services that are better aligned with the current needs of older adults and their families.

What Japan has gone through for the past several decades with its rapidly aging population tells us that families remain important in the lives of older adults, yet their capabilities, availability, and willingness are not constant. Meeting the needs of an aging population should be achieved with careful consideration of the changes in demographics and the culture of intergenerational family relationships.

CRITICAL THINKING QUESTIONS

1. *Do you think families are now less able to take care of their older members? Why or why not?*

2. *What do you think is the government's role in caregiving for older adults in the United States? How do you think public caregiving services for older adults should be either expanded or limited in the United States?*

Our next researcher/educator is Dr. Keren Brown Wilson who is the chief executive officer (CEO) of the Jessie F. Richardson Foundation (JFRF) in Portland, Oregon. Dr. Brown Wilson describes her efforts to design a program that offers students both a service experience and a way to support the elders in one of the poorest countries in the Western Hemisphere. Life expectancy in Nicaragua is 74 years.

PERSPECTIVES

NICARAGUA

Keren Brown Wilson, PhD
President and Founder
Jessie F. Richardson Foundation
Clackamas, OR

Reflections About Gerontology and International Service Learning

Over the past decade, it has become increasingly common for gerontology programs in the United States to offer a service-learning opportunity to students in addition to traditional internship experiences. During that period of time the JFRF developed an ongoing international service-learning program in partnership with four universities. Each of these programs, although different in structure, duration, and discipline, adheres to the basic principles of domestic gerontologically focused service-learning programs:

1. Face-to-face interaction with older adults and organizations that serve them in structured community activities

2. Academic credit for course work that is integrated with service, a reflective component, and work that is assessed and evaluated

3. Service meets a community need and is meaningful to participants

The country of focus for this international effort is Nicaragua, selected based on its status as one of the poorest countries in the Western Hemisphere. Over a decade more than 400 undergraduate and graduate students have worked in six departments (e.g., provinces) on projects identified using an asset-based community development model (ABCD) to identify and prioritize projects.

(continued)

They have been enrolled as nursing, engineering, allied health, community health, social work, business, and gerontology students. Some of the classes involved satisfying clinical fieldwork requirements (e.g., nursing, engineering); others address growing interest in interprofessional training (e.g., physician assistant, physical therapy, occupational therapy, pharmacy, dental, psychology). Still others are "capstone" classes that include a mix of students (e.g., community health, social work) to fulfill a graduation requirement and some are gerontology students working on certificates or advanced degrees. The service-learning experience ranges from 10 days to 14 weeks with both faculty and JFRF staff supervision in groups ranging in size from 6 to 24 participants.

All of the experiences are part of a long-range plan to improve conditions of older adults living in Nicaragua. Because Nicaragua, like many developing areas of the world, historically has primarily focused on child and maternal health, few resources are available to address issues associated with older adults. Few (12%) older Nicaraguans have pensions and there is no system like Social Security. For those unable to work or whose families are unable to care for them, life is very difficult. These elders often are homeless or live in homes for the indigent "hogares." Many of the service-learning projects have focused on these institutions. Twenty-four thousand hours of community service have been performed by these service-learning students.

Some projects involved using clinical skills, such as nursing assessments, creating occupational or physical therapy plans, or treatment of chronic and acute conditions of residents of these hogares. Other projects address physical conditions of the hogares and the community, such as improved water supplies, repaired sidewalks, and hand-rail installation. Education of caregivers, older adults and their families, and community leaders has been a focus. Topics have ranged from diabetes to dementia care to first aid for first responders. In a typical year, service-learning participants provide 60 different trainings in the communities where they work.

In a world where 80% of older adults live in developing areas and where the emphasis of most aid and policy work is on acute disease and child and maternal health, gerontologically focused service-learning programs offer a way to develop the capacity of countries with few resources. It also offers students the opportunity to become attuned to their own sense of civic engagement and become sensitized to culturally diverse responses to aging.

FAMILY CAREGIVING AROUND THE WORLD

Regardless of the income of specific nations, families provide essential and important support for elders. In the United States, family caregivers are the default long-term care system. Millions of Americans, an estimated one in five households, are involved in providing care and assistance to a family member or friend on a regular basis (National Alliance for Caregiving [NAC]/AARP, 2009). Caregiving for a family member is a normative behavior and one that families organize based on their ability to provide services directly or purchase goods and services. The care recipients benefit from family caregiving in a number of ways, including the receipt of services by someone who loves them and who knows their preferences and priorities. Gail G. Hunt—who is the CEO of the NAC in the Washington, DC, area—provides information about a new international organization.

PERSPECTIVES

CAREGIVING: AN INTERNATIONAL ISSUE

Gail G. Hunt
President and CEO
National Alliance for Caregiving
Bethesdsa, MD

Caring for an older parent, sibling, other relative, or friend is a common activity in the United States. It is estimated that 39% of U.S. adults are caring for either an adult or a child with serious health issues. This is an increase from the 30% estimated in 2010 (Pew Research Center, 2013). Family caregiving is a ubiquitous activity in all nations internationally. The first international conference devoted to family caregiving was convened in 1998 by Baroness Jill Pitkeathley who, at that time, was the head of Carers UK, an advocacy group focusing on caregiver issues in the United Kingdom. Two years later, Carers Australia hosted the second

(continued)

international conference and in 2002 the NAC convened the third international conference in Washington, DC. These conferences allowed advocates, researchers, and support professionals to begin a dialogue on shared interests and common concerns.

In 2012, NAC incorporated a nonprofit group in the United States to create an international organization focused on the issues of family caregivers. In May 2013, the International Alliance of Carer Organizations (IACO) was launched. To date, the members of IACO include Carers Australia, Carers New Zealand, Canadian Home Care Association, Care Alliance Ireland, Carers Sweden, Carers UK, EuroCarers, and the NAC.

The mission of the IACO is as follows:

■ To increase the visibility of family caregiving across the life span as an international issue

■ To promote the sharing of best practices in caregiving programs between countries

■ To encourage and provide assistance to countries interested in developing family carer organizations

At the June 2014 meeting of IACO, eight countries agreed to focus on carer's health and well-being. Governments are facing economic pressures that make it difficult to continue funding social welfare programs for carers. In partnership with employers, supplemental support and information that address the burden of caring for an aging or disabled loved one are possible.

We plan to continue our individual advocacy in our own nations and strengthen our efforts through collaborative work in the eight nations represented in IACO. IACO plans to provide technical assistance and support in the development of other caregiving advocacy organizations internationally. Although the culture, policies, and resources vary from nation to nation, there is a strong commonality among all nations when it comes to caregiving for a loved one. It is our intent to capitalize on that commonality to strengthen caregiving around the world and to ensure that everyone understands that caregiving activities are important not only to the individual who needs care, but to the society as well. Finally, IACO is in an ideal position to conduct international research that increases our understanding about caregiver health and well-being as well as best practices globally.

INTERNATIONAL RIGHTS OF ELDERS

The United Nations passed a set of principles for older persons in 1991 that were based on the International Plan of Action on Aging passed in 1982 and the Declaration of Rights and Responsibilities of Older Persons developed by the International Federation of Ageing (Administration on Aging [AoA], 2001). The principles included the following:

- Independence
- Participation
- Care
- Self-fulfillment

Similar to the objectives of the Older Americans Act, which specified the policy objectives for older Americans, the UN principles include statements about economic independence and community living, integration and participation in society, as well as the ability to form associations of older adults, provide care that conforms with cultural norms of society, pursue opportunities to develop their potential, and foster the ability to live in dignity and security.

THE OLDEST-OLD

The oldest-old are elders older than 85 years or 90+ depending on the researcher and the nation being considered. The importance of this group is that it is a rapidly growing group of elders and it also is a population most likely to need help and support. In 2010, the number of elders who were 85+ was 42 million globally with an expected increase to 147 million by 2050, or a 350% increase in 40 years. Centenarians, individuals older than 100 years, are also a rapidly growing, if relatively small, group of elders. That age group is anticipated to increase by 10 times to 3 million people in 2050, and the extent to which different societies provide high-quality lifestyle options to this group is a marker of social justice (Sadana, Foebel, Williams, & Beard, 2013). More research about the oldest-old is ongoing and will provide guidance and better understanding about this stage of life. The SAGE study described earlier in this chapter is one of the ongoing research efforts that will provide better understanding. Of particular interest to the provision of community services is the extent to which these long-lived people willingly and accurately identify their needs. Attitudes about service use and dependency will obviously play an important role in help seeking. On the provider side, it is essential that a needs assessment of the oldest-old be a strength-based assessment that is carefully structured to eliminate any provider bias that might arise when dealing with the very old.

Buettner (2008) has visited and written about the "blue zones" identified by researchers as locations where a high percentage of people have unusually long lives. His work included visits to and analysis of the blue zones in Sardinia, Costa Rica, Okinawa, and Loma Linda, CA. Some common themes among those who live and age in blue zones include a tight community of peers, life with a mission, vegetable-based diets, and a conscious and purposeful connection with others who share their values. The work of Buettner has fostered interest in the development of blue zone states and communities. Iowa Governor, Terry Branstad, started the Healthiest State Initiative in 2011 based on evidence-based approaches that foster blue zone elements. Communities incorporate these approaches into their community planning on exercise, parks, and workplaces. The Gallup Healthways Well-Being Index (www.gallup.com/poll/wellbeing .aspx?ref=b) is being used to measure change over time and compare communities with each other as they seek to develop a blue zone approach (Healthiest State Initiative Blue Zones Project, 2013).

CONSUMER VIEW AND CASE STUDY

Rosa R. left El Salvador for the United States during the Salvadoran Civil War in the 1980s. She left her native country with two small children and a heart filled with optimism about their future. In 2014, she is now a U.S. citizen as are her two children. Her two children are college graduates and hold professional positions in the United States. However, her mother did not come to the United States with Rosa. She preferred to remain behind with her extended family and is now in her 90s. For many years after Rosa became a U.S. citizen, she was able to get permission for her mother to visit during the summer. However, as Rosa's mother entered old age, the travel to the United States became a struggle for her. It was difficult to get on an airplane, difficult to get from her house to the airport, and she began to get confused about the transfers she needed to make from one plane to another in the strange airports. Rosa knew that if she was to see her mother on a regular basis she would need to identify an escort for her and help that escort get a visa to visit the United States. Luckily, a niece lived near Rosa's mother and wanted to take the trips to facilitate the visits.

However, before the new visa could be used, someone began to use the identity of Rosa's mother. This realization created a problem for the travel and it was 2 years before Rosa could see her mother.

It is a small world, but that world becomes very large when one of the travelers needs help traveling and two governments have to straighten out a stolen identity.

POLICIES AND PRACTICES TOWARD THE OLDER POPULATION

The policies and practices surrounding elders vary around the world. Nonetheless, how older adults are treated by these policies and practices is a good barometer of the levels of social justice found in each nation. The oldest-old are a particularly vulnerable population and the definitive litmus test of the policies in place and their adequacy to support the most vulnerable residents. High-income nations have social insurance programs in place to replace lost income when an older adult retires—the adequacy of this replacement varies dramatically with country. In the United States replacement value is lower for Social Security than in other high-income nations, and the individual is expected to have other sources of income to replace what is lost after leaving the workplace. Nonetheless, all of the high-income nations will be faced with a similar dilemma as the percentage of elders increase during the upcoming decade or two: How to continue to provide the same level of support to a much larger group of individuals? It is not just a retirement program that is a factor in the overall well-being of an older adult. Other policies are of importance as well. For example, do policies affecting the "livability" of the cities and suburbs support an older person's independence after he or she ceases driving an automobile? Is the medical care system affordable, responsive, and of high quality?

In lower income nations, the development of systems that address income, health, and independence of the increasing population of older adults is still in progress. Bodogai and Cutler (2014) describe the situation in Romania in a recent article and point out that, in addition to a scarcity of research on aging in Romania, persistent policy and practice issues need to be addressed to ensure that older Romanians in the future are able to sustain a preferred quality of life. For example, there are disincentives to continuing to work after a relatively low retirement age of 57 years for women and 62 years for men. These retirement ages will increase in 2015 to 60 years for women and 65 years for men but are still relatively low con- sidering the fact that life expectancy is increasing and, for some, continuing to work would be a preference. Bodogai and Cutler suggest that a policy change that would allow Romanians to have higher pensions if they work longer would benefit both the individual and society. In addition, there are gender disparities that adversely affect women due to relatively low wages during their working years and there is no consideration for years that the women were out of the workforce managing family caregiving. These issues sound very similar to some of the debates that are going on in the United States where, although considered a high-income nation, gender disparities exist and there are no provisions for consideration of family responsibilities in the Social Security program. Other nations, such as India, are further behind in the development of "safety net" programs for elders. Despite the level of development in nations around the world, we all face a common challenge: How can we best modify our culture and social norms to accommodate the dramatic increase in elders?

LTSS AROUND THE WORLD

In Chapter 2 of this book, we spend a good deal of time addressing the issues surrounding long-term supports and services (LTSS) in the United States. As population aging occurs around the world, LTSS is a serious issue for all nations, and decisions regarding LTSS policies will be a life-or-death matter for millions of elders, not just a matter of personal preference or lifestyle. Applebaum, Bardo, and Robbins (2013) examined international methods of managing LTSS and identified a typology of LTSS that varies by nation. The universal definition of LTSS used in this analysis was that consumers of LTSS were those who needed assistance and support in basic tasks of daily living. This support can be provided in a wide array of settings or, as is the case in some countries, not at all on a national policy level, leaving the LTSS task entirely up to family and friends. Their typology included five classifications that are descriptive and also related to the support available for each classification. A description of these five classifications follows.

Group 1: Universal Coverage

This classification offers public support for everyone, regardless of age, using a screening mechanism and a range of funding sources. Individuals are assessed and assigned to one of three levels of care and/or support. As is the case in the United States, the nations that offer universal coverage favor community-based settings and the individual who needs institutional care must cover a "significant co-pay."

Examples of nations with universal LTSS coverage are Germany, Japan, Korea, and the Netherlands.

Group 2: Mixed Public and Means-Tested Funding

In this category, there is mixed funding and some countries provide public funding for nursing homes but not for assisted-living facilities, and consumers have choices of specialized housing, community-based services, and other models of support. Informal care (care provided by family and friends) is a component of the LTSS network and the options are self-directed by the consumer. Examples include Australia, Canada, France, Ireland, Spain, and Switzerland.

Group 3: No Public Funding

Countries in this category offer a range of choices, including institutional care, supportive housing, and home- and community-based services but no public insurance or fund to cover the costs of these choices. In contrast to mixed funding, all LTSS are means tested, and support is available only after an individual exhausts all of his or her resources. Examples include the United States, Estonia, Italy, Poland, and Romania.

Group 4: Few Public Funds

Countries in this category have restricted funding to help consumers who need long-term care (LTC) and must rely on family and friends for the majority of support needed. However, these countries share an LTSS element—there are private developers who are beginning to put up nursing homes and provide home health services. The countries in this category include China, Argentina, Brazil, Egypt, India, Mexico, South Africa, and Thailand.

Group 5: No Funding and Few Services

In this category, the countries have no or few services available for LTSS and no public funding. Families are relied on for the majority of services needed by consumers. Examples include Bangladesh, Ghana, Kenya, and Nepal.

CONCLUSION

As discussed earlier in this chapter, the reliance on family care is becoming more problematic in certain countries. This is not a good sign for those countries that fall in Groups 4 and 5. Even Group 3 nations, such as the United States, are being warned by researchers that the reliance on informal support is unlikely to persist over time as the demand for LTSS grows.

OUR SHARED AGING FUTURE

In the recent past, there have been many differing perspectives on global aging and its effect on our collective lives, economy, and literally everything about how we live our lives. Much of the narrative has a "doomsday" quality about it and is described in dire language with words like "tsunami" and concepts like "the dependency ratio." Regardless of how this phenomenon is described, it is playing out all around the world. In the United States, we inadvertently benefit to some extent by our immigration policies when it comes to our population distribution. In contrast to a country like Japan, which is not welcoming to immigrants, the United States has continued to follow a path of immigration that, although not an open door, continues the opportunities for many immigrants to come to the United States and stay there. These immigrants are of all ages, but many are young people who can offset some of the imbalance between old and young that we see emerging in the future as population aging continues. Myers (2012) suggests that if the United States added 1.5 to 2 million immigrants a year to its existing immigration rate, the increase in a "senior ratio" (number of older Americans compared to younger) would decrease by 25%. Politics being what it is today, it is unlikely that there will be the support needed to increase the immigration rate. Absent that support, the United States will need to shore up Social Security, rethink the role of education in an aging society, and reexamine the role of older Americans in society (Bloom, 2012). While policy makers are delaying the inevitable reality of an aging society in favor of the status quo, increased economic inequities and health disparities will continue to affect Americans. What is a more troubling future than fearing the worst and adding age discrimination to our national vocabulary is a future in which, as is the case in India, there are mandatory laws passed requiring family members to financially support their elder relatives. The support of the oldest-old and those who require LTSS earlier in life will be the most pressing issue for all nations going forward—rich and poor alike. We can learn from one another as our culture and policies change and adapt to our aging future. This, in and of itself, is a great reason to participate and learn about international issues and global aging.

CRITICAL THINKING QUESTIONS

1. *What effect do different national policies on health care, income programs, and housing have on the quality of life in old age around the world?*

2. *Can longevity occur in a society with limited resources and few support programs or policies? If so, what are the implications for the oldest-old?*

3. *Do you think that family members should be required to provide maintenance and support to older family members who lack the resources to do so for themselves? Why or why not?*

4. *What would be your plan to deliver and support LTSS to a growing old-old population around the world?*

REFERENCES

Administration on Aging (AoA). (2001). *International aging.* Retrieved from http:// www.aoa.gov/AoA_programs/Special_Projects/Global_Aging/resources_ rights_int_01.aspx

Applebaum, R., Bardo, A., & Robbins, E. (2013). *International approaches to long-term services and supports. Generations, 37*(1), 59–65. Retrieved from http://asaging. org/blog/international-approaches-long-term-services-and-supports

Bloom, D. E. (2012). Viewing U.S. economic prospects through a demographic lens. *The Reporter, 44*(4), 12–17.

Bodogai, S., & Cutler, S. (2014). Aging in Romania: Research and public policy. *The Gerontologist, 54*(2), 147–152.

Buettner, D. (2008). *The blue zones: Lessons for living longer from the people who've lived the longest.* Washington, DC: National Geographic Society.

Carstensen, L.L. and Fried, L. (2012). *The meaning of old age.* In Global Population Ageing: Peril or Promise? Monograph of the World Economic Forum.

He, W., Muenchrath, M., & Kowal, P. (2012). *U.S. bureau, shades of gray: A cross-country study of health and well-being of the older populations in SAGE countries, 2007–2010.* Washington, DC: U.S. Government Printing Office.

Healthiest State Initiative Blue Zones Project. (2013). Retrieved from http://www .iowahealthieststate.com/blue-zones

HelpAge India. (2013). *Elder abuse in India 2013.* Retrieved from http://www .helpageindia.org

Myers, D. (2012). The contribution of immigration to reducing aging in America: Application of the senior ratio to census projections. *Public Policy and Aging Report, 22*(2), 1–7.

National Alliance on Caregiving/AARP. (2009). *Caregiving in the U.S.* Retrieved from http://www.caregiving.org/pdf/research/Caregiving_in_the_US_2009_full_report.pdf

National Institute on Aging (NIA), National Institutes of Health, U.S. Department of Health and Human Services, U.S. Department of State. (2007). *Why population aging matters: A global perspective.* Retrieved July 4, 2013, from http://www.nia.nih.gov

Olshansky, J., Antonucci, T., Berkman, L. Binstock, R., Boersch-Supa, A., Cacioppo, J., ... Rowe, J. (2012). Differences in life expectancy due to race and educational differences are widening, and many may not catch up. *Health Affairs, 31*(18), 1803–1813.

Organization for Economic Co-operation and Development (OECD) & G20 Indicators. (2013). *OECD pensions at a glance.* Retrieved from http://dx.doi.org/10.1787/pension_glance-2013-en

Pew Research Center. (2013). *Pew research internet and American life project.* Retrieved July 15, 2014, from http://www.pewinternet.org/2013/06/20/family-caregivers-are-wired-for-health/

Sadana R., Foebel, A., Williams, A., & Beard, J. (2013). Population aging, longevity, and the diverse contexts of the oldest old. *Public Policy & Aging Report, 23*(2), 18–25.

United Nations Department of Economic and Social Affairs, Population Division. (2012). *World population prospects: The 2011 revision.* New York, NY: Author.

United Nations, Department of Economic and Social Affairs, Population Division. (2013). *World population ageing 2013.* New York, NY: Author.

World Health Organization (WHO). (2014). *World health statistics: 2014.* Retrieved from http://www.who.int/mediacentre/news/releses/2014/world-health-statistics-2014/en/

CHAPTER NINE

Our Aging Future—
Persistent and Emerging Issues
for the Aging Network

A Call to Action

The years teach much which the days never knew.
—*Ralph Waldo Emerson*

As we near the end of our discussion of the networks dedicated to improving the lives of older adults, we will address emerging and persistent issues that need attention for the benefit of today's elders and the elders of tomorrow. Although not all of the persistent or emerging issues are readily addressed by public policy or practice standards, our hope is that as we move through the 21st century they will become an integral part of discussions and, when appropriate, that discussion will result in programming and practice changes. At some point, if we are to address the diversity of aging and support the aging process for all, there will need to be a multidisciplinary approach to policies, programs, and practice. Just as we need to work toward the integration of health care in a multidisciplinary way, we need to also look toward integrating programs and services that address the whole of who we are. We are not just connected to society and our local communities by our desire to age well and help others do the same, but by the very humanness of who we are. It is critical that we begin to see aging as normative. We do this by acknowledging the following World Health Organization (WHO, 2007) principles:

- Recognizing the great diversity among older persons
- Promoting older persons' inclusion and contributions in all areas of community life
- Respecting older persons' decisions and lifestyle choices
- Anticipating and responding flexibly to aging-related needs and preferences

This should be the vision for our aging future and this is our challenge. How will we achieve this? What will your role be? The process begins by embracing the aging process and the meaning of aging in a diverse world. Our aging future depends on our willingness to not only embrace aging but to see it as a normative part of the life span, not something to fear or pity. The way we integrate the human with the professional in our aging networks will be the measure of our success, or our failure. The "old as other" can no longer be the foundation for the development of programs and services. The old as part of a normative life-span existence is our future.

At the end of this chapter, we hope you will be curious about the following topics:

(a) What is the nature of cohort changes that will be facing us as future professionals in the field of aging?

(b) The persistent and emerging issues are many. But, are they the most important and pressing issues to address at this time?

(c) How can we respect the heterogeneity of the older population while developing fair and systematic approaches to long-term services and supports (LTSS)?

(d) Where will the leadership come from to manage the changes that are needed as we evolve into an aging society?

(e) What is the role of social media in perpetuating ageism?

PERSISTENT AND EMERGING ISSUES

We have identified several persistent and emerging issues that will need to be addressed by the aging networks and by the field in general. Each of these issues is discussed in this chapter.

The persistent issues faced by the aging networks are:

- Ageism
- Professional competencies
- The aging workforce on all levels
- LTSS in the community

The emerging issues that must be considered are:

- Goodness of fit and changing cohorts
- Diversity
- Innovation and the aging networks

Persistent Issues

Ageism

One of the biggest challenges to the aging networks of services and supports for a growing and expanding older population is to educate younger members of society and policy makers about population aging and directly confront misperceptions about the negative effects of aging and older adults on society. Today's older population is different from the past, and tomorrow's older population will be different from those we see today. The highly educated older adults of tomorrow will enter old age not only with the higher expectations that come with education but also with skills and interests that will be directed at solving problems faced by society. It will largely fall on the aging networks to communicate that fact to the larger population and to do their part in seeing that the negative effects of ageism and other stereotypes are directly confronted with facts.

Schulz and Binstock (2008) remind us that the voices of the "merchants of doom," those individuals who are loud and carry a damaging message, may act to not only perpetuate the stereotypes of old age but to create intergenerational divides, particularly in an era of limited resources. Specifically, these voices warn of the *problems* that an aging nation will have to deal with in the face of population aging. This problem-focused view of aging led us to the development of policies for older adults that are now considered patriarchal. However, this "compassionate ageism" served a purpose and moved us into an era of historic policy and program development, including Medicare and the Older Americans Act (OAA).

The challenge for the aging networks is to move from the problem-based view of aging to an active aging model that integrates the whole person: an empowerment model of services and supports. In general, policy makers and program developers have viewed age as a deciding factor in the development of programs and services in the United States. The prevailing service philosophy of the aging network of services in the United States has been that older adults are, by virtue of age, in need of intervention. The network in some ways can limit the autonomy of the older person in favor of "professional" judgments (Niles-Yokum, 2006).

Ageism results in age discrimination and age discrimination fosters ageism. The workplace has long been an environment of ageism. Only today when some components of the workforce are increasingly "gray" do we see some easing of the persistent ageism that was present 30 years ago. This was made possible by the elimination of many mandatory retirement policies that were in place in almost all work sectors until recently. McNamara and Williamson (2012) describe "acceptable" ageism that is institutionalized, including mandatory retirement policies (for specific occupations), senior discounts, age-restricted communities, retesting requirements for driver's licenses, and using age as a basis for organ transplants. They point out that these "acceptable" age-based practices are considered "normal" but, if they were only applied to Hispanics or women, they would not be seen as "acceptable" and actually viewed as discriminatory. The authors suggest that, although conventional wisdom might hold that age is a factor that is similar to gender, race, or ethnicity, it is actually treated differently from any other social factor.

Ageism is ingrained in our collective psyche even for those who believe that they are immune to this form of discrimination. An age-neutral attitude may be, for example, challenged by the individual growing gray or wrinkled with age. Is hair coloring or using cream "guaranteed" to remove wrinkles an indicator that this age-neutral person is an ageist person after all? Are aging network services practicing ageism when they are based on age eligibility? There are no quick or easy answers about exactly how much ageism affects the individual elder or societal responses or how insidious it is. We definitely need to keep thinking and talking about this to explore the concept to its fullest and to ensure that as professionals working in the field of aging we do not blatantly succumb to ageism practices and assumptions.

There are those who suggest that the United States is the most ageist society in the world as a result of our age segregation policies and practices. Age is the primary determinant of not only educational settings but social settings as well. We allow 55+ housing to exclude children and younger adults as a legal right. Senior centers provide an age-appropriate social setting once the work role has been phased out. In a 2008 ethnographic study, Dobbs et al. (2008) observed ageism, a stigma related to disease and illness, and the residential care setting as a stigmatizing environment. In conducting the study, the research team observed stigmatization along a continuum that included creating a "them" and "us" along age and functional capacity levels and labeling that was in itself ageist. In a recent study, Levy, Chung, Bedford, and Navrazhina (2014) examined Facebook in terms of ageism. Their analysis predicted that Facebook entries would include ageist content for a number of reasons, including the use of this social media site by younger people, increasing contact with media that increases stereotypes, the tendency to use negative stereotypes to reinforce a positive identity for the "in group," and Facebook's community standards, which are silent on age. They found that the majority of content related to aging was negative. Nearly half (41%) mentioned physical problems, 27% cognitive limitations, and 13% both physical and cognitive issues in older adults. Surprisingly, 37% of the groups examined suggested banning older adults from public activities such as driving and shopping. All of the groups included in the study were created by individuals younger than 60 years. The researchers end their very interesting article with the statement that: "there is a need for Facebook not only to recognize that older individuals are at risk of being targeted, but also to provide a buffer against the promotion of negative age stereotypes (Levy, 2014, p. 175).

Professionalism of the Aging Network

The project undertaken by senior centers described in Chapter 4 that allowed them to take a look at their future in a strategic fashion was possible because of professionalism in the leadership of senior centers and professional linkages that were supported by National Council on Aging (NCOA), their parent organization. The aging network today is staffed by millions of workers, many of whom entered the network accidentally. In the United States today, we have about 200 academic programs in gerontology that offer graduate degrees and an additional number that offer undergraduate degrees or certificates in aging. The aging network can increase its professional standing and benefits that accrue from that standing by placing a priority on hiring staff with gerontology degrees or training. Participation in associations that support this professionalism and foster networking is also an essential element to preparing for the future.

In addition, the direct-care workforce—those personal care workers who form the backbone of the long-term care system—are members of the aging network. More important, these workers are sometimes the only members of the aging network with whom an older person comes into contact on a regular basis. Yet, we continue to deny this sector access to education and training that might provide them with a professional "ladder" to climb to higher income and professional skills.

In order to "professionalize the aging network," there needs to be an understanding of the importance of academic degrees in gerontology and related fields as an entry-level criterion. The majority of people working in the field of gerontology and within the aging network have never had a class in gerontology. A recent research brief prepared and disseminated by the Aging Network Workforce Competencies Partnership (ANWC), which is made up of the National Association of Area Agencies on Aging (N4A), the National Resource Center on Participant-Directed Services (NRCPDS), and the Council on Social Work Education National Center for Gerontological Social Work Education (CSWE Gero-Ed Center), conducted a survey of Area Agencies on Aging (AAA) directors and staff to examine competency-based workforce needs within the aging network. The majority of AAA directors reported that they had inadequate time and resources to engage in competency-based training of staff to meet the new demands of the profession despite the awareness of the needs for competency-based training to manage the increasingly complex service environment in which they are operating (ANWC, 2014).

The Long-Term Care Challenge

Services and programs of the aging network are components of the home- and community-based care system that, by definition, is a long-term care system. No longer is long-term care synonymous with a nursing home. Senior centers, adult day service programs, congregate and home-delivered meals, transportation, and the other aging network sectors all play a role in long-term care and will continue to do so into the future.

The most pressing and most costly initiatives faced by the aging networks in the next few decades will be for long-term care services needed by frail and disabled elders, including patients with Alzheimer's disease. Paying for these services is one challenge. A more pressing challenge for the aging network is the adequacy and quality of the services and the training and ability of the workforce. Assisted-living facilities (ALFs) are playing an important role in supporting this frail and disabled population in the community. Most ALFs and personal care homes are freestanding and have little to do with other parts of the aging network. However, there is a good argument to be made for integrating community services with residential settings. As the old-old population increases, so does the incidence of Alzheimer's disease and related dementias, frailty, and disability. Crossover services offered by senior centers and adult day services will be needed. It will also be important for the aging network to build strong coalitions among all of the participants in the home- and community-based care sector in order to acquire adequate funding and access for those who need the services and for addressing any regulatory barriers to integrating service models.

Coalitions and collaborative efforts are critical to the success of the provision of the services and supports in terms of adequacy and quality, as was mentioned previously. There are many efforts underway to address the workforce issue. For example, Leutz (2012) writes about the employment of foreign-born workers in LTSS, including pathways to LTSS jobs. It may be that population aging will provide opportunities for foreign-born workers and for consumers as well. Leutz (2012) and others (Martin, Lowell, Gozdziak, Bump, & Breeding, 2009; Redfoot & Houser, 2005) suggest that cultural differences could be transformed from a handicap to an asset by involving immigrants, employers, coworkers, and even clients in tailored training programs. Additionally, other approaches have been suggested, including upgrading the professionalism of direct-care workers to improve quality of care and, as a result, increasing wages (Institute of Medicine [IOM], 2008; Leutz, 2012). This brings us back to the importance of partnerships, particularly around education. It has been suggested that community colleges may play a vital role in this area as well as program providers and practitioners and the public sector (i.e., the aging networks).

One partnership that is delving deep into issues of the direct-care workforce, aging-related competencies, and quality of life for older adults is the Partnership for Health in Aging (PHA), a coalition of organizations representing health care professions caring for older adults. A variety of organizations came together in 2008 to review the Institute of Medicine (2008) report. The PHA was created to address the recommendations put forth in the IOM report to improve the capacity of the direct-care workforce and improve the quality of care provided to consumers. The PHA should be seen as a model for other organizations acting on local and national levels interested in working together to improve quality of care and the workforce as well.

Emerging Issues/Challenges

Goodness of Fit: Adjusting to the Changing Face of Aging

The latter part of the 20th century saw an enormous growth in the number and quality of programs and services oriented to older Americans. The early part of the 21st century is witness to the incredible phenomenon that is population aging, a journey that will take us to places heretofore unseen. There are many challenges associated with population aging for both the larger society and the aging networks. The aging networks should take a leadership position in addressing these challenges, which means that, in order to remain a vital network, its members must be up to the task to examine things according to what they might be, rather than what they have been. The lives of older Americans will be different from those who preceded them into old age, and the changes that will occur both as a function of the new cohorts entering late life and by the force of their numbers will reshape society and redefine the role of the aging network.

As new elders enter old age, the aging network will be challenged to adapt to changing attitudes, preferences, and lifestyles. Programs will need to accommodate the needs and preferences of changing cohorts. All over America, "aging in place" is taking on many forms. Whether it be a continuing care retirement community (CCRC) with a resident average age of 85 years and a limited ability to attract younger replacements, or a membership organization that, as a result of aging and death of members, is shrinking in size, aging in place has many consequences. The challenge to the aging network is twofold: to keep providing meaningful programs they find worthwhile and to develop programs and services that will be attractive to the baby boomers and the cohorts of older people who will follow them. The success of initiatives such as Road Scholar indicates that many alternatives are available.

In 1995, under a grant from the Administration on Aging (AoA), the National Institute of Senior Centers (NISC), a constituent unit of NCOA, developed a blueprint for the future of senior centers. The process they used in the development of this blueprint is a useful one for any sector of the aging network. They convened a group of experts and providers and discussed the challenges they would be facing as an aging network program in the future. Out of this consensus conference, a series of recommendations were developed and acted on. The group recommended that senior centers promote professionalism and high standards through accreditation and certification of staff, develop strategic plans for the future that involved community partnerships, redefine their position within the system of home- and community-based services, and incorporate technology into their work and programming.

There were also a series of policy recommendations and approaches to funding in their blueprint. Today, those senior centers that embraced some of these recommendations are offering a new and improved array of features that have attracted younger participants to the centers and continue to be seen as a vital part of the community.

Since 2000, for example, an increasing number of older Americans have either remained in the workforce or returned to it. In the first decade of the millennium, we have seen a gradual erosion of the expectation that old age is a time of rest, relaxation, and retirement. Many retirees spent their retirement engaged in their communities and in activities that they had postponed while working. Increasingly, older adults will require a wider range of options and a different approach to this phase of life. The aging network of programs and services could play an important role in helping older Americans plan and implement their own approach to late life at this time of changing realities and opportunities.

As was discussed earlier, during the recession in the United States that began in 2008, the labor force participation of older workers increased. This increase is important not only because it occurred during an economic recession but also because it reversed a decade-long pattern of earlier retirement among American men. Another indicator of changing times comes from the U.S. Bureau of Labor Statistics (BLS, 2014). They project an 84% increase in workers older than 75 years between 2006 and 2016 and an 83% increase in workers between the ages of 65 and 74 years in that same time period. Therein lies another very important challenge to an aging society—how can we provide the tools and support needed for older Americans to continue to play a meaningful role in the workforce?

Innovation and adaptation to the changing face of aging is the key to survival for the aging networks. Patricia Moore, President of Moore Design Associates, a gerontologist and universal designer who spent 3 years of her life disguised as older woman in New York City (NYC) reminds us of the importance of innovation and universality in design as defined broadly whether it be programming, service delivery, or day-to-day inclusivity and respect for persons.

PERSPECTIVES

DESIGN FOR AGING, DESIGN FOR ALL

Patricia Moore, FIDSA
Moore Design Associates
Phoenix, AZ

The distinctions of family structure, levels of financial and health wellness, and the communities in which we live define the quality of our individual lives. When a delicate balance of the trilogy of people, places, and products appropriate to meeting and sustaining the requirements of daily living is achieved, we have a *quality* lifestyle. Disruption or removal of reasonable support from any of these vital elements will put life at risk.

In 1979, as an industrial designer at Raymond Loewy's NYC offices, I was often frustrated in my efforts to promote design solutions that met the requirements of all consumers as equals. Whenever a project was in development and I raised an issue about the level of usefulness for someone who "saw" with his or her fingertips, "walked" with a wheelchair, or "heard" with his or her eyes, I was told that we did not design for "those" people.

They referenced "those" people as if the world could be divided into disparate groups of "them" and "us," "normal" and "abnormal," and "regular" and "irregular." So outrageous was this declaration to me that I challenged the blatant discrimination and separatism with an "empathic experience" that has defined my life as a designer.

Using prosthetics, which reduced my abilities as a woman, in conjunction with the face mold I was wearing and other outward appearances that included a full range of obvious health and socioeconomic indicators (from homeless to wealthy persons), I was catapulted into the future. I became a woman who appeared to be more than 80 years of age.

In these guises, I traveled to 116 cities throughout the United States and Canada, learning firsthand how it felt to be perceived

(continued)

as an elder in a youth-obsessed culture and as someone who dealt with physical limitations in a wellness-oriented world. Each day I faced the dilemma of being made "not able" by the things that surrounded me, by the environments in which I was forced to exist, and most important, by the impatience and ridicule of those who rejected me because of what they viewed as my failures.

After nearly 4 years of living as elders, I reemerged as my younger self, convinced that a mandate of "universality" in design was the mandate of our time. By creating a consumer existence that celebrated individual capacity with inclusive solutions for the life span, design could be celebrated as the life force it is meant to be.

Recognizing that every person has a level of ability is the primary directive of design. It is the designer's mission to accommodate individual abilities with solutions that embrace every individual's needs. When a product cannot be used as intended or when a setting is hostile to the presence of a person, it is the failure of the design and not the individual.

With a universal approach—an inclusive agenda—for the creation of the products that we use each day and the places in which we live, work, and play, perhaps the critical variable of people, capable of viewing each other as vital and important individuals, regardless of age or ability, will actually come to pass.

Until that time, and as long as manufacturers and politicians mollify themselves, dismissing the ever-growing mass of people deliberately made unable, we will all exist as the potential victims of inadequate and discriminatory design. Not only is now the time for design inclusivity and universality, it is the only reason for *design*.

MOORE'S SUGGESTED READINGS FOR STUDENTS OF GERONTOLOGY

1. Murphy, A. D. (2014). *Aging in place: 5 steps to designing a successful living environment for your second half of life*. Poulsbo, WA: Entrepreneur Publising.

2. Hoffacker, S. (2013). *Universal design and aging: Keeping our homes safe, accessible and comfortable as we age in place*. West Palm Beach, FL: Hoffacker Associates, LLC.

(continued)

3. The American Institute of Architects. (2011). *Design for aging review: AIA design for aging knowledge community by AIA.* Washington, DC: The American Institute of Architects.

4. Anderzhon, J. W., Hughes, D., Judd, S., & Kiyota, E. (2012). *Design for aging: International case studies of building and program.* Hoboken, NJ: Wiley.

5. Null, R. (2013). *Universal design principals and models.* Boca Raton, FL: CRC Press.

6. Brawley, E. (1997). *Designing for Alzheimer's disease.* Hoboken, NJ: Wiley.

Increasing Diversity

The challenge to programs and services is how to use the vitality of new cultural infusions while maintaining individual cultural diversity that makes us who we are. The United States of the 1960s was a country of White descendants from Western Europe. Added to this group was a substantial population of Black residents with African roots; Native Americans whose numbers had been depleted through almost two centuries of warfare and impoverishment; Latino residents whose roots could often be traced to periods before the annexation of the Southwest into the United States; and a small population of Asians, predominantly from Japanese and Chinese backgrounds.

The United States in 2014 is considerably different from the United States of 1960. The Latino population is rapidly growing through immigration and a high birth rate. Latinos are now the largest minority population in the United States, coming from a variety of countries in Latin America, with a diversity of cultural backgrounds and beliefs. The African American population continues to grow, but not as rapidly as the Latino population.

The Asian population is also growing rapidly, and is very visible in its concentration in a number of urban areas. This population growth, spurred on by immigration reform of 1965 and the end of the Vietnam War, now includes not only substantial numbers of Chinese and Japanese but also Vietnamese, Cambodians, Laotians, Filipinos, Indians, and Koreans. Political conditions in countries such as Haiti have also promoted immigration to the United States. Political problems in other areas of the world, including Eastern Europe and Hong Kong, promise to continue the United

States' role as the destination of choice of individuals suffering economic or political problems.

An additional piece of the diversity picture includes sexual orientation and the need for education and increased awareness of related issues. As was mentioned previously, between 1.75 and 4 million Americans who are 60+ are lesbian, gay, bisexual, or transgender (LGBT; AoA, 2010). Finding ways to address the challenges and opportunities for LGBT elders is critical as we work toward a more inclusive and diverse aging society.

Some of the seniors who will need services in the coming decades arrived in the United States as adults of various ages. Others arrived as children. Some speak English fluently; others do not. Some will have strong connections to family in this country. In other cases, families would have been split by immigration—some remaining in the home country while others immigrated to the United States. Some older adults have spent their lives struggling with identity not only with their race and ethnicity but also with sexual orientation. The aging network faces the challenge of developing a variety of programs that effectively address the needs and desires of all of these groups. Many aging network organizations are experimenting with different models of services, such as ethnic-specific meals in meal programs, child day care for Hispanic elders who are caring for grandchildren and great-grandchildren during the day, which prevents them from using the meal programs. The adaptations to a changing cultural consumer will require innovations and creativity and are necessary to keep the aging network relevant to all elders.

Innovation in the Aging Networks

The role of the public aging network in long-term care and in the provision of programs and services to older people is more in question now than it has ever been since the passage of the OAA in 1965. As Hudson and Kingson (1991) reaffirmed almost a quarter century ago, there can be no question that the intent of the OAA was to serve all older persons, regardless of their situation. Over time, as the economic situation of the older population has improved, it has seemed more important to stress the needs of older persons who have the most pressing needs, including economic, social, and health-related issues.

To some extent, the growth of provisions in the OAA is a positive reflection of the growth of the field of aging and groups concerned about specific issues. It is questionable, however, whether one major piece of legislation based on the administrative structure of State Units on Aging and AAAs can effectively embody all of these concerns. There are arguments that AAAs should become coordinators of all community programs and services. However, coordination is a difficult task because of the myriad administrative arrangements that exist to provide and fund services at state and local levels. Many of the most crucial programs and services for the aged are not under the control of AoA. These include transportation, housing, education, and health care.

Because the American social welfare structure is organized along these functional lines (e.g., transportation), an agency concerned with a specific population group (e.g., the aged) has difficulty pulling together these sources and overcoming the "turf" issues that will enable it to mount effective methods. In the 1960s, the Federal Office of Economic Opportunity, organized to coordinate programs for the poor, encountered the same obstacles. Even if it were possible to implement, a coordination of programs and services for older people by the AAA would not necessarily reduce costs for long-term care, delay nursing home placement, or lead to positive changes in functioning among older people (Fortinsky, 1991).

The expansion of the field of aging has also brought many new groups into the service provision arena. Hence, we use the term "aging networks" as plural. Hospitals, concerned about reduced numbers of inpatients, are promoting outpatient and in-home services. Private firms have begun to develop products specifically geared to older people, and the housing industry has become extensively involved in the potential retirement and life-care community markets. Voluntary and faith-based agencies now provide services similar to those offered through public agencies. Employers are beginning to offer elder care programs for employees. Private case managers have developed a network around the country to serve families who can afford these services; private adult day care programs have also begun to appear in some locales. The public sector, which involves State Units on Aging and AAAs, is now only one element in an enlarged service delivery complex concerned about older people (Quirk, 1991). The failure of growth in federal funding has made it difficult for AoA to maintain its past programs at an adequate level.

A change in direction cannot be made without extensive discussion and evaluation of the effectiveness of programs operated through the aging network. Unfortunately, evaluation of these programs is weak, partly due to a lack of standards. Rather than the effects of a program on any number of criteria, reports by AAAs, the State Units on Aging, and the AoA stress numbers of participants, numbers of meals served, or numbers of older workers placed in jobs. Kutza's views from 1991 are still relevant today, including what she termed as these "failures to be self-critical" (Kutza, 1991, p. 67) acting to weaken the aging network. The reluctance to be self-critical, however, also reflects the maturity of the aging network, and the self-protective desire of agencies to ensure their continued funding and existence. Full-scale valid evaluations of aging network programs now confront an aging network less concerned about innovation than survival, particularly in a period of economic uncertainty. The dilemma of increased demands, but limited resources, may force an intensive reexamination of the effectiveness of programs, the simplification of access to important programs and services, and the development of programs designed to deal with some of the most difficult remaining problems, such as how we can support an aging society in a way that honors the individual and addresses the societal impact?

These goals cannot be accomplished in a framework that views programs and services for the aged as separate from those for other populations. Social welfare advocates and human services professionals must unite in a framework that sees the needs of children, the aged, minority populations, and other groups as interrelated rather than competitive. A failure to bridge seeming differences in needs will mean continued competition for social welfare dollars—a competition that will eventually defeat the best intentions of all advocacy groups.

Taking an innovative approach to services and supports that are provided by the vast expanse of the aging networks is going to require a proactive approach rather than a reactive approach. Throughout this book we have addressed a whole host of issues of importance but for this section in particular we look back to the social determinants of health, including the structural forces that underscore poverty, health, and education in the context of social isolation and other related demographic factors—age, family size, social networks, and living arrangements—to highlight an emerging public health crisis in the United States, dying alone. Other countries are addressing this issue, namely, the United Kingdom, Australia, and Japan. Certainly, the systems of health care in those countries allow a different sort of access in terms of who, what, where, and when. In this country, would we allow for a program in which frontline workers knock on doors to check on older adults to ensure they are still alive? Maybe, but until then it will take cooperation and innovation to address this emerging issue, which promises to be part of our landscape.

CONCLUSION

As we close our final discussion related to challenges within the aging network and look to the future, it is important to consider issues that play a role across disciplines and have an impact on the aging network at every level. As the field of gerontology grows and the population of older adults continues to increase, the need for a gerontologically educated workforce becomes a critical factor in our ability to provide a good old age for everyone in our society. We have made great strides in our programs, services, and educational opportunities for those interested in the aging of our society. In order to continue to add to our successes, we must also make room for those who have a background in gerontology, whether it is in the classroom, on the frontlines, or developing policies and programs.

Dr. Butler, in his book, *Why survive: Growing old in America,* asks, "Why study the elderly? Why spend research money on old people when there are compelling priorities for other age groups, particularly the young?" (Butler, 1975, p. 18). Butler puts forth many of his own compelling reasons but one stands out for our purposes, "a greater understanding and control over the diseases and difficulties of later life would hopefully make old age less frightening and more acceptable as a truly valuable last phase of life. The relief of human suffering has merit in itself, but it also releases human beings from the fears and defenses they build up around it" (p. 19). With that in mind, related questions remain and we pose these to our colleagues in the field of gerontology.

CRITICAL THINKING QUESTIONS

1. *How can policy and practice continue to support the health care and social needs of older adults in a way that recognizes heterogeneity of individuals, despite the societal biases of various groups (including the elderly themselves)?*

2. *How can gerontological education at all levels—from elementary schools through doctoral programs—embrace the rich and complex history of "old age" throughout the centuries to help rediscover and perhaps even redefine what it means to grow old and consider the implications for the individual and society?*

3. *How can we move forward with scientific advances in gerontology research without privileging complex statistical models over individual experience?*

REFERENCES

Aging Network Workforce Competencies Partnership (ANWC). (2014). *Aging network workforce competences research brief.* Retrieved from http://www.cswe.org

Butler, R. (1975). *Why survive? Being old in America.* New York, NY: Harper & Row.

Dobbs, D., Eckert, J. K., Rubinstein, B., Keimig, L., Clark, L., Frankowski, A., & Zimmerman, S. (2008). An ethnographic study of stigma and ageism in residential care or assisted living. *The Gerontologist, 48*(4), 517–526.

Fortinsky, R. (1991). Coordinated, comprehensive community care and the Older Americans Act. *Generations, 15,* 39–42.

Hudson, R., & Kingson, E. (1991). Inclusive and fair: The case for universality in social programs. *Generations, 15,* 51–56.

Institute of Medicine. (2008). *Retooling for an aging America: Building the health care workforce.* Washington, DC: National Academies Press.

Kutza, E. (1991). The Older Americans Act of 2000: What should it be? *Generations, 15,* 65–68.

Leutz, W. (2012). Foreign-born workers in long-term supportive services. *Public Policy & Aging Report, 22*(2), 1–11.

Levy, B., Chung, P., Bedford, T., & Navrazhina, K. (2014). Facebook as a site for negative age stereotypes. *The Gerontologist, 54*(2), 172–176.

Martin, S., Lowell, B. L., Gozdziak, E. M., Bump, M., & Breeding, M.E. (2009). *The role of migrant care workers in aging societies: Report of research findings in the United States.* Washington, DC: Institute for the Study of International Migration, Walsh School of Foreign Service, Georgetown University.

McNamara, T., & Williamson, J. (2012). Is age discrimination ever acceptable? *Public Policy and Aging Report, 22*(3), 9–13.

Niles-Yokum, K. (2006). *Older adults and consumer-direction: Factors that play a role in choice and control* (Doctoral dissertation, University of Maryland).

Quirk, D. (1991). The aging network: An agenda for the nineties and beyond. *Generations, 15,* 23–26.

Redfoot, D. L., & Houser, A. N. (2005). *"We shall travel on": Quality of care, economic development, and the international migration of long-term care workers.* Washington, DC: AARP Public Policy Institute.

World Health Organization (WHO). (2007). *Global age friendly cities: A guide.* Geneva, Switzerland: WHO Press.

State Units on Aging

Alabama Department of Senior Services
  http://www.adss.state.al.us
Alaska Commission on Aging, Department of Health and Social Service
  http://www.alaskaaging.org
American Samoa Territorial Administration on Aging
  http://americansamoa.gov/departments/agencies/taoa.htm
Arizona Division of Aging and Adult Services
  https://www.azdes.gov/common.aspx?menu=36&menuc=28&id=190
Arkansas Division of Aging and Adult Services, Department of Human
  Services
  http://www.arkansas.gov/dhs/agingindex.html
California Department of Aging
  http://www.aging.ca.gov
Colorado Division of Aging and Adult Services, Department of Human
  Services
  http://www.cdhs.state.co.us/aas
Connecticut Bureau of Aging Community & Social Work Services,
  Department of Social Services
  http://www.ct.gov/dss/site/default.asp
Delaware Division of Services for Aging and Adults with Physical
  Disabilities, Department of Health and Social Services
  http://www.dhss.delaware.gov/dsaapd
District of Columbia Office on Aging
  http://dcoa.dc.gov/dcoa/site/default.asp
Florida Department of Elder Affairs
  http://elderaffairs.state.fl.us/index.php

Georgia Division of Aging Services
  http://www.aging.dhr.georgia.gov
Guam Division of Senior Citizens, Department of Public Health and Social
  Services
  http://www.dphss.guam.gov/about/senior_citizens.htm
Hawaii Executive Office on Aging
  http://hawaii.gov/health/eoa/index.html
Idaho Commission on Aging
  http://www.idahoaging.com
Illinois Department on Aging
  http://www.state.il.us/aging
Indiana Division of Aging, Family, and Social Services Administration
  http://www.indiana.gov/fssa/2329.htm
Iowa Department on Aging
  http://www.state.ia.us/elderaffairs
Kansas Department on Aging
  http://www.agingkansas.org
Kentucky Department for Aging and Independent Living, Cabinet for
  Health & Family Services
  http://chfs.ky.gov/dail
Louisiana Governor's Office of Elderly Affairs
  http://goea.louisiana.gov/
Maine Office of Elder Services, Department of Health and Human
  Services
  http://www.maine.gov/dhhs/oes
Maryland Department of Aging
  http://www.mdoa.state.md.us
Massachusetts Executive Office of Elder Affairs
  http://www.mass.gov/?pageID=eldershomepage&L=1&L0=Home&
  sid= Elders
Michigan Office of Services to the Aging
  http://www.michigan.gov/miseniors
Minnesota Board on Aging, Department of Human Services
  http://www.mnaging.org
Mississippi Council on Aging, Division of Aging and Adult Services
  http://www.mdhs.state.ms.us/aas.html
Missouri Division of Senior and Disability Services, Department of Health
  and Senior Services
  http://www.dhss.mo.gov/
Montana Office on Aging, Senior and Long Term Care Division,
  Department of Public Health and Human Services
  http://www.dphhs.mt.gov/sltc

Nebraska Health and Human Services—State Unit on Aging
    http://www.hhs.state.ne.us/ags/agsindex.htm
Nevada Division for Aging and Disability Services, Department of Health
    and Human Services
    http://aging.state.nv.us
New Hampshire Bureau of Elderly and Adult Services
    http://www.dhhs.state.nh.us/DHHS/BEAS/default.htm
New Jersey Division of Aging and Community Services, Department of
    Health and Senior Services
    http://www.state.nj.us/health/senior
New Mexico Aging and Long-Term Services Department
    http://www.nmaging.state.nm.us/
New York State Office for the Aging
    http://www.aging.ny.gov
North Carolina Division of Aging and Adult Services, Department of
    Health and Human Services
    http://www.dhhs.state.nc.us/aging
North Dakota Aging Services Division, Department of Human Services
    http://www.nd.gov/dhs/services/adultsaging
Ohio Department of Aging
    http://aging.ohio.gov/home/
Oklahoma Aging Services Division, OK Department of Human Services
    http://www.okdhs.org/divisionsoffices/visd/asd/
Oregon Seniors and People with Disabilities, Department of Human
    Services
    http://www.oregon.gov/DHS/aboutdhs/structure/spd.shtml
Pennsylvania Department of Aging
    http://www.aging.state.pa.us
Puerto Rico Governor's Office for Elderly Affairs
    http://www.gobierno.pr/OGAVE/Servicios/ProgramaEstatalAsisten-
    cia.htm
Rhode Island Department of Elderly Affairs
    http://www.dea.state.ri.us
South Carolina Bureau of Senior Services
    http://www.dhhs.state.sc.us/dhhsnew/seniors.asp
South Dakota Office of Adult Services & Aging, Department of Social
    Services
    http://dss.sd.gov/elderlyservices
Tennessee Commission on Aging and Disability
    http://www.tennessee.gov/comaging
Texas Department of Aging & Disability Services
    http://www.dads.state.tx.us

Utah Division of Aging and Adult Services, Department of Human Services
http://www.hsdaas.utah.gov

Vermont Department of Disabilities, Aging and Independent Living, Division of Aging and Disability Services
http://dail.vermont.gov

Virgin Islands Senior Citizen Affairs Administration
http://www.dhs.gov.vi/seniors/index.html

Virginia Department for the Aging
http://www.vda.virginia.gov

Washington Aging and Disability Services, Department of Social & Health Services
http://www.aasa.dshs.wa.gov

West Virginia Bureau of Senior Services
http://www.wvseniorservices.gov/

Wisconsin Bureau of Aging and Disability Resources, Department of Health Services
http://dhfs.wisconsin.gov/aging

Wyoming Aging Division, Department of Health
http://wdh.state.wy.us/aging/index.html

Administration on Aging Regional Support Centers

Region I   Connecticut, Massachusetts, Maine, New Hampshire, Rhode Island, Vermont
                Regional Office: Boston, MA
                617-565-1158

Region II/III   Delaware, Maryland, New Jersey, New York, Pennsylvania, Virginia, West Virginia, Washington, DC, Puerto Rico, Virgin Islands
                Regional Office: New York, NY
                212-264-2976/2977

Region IV   Alabama, Florida, Georgia, Kentucky, Mississippi, North Carolina, South Carolina, Tennessee
                Regional Office: Atlanta, GA
                404-562-7600

Region V   Illinois, Indiana, Michigan, Minnesota, Ohio, Wisconsin
                Regional Office: Chicago, IL
                312-353-3141

Region VI   Arkansas, Louisiana, Oklahoma, New Mexico, Texas
                Regional Office: Dallas, TX
                214-767-2951

Region VII   Iowa, Kansas, Missouri, Nebraska
                Regional Offices: Kansas City, MO/Chicago, IL
                312-353-3141

Region VIII   Colorado, Montana, Utah, Wyoming, North Dakota, South
               Dakota
               Regional Office: Denver, CO
               303-844-2951
Region IX   Arizona, California, Nevada, Guam, CNMI (Mariana
               Islands), American Samoa
               Regional Office: San Francisco, CA
               415-437-8780
Region XI   Alaska, Idaho, Oregon, Washington
               Regional Office: Seattle, WA
               206-615-2298

National Aging Network Organizations and Resources

Advocacy Organizations

Organization	Website
AARP	www.aarp.org
Aging and Disability Resource Center	www.adrc-tae.org
Alliance for Aging Research	www.agingresearch.org
Alzheimer's Association	www.alz.org
American Society of Aging	www.asaging.org
Association of Gerontology in Higher Education	www.aghe.org
Generations United	www.gu.org
Gerontological Society of America	www.geron.org
Gray Panthers	www.graypanthers.org
Leadership Council of Aging Organizations	www.lcao.org
Leading Age	www.leadingage.org
National Adult Day Services Association	www.nadsa.org
National Adult Protective Services Foundation	www.napsa-now.org
National Asian Pacific Center on Aging	www.napca.org
National Association of Area Agencies on Aging	www.n4a.org
National Association of State Units on Aging	www.nasua.org
National Caucus & Center on Black Aged	www.ncba-aged.org
National Center on Creativity and Aging	www.creativeaging.org
National Committee to Preserve Social Security and Medicare	www.ncpssm

Organization	Website
The National Consumer Voice for Quality LTC	www.theconsumervoice.org
National Council on the Aging	www.ncoa.org
National Gay and Lesbian Task Force	www.thetaskforce.org/issues/aging
National Hispanic Council on Aging	www.nhcoa.org
OWL—The Voice of Mid-life and Older Women	www.owl-national.org
SAGE Services and Advocacy for Gay, Lesbian, Bisexual and Transgender Elders	www.sageusa.org

Federal Resources

Organization	Website
Administration for Community Living	www.acl.gov
Administration on Aging	www.aoa.gov
Centers for Disease Control and Prevention	www.cdc.gov
Centers for Medicare and Medicaid Services	www.cms.gov
Corporation for National and Community Service	www.nationalservice.gov
Department of Health and Human Services, Office of Minority Health	http://minorityhealth.hhs.gov
Department of Housing and Urban Development (HUD)	www.hud.gov
Employment and Training Administration/Department of Labor	www.doleta.gov
Federal Transit Administration	www.fta.dot.gov/
Health Resources and Services Administration, Cultural Competence Resources for Health Care Providers	www.hrsa.gov/ culturalcompetence
Medicare (CMS)	www.medicare.gov
National Institute on Aging	www.nia.gov
National Institute of Mental Health	www.nimh.nih.gov
National Women's Health Information Center	www.womenshealth.gov
Social Security Administration	www.ssa.gov
Substance Abuse and Mental Health Services Administration	www.samhsa.hhs.gov
Veterans Administration	www.va.gov

Resources

Organization	Website
ARCH National Respite Network	www.archrespite.org
AARP Public Policy Institute	www.aarp.org

Organization	Website
Alzheimer's Disease Education and Referral Center/NIA	www.nia.nih.gov/alzheimers
American Bar Association, Commission on Law and Aging	www.aba.org
Center for Retirement Research at Boston College	http://crr.bc.edu
Compassion and Choices	www.compassionandchoices.org
Elder Economic Security Index Wider Opportunities for Women	www.wowonline.org
Independent Transportation Network America	www.itnamerica.org
Intentional Communities	www.ic.org
National Academy on an Aging Society	www.agingsociety.org
National Academy of Social Insurance	www.nasi.org
National Alliance for Caregiving	www.nac.org
National Center on Caregiving/Family Caregiver Association	www.fca.org
National Coalition for the Homeless	www.nationalhomeless.org
National Committee for the Prevention of Elder Abuse	www.preventelderabuse.org
National Center on Elder Abuse	www.ncea.org
National Hospice and Palliative Care Organization	www.nhpco.org
National Long Term Care Ombudsmen Resource Center	www.ltcombudsman.org
National Resource Center on Native American Aging	www.nrcnaa.org/
National Senior Citizen Law Center	www.nsclc.org
Naturally Occurring Retirement Communities	www.norcblueprint.org
Network on Multicultural Aging	www.asaging.org/NOMA
Urban Institute	www.urban.org
Women's Institute for a Secure Retirement	www.wiserwomen.org

TOOLS FOR THE AGING NETWORK

Consumer's Tool Kit for Health Care Advance Planning
    www.abanet.org/aging/toolkit
MedlinePlus Gay, Lesbian and Transgender Health Resources
    www.nlm.nih.gov/medlineplus/gaylesbianandtransgenderhealth
    .html
U.S. Administration on Aging's: A Toolkit for Serving Diverse Communities
    www.aoa.gov/AoARoot/AoA_Programs/Tools_Resources/DOCS/
    AoA_DiversityToolkit_Full.pdf

TOOLS FOR PROTECTING YOUR
HEALTH CARE WISHES

"Good to Go" Toolkit and Resource Guide
    www.compassionandchoices.org/g2g
Outing Age 2010: Public Policy Issues Affecting Lesbian, Gay, Bisexual
and Transgender (LGBT) Elders
    www.thetaskforce.org/reports_and_research/outing_age_2010

LGBT SERVICES AND SUPPORTS

www.n4a.org/files/programs/resources-lgbt-elders/Inclusive
    ServicesGuide2012.pdf

www.asaging.org/national-resource-center-on-lgbt-aging-aia

www.lgbtagingproject.org

www.sageusa.org/nyc/thesagecenter.cfm

EXAMPLES OF BEST PRACTICES
IN COMMUNITY LIVING

Village Movement

www.beaconhillvillage.org

www.sbvillage.org

vtvnetwork.org/content.aspx?page_id=0&club_id=691012

www.aarp.org/home-garden/livable-communities/info-04–2011/villages-real-social-network.html

dailynightly.nbcnews.com/_news/2014/01/24/22432854-it-takes-a-village-seniors-thrive-while-living-at-home

WHO: Age-Friendly Cities Model

www.agefriendlyportland.org

www.who.int/ageing/age_friendly_cities_guide/en

Model and Evidence-Based Programs

FOSTER GRANDPARENT PROGRAM

The Foster Grandparent Program connects older adults (55+) with the youth in their community. Older mentors act as positive role models to children and youth and also report positive benefits from volunteering.

www.nationalservice.gov/programs/senior-corps/foster-grandparents

RETIRED SENIOR VOLUNTEER PROGRAM

The Retired Senior Volunteer Program (RSVP) is authorized under Title II, Part A, of the Domestic Volunteer Service Act of 1973, as amended (Public Law 93–113)

www.nationalservice.gov/programs/senior-corps/rsvp

SENIOR COMPANION PROGRAM

The Senior Companion Program is authorized under Title II, Part C, of the Domestic Volunteer Service Act of 1973, as amended (Public Law 93–113)

www.nationalservice.gov/programs/senior-corps/senior-companions

EXPERIENCE CORPS

The Experience Corps was first piloted in 1993 and included lead agencies in select cities, such as the Foster Grandparent Program and RSVP. The program was later expanded through funding from the Corporation for National and Community Service. Civic Ventures (Encore) helped to further expand the program. Experience Corps later teamed with AARP to further address the intergenerational component.

AARP Experience Corps places older adult mentors in the schools to work with K–3 students in disadvantaged schools.

www.aarp.org/experience-corps

HEALTHY IDEAS

Approximately 20 states have programs replicating Healthy IDEAS (Identifying Depression, Empowering Activities for Seniors). The Healthy IDEAS "is an evidence-based community depression program designed to detect and reduce the severity of depressive symptoms in older adults with chronic health conditions and functional limitations through existing community-based case management services" (www.NCOA.org).

www.careforelders.org/default.aspx?menugroup=healthyideas

THE PEARLS PROGRAM

Developed by researchers at the University of Washington, led by Dr. Ed Wagner in the late 1990s, the Pearls Program is an evidenced-based treatment for depression in the elderly. The program is geared toward older adults (60+) who have symptoms related to minor depression and dysthymic disorder.

www.pearlsprogram.org

ARTS FOR THE AGING PROGRAM

Arts for the Aging Program (AFTA) is a nonprofit organization in the Washington, DC, metro area founded in 1988 that "provides visual, performing, literary, and intergenerational art outreach programs specially designed to enhance the health and well-being of seniors." The focus of AFTA is on older adults in underserved settings (adult day, skilled nursing) who have cognitive and/or physical impairments. Programs are led by professional artists.

www.aftaarts.org

Classroom Assignments

Engaging students in the classroom—whether it is a face-to-face class or a virtual class—is the key to a successful semester. The assignments we have included for each chapter are activities that can be used in both settings. Because students are often less than enthusiastic about studying gerontology, activities and assignments are particularly important as a vehicle for capturing their imagination and making the field come alive for them. We include these assignments as a starting point for your use. We hope you find them useful.

CHAPTER ONE: THE DEMOGRAPHICS OF AGING TODAY

Exploring Your Own Community

Using the most recent census data, examine the number and proportion of elders in your community. Include lifestyle factors such as the following:

- Number/percentage of elders living alone

- Number/percentage of old-old and their living situation

- Proportion of men to women

- Number/percentage of grandparents raising grandchildren

- Number/percentage of elders living in assisted-living facilities and nursing homes. (This analysis will require using some data other than census data and will require a little sleuthing on the part of students to identify facilities and their licensed capacity/census.)

▓ Determine whether the number of elders in your community is increasing or decreasing. If there is a trend, speculate on reasons why this is occurring.

Prepare a paper with your findings. You can use these data to supplement the team assignments prepared for Chapter 3.

CHAPTER TWO: OLDER AMERICANS ACT LEGISLATION AND THE EVOLUTION OF A NETWORK

Assignment A: Exploring the White House Conference on Aging

Examine the 2005 White House Conference on Aging (WHCOA) report. Prepare a set of recommendations for the upcoming 2015 WHCOA. Because the WHCOA is a one-time event that occurs every 10 years or so, the office of the WHCOA closes after the event and the recommendations are prepared. The only site we could find that included the full report of the WHCOA—2005 is given below. You will find the pdf of the report at the National Indian Center on Aging (NICOA) website: nicoa.org/wp-content/uploads/2012/04/2005-WHCOA-Final-Report.pdf

An additional online document that you will find useful is an analysis by Dr. Moody who suggests an agenda for the 2015 WHCOA: assets .aarp.org/www.aarp.org_/articles/research/oaa/whconf_2015.pdf

Assignment B: Exploring Your Community Resources

▓ Identify an aging network organization in your community, such as a senior center, meal program, or an Area Agency on Aging. Make an appointment with a staff member of the organization (director, community liaison, etc.) and visit the agency.

▧   Alternatively, you can arrange a visit to a senior center and interview a few participants about the reasons they attend the center, how long they have been attending, and what the senior center means to them. This consumer-focused activity can provide some important insight into the importance of the program(s) to the users.

    ●   Be sure to check with your professor about the Institutional Review Board (IRB) regulations of your school to ensure that you adhere to them before your interview.

For either of the activities above, prepare a brief paper and share your insights with the class in an online PowerPoint or classroom presentation.

CHAPTER THREE: COMMUNITY-BASED SERVICES

In Chapter 3, there is a case study of a hypothetical case—a woman named Ethel. Using the Internet and any printed information you can find about your community services, develop a plan for Ethel in your community. Review your plans in small groups or by posting online to get critical feedback from your fellow students. Discuss the following topics:

▧   How difficult was it to get specific information about community resources?

▧   Were there resources that were applicable to Ethel's status and needs?

▧   What were the specific recommendations you made after reviewing community resources?

▧   What was missing in the community?

CHAPTER FOUR: COMMUNITY SUPPORTS
FOR AGING IN PLACE

Note: This assignment is a semester-long assignment and can include the work that students have done in other assignments described earlier. This assignment works best in a face-to-face class but can be modified for online classes.

Aging Well in Your City

Preliminary Project Background

Aging Well in City Domains

The Aging Well project allows students the opportunity to work together in teams to assess how age-friendly their community is. Working within the domains suggested by the World Health Organization, students will learn about the importance of community from a variety of perspectives, the role social determinants of health play on the course of life, the role we all play in our communities, and how we can make a difference.

 I. Housing

 II. Transportation

 III. Culture and lifelong learning

 IV. Civic engagement and volunteer opportunities

 V. Health and support services

 VI. Public safety

Student Teams

 I. Housing

 II. Transportation

 III. Culture and lifelong learning

 IV. Civic engagement and volunteer opportunities

 V. Health and support services

 VI. Public safety

Preliminary Project Phases

 I. Research domain area—your city

   a. Census

   b. Area agency on aging

   c. Public- and private-sector service agencies

II. Walkability audit[1]

III. Site interviews with older adults

IV. Prepare findings/paper, and presentation

Community Project Details

For this team project you will be expected to explicitly use and draw off concepts and topics from class and your own outside research. You will become an expert in your particular domain area and be able to discuss both local and national programs. *Note*: You are expected to work together as a team—this is a team experience and all members should make a concerted effort to actively participate, be responsive, and contribute in a meaningful way. The team component will be an important part of your grade and will include a peer evaluation.

Paper

You are to write a six- to eight-page paper, double-spaced, title page (not included in page count), 12-point font, 1-inch margins on the upper, lower, and right side of the paper. It is expected that each member of the group will have input and actively participate in the development and writing of the paper. The paper should be developed following the outline that was created in terms of headings and content. I expect to see a final section on lessons learned and recommendations for how York can become a more aging-friendly city specific to your domain. Follow American Psychological Association (APA) publication guidelines.

Presentations

Your team will present its findings in a 15- to 20-minute presentation. How you decide to coordinate the presentation is up to you as a team. This should be a democratic process and include all team members. Presentations should include all members of the team and flow in a way that brings all the pieces together. It should be clear that team members worked together, not separately. Presentations should be drawn from the paper and follow the outline

---

[1] There are many walkability assessment tools online. Here is one we like. Remember to conduct your walkability inventory with an elder in mind.
www.idph.state.ia.us/iowansfitforlife/common/pdf/access_your_community.pdf

that was used in assigning research tasks and developing the paper. I expect to see a final section on lessons learned and recommendations for how York can become a more aging-friendly city specific to your domain.

General—(may use one or more members) Introduction to the domain. Project background as it relates to your domain area and introduction to York/National.

Individual members—Members should follow the outline that they followed for the assigned research tasks and for the paper. Describe personal experience related to working on the project and lessons learned from a gerontological perspective as well as a personal perspective. Interviews should be included in some form.

Peer evaluation—This is a group project and as such you will be expected to work together as a team. As a part of this process, you will be asked to evaluate your group members on a number of issues, including participation, cooperation, and others. These will be similar to the class evaluations you are familiar with.

Your grade will be based on the following:

- How well your project conveys the domain and stays on track within the domain throughout the research (most important).

- How accurate the information is that you present (integration of gerontological perspectives/concepts, including text/lecture/WHO/movie material).

- How thorough your project is. (Does it cover all the important aspects of the domain and related health concepts?)

- Teamwork—This is a 400-level class; I have very high expectations with regard to this component and very little tolerance for problems in this area (based on peer evaluation and my own evaluation).

- Recommendations

- Clarity

- Organizational structure of paper and presentation (including evidence of teamwork)

- Originality

- Creativity

Due Dates

■ Week 1 of project time—Outline due and brief report due. Your outline is intended to allow you to get focused on your particular domain. Examine the World Health Organization (WHO) and National Association of Area Agencies on Aging (N4A) documents and research your domain area. What topics within will you be examining? In addition to the outline, you are to submit a brief report that includes information about who will be assigned to what piece and any related details. Follow proper outline format. See links below for information:

● www.albany.edu/eas/170/outline.htm

● www.owl.english.purdue.edu/owl/resource/544/02/

■ Week 2—Submit summary of group activities to date as a brief report (including specific details about work assignments). This should include current findings and future directions and project activities.

■ Week 4—Submit summary of group activities to date as a brief report (including specific details about work assignments). This should include current findings and future directions as well as project activities.

■ Week 5—Presentation plan due. This can be in outline format and should specify the role of each team member in presenting content (be specific).

■ Week 6—Draft paper due.

■ Week 7—Final paper due and peer evaluations due.

CHAPTER FIVE: INCOME SECURITY IN OLD AGE

Assignment A

Provide students with a Social Security payment amount (e.g., $1,300 a month or less depending on your focus) and ask that students prepare a monthly budget based on that amount. The following items should be included:

■ Rent/mortgage including utilities

■ Medicare and Medigap payments

- Food
- Transportation
- Clothing
- Personal care expenses

Would the individual have eligibility for any public benefits such as the Supplemental Nutrition Assistance Program (SNAP), subsidized housing, or energy assistance? This would require the students to explore each program.

Assignment B

Using information found on the Web, have students prepare a paper that addresses the following question: Is Social Security going broke? Why or why not?

CHAPTER SIX: PROTECTING THE RIGHTS AND WELL-BEING OF OLDER AMERICANS: ELDER JUSTICE AND DISASTER PREPAREDNESS

Assignment A

Prepare a paper about the emergencies that might occur in the students' community (earthquakes, floods, tornado, etc.) and the provisions in place in the community to help residents. Are there special provisions for older adults and if not, what should be added to this planning?

Assignment B

Prepare a paper on one type of elder abuse and, using the information prepared for the Elder Justice Coalition (www.elderjusticecoalition.com), identify the strategies that could be used to reduce the incidence/prevalence of this abuse.

CHAPTER SEVEN: WORKFORCE ISSUES OF THE AGING NETWORKS

Literature Review and Interviews

Encourage students to consider the future of the aging networks and with a perspective that is informed by research and experts. Have students research the development of the aging networks and the professionals who work in them. They should conduct a literature review on the competency work currently being undertaken in the field (Association for Gerontology in Higher Education [AGHE], Partnership for Health and Aging [PHA], Institute of Medicine [IOM], etc). As a final component of this project, students should make contact with an aging network professional and conduct an informational interview that explores the following: What is their educational background, what are their career trajectories, how did they get interested in aging, and what are their views on aging-related competencies? Students should be encouraged to develop their own interview and related domains together as a class as part of the learning process.

CHAPTER EIGHT: GLOBAL AGING

Semester Project

Identify a few countries that are low income, middle income, and high income and assign student teams (three to four students is ideal) to a country. The semester assignment is to use a quality-of-life index, such as the Organisation for Economic Co-operation and Development (OECD) index, to explore their country. They will need to look at some elements specific to old age in that country using Internet sources and, at a minimum, explore:

- Social insurance benefits for income or other income programs for elders
- Health benefits and resources
- Life expectancy compared to other nations
- Other support programs, if any, in place
- Role of family in the support of elders

▓ Laws and policies about older adults (retirement, family responsibility, control over their own resources, elder abuse and exploitation, etc.)

www.oecdbetterlifeindex.org

Each team should work during the semester on a schedule as appropriate for your semester with brief reports on specific topics during the semester. The final project outcome is a presentation to the class about the status of elders in their country. Specifically, in addition to a description of the status of elders in the country, how does this compare to the overall index of the country for all residents?

Index